LEADERSHIP
LESSONS

LEADERSHIP
LESSONS

AVOIDING THE PITFALLS
OF KING SAUL

Ralph K. Hawkins, Ph.D.
and
Richard Leslie Parrott, Ph.D.

THOMAS NELSON
Since 1798

NASHVILLE   DALLAS   MEXICO CITY   RIO DE JANEIRO

Published in Nashville, Tennessee, by Thomas Nelson. Thomas Nelson is a registered trademark of Thomas Nelson, Inc.

Thomas Nelson, Inc., titles may be purchased in bulk for educational, business, fund-raising, or sales promotional use. For information, please e-mail SpecialMarkets@ThomasNelson.com.

ISBN: 978-1-4016-7728-2

Printed in the United States of America

13 14 15 16 17 18 RRD 6 5 4 3 2 1

Ralph K. Hawkins

To my leadership heroes . . .
 Mike and Judy Beatty
 Jimmy and Kay Shirer
 Jerry and Peggy Boggus
 Dexter and Birdie Yeager

Richard Leslie Parrott

To the members of my Sunday school class, the Koinonia class. Each week we gather to study the Scripture and encourage one another as we live, love, and learn together with the same mindset as Christ Jesus (Phil. 2:5).

Contents

Part I

Studying Failure

Chapter 1

Why Study a Failed Leader?

What kind of leader blows up and throws a spear at one of his most trusted commanders? What kind of leader attempts to kill his own son, his designated successor, in the middle of a conference? What kind of leader customarily sits with his back to the wall so that he cannot be taken by surprise? What kind of leader slaughters the inhabitants of an entire town because they have harbored someone whom he perceives to be threatening his leadership? What kind of leader would do these terrible things, and more? Believe it or not, the leader who did these things is a biblical character, and one anointed by the famous prophet Samuel as Israel's first king—Saul of Kish.

Do these foibles sound extreme? Are they so far removed from present-day concerns as to be irrelevant? We do not think so, as our own encounters with problematic leaders both in church and in business seem to verify:

- a church leader works against the pastor and other staff, seeking to divide the church because he cannot "get his way";
- a pastor seeks to impose his agenda on the church, regardless of how many people protest the changes;
- the manager of a retail store secretly wears merchandise home without paying for it;
- a department head threatens and cajoles those under his supervision.

Each of these examples involves men and women who may indeed be "basically good and honest people," but who, like most leaders, struggle with shortcomings in their leadership.

When seen in perspective, many of Saul's foibles are not so exceptional. Leaders everywhere struggle with the tendency

3

toward manipulation of others, the utilization of "spin," inappropriate behavior, and self-promotion. In *Leadership Lessons: Avoiding the Pitfalls of King Saul*, leaders will have the opportunity to lay bare the life of a "basically good and honest person" to see the ways he struggled to live and lead with integrity, and learn from the times when he succeeded in that endeavor—as well as from the times in which he failed.

Leadership books—both in general and business categories—have traditionally focused on "best practices," while our concentration will be on seeking to learn from someone else's shortcomings. Our approach of using the "worst practices" of a historical figure in order to teach positive leadership habits may seem unusual to some, though it is actually an emerging trend in leadership studies. When Sydney Finkelstein, a professor at Dartmouth College's Tuck School of Business, began to teach management by focusing on "worst practices," his students were skeptical. He offered "Learning from Corporate Mistakes" as an elective and, ultimately, the class became so popular that Tuck reworked its MBA program with this class as a required first-year course. Abandoning traditional management offerings, Finkelstein has raised eyebrows with his unconventional research. Students, however, have responded extremely well, and appreciate the profundity of real-life examples of leadership failures. Finkelstein published his findings in 2003 in *Why Smart Executives Fail: And What You Can Learn from Their Mistakes*,[1] and the book has become a leadership classic.

While it may seem counterintuitive to focus on "worst practices," this approach is essentially saying: "Here is how people messed up. Don't do what they did." Everyone has heard the old adage, "It's good to learn from our failures, but it's an even better thing to learn from someone else's failures." This approach makes perfect sense; what could be more valuable than learning from someone else's failures? Professor Finkelstein, author of *Why Smart Executives Fail*, went on to create a management tool, in conjunction with Jackson Leadership Systems, called the SMART Early Warning System,™ that company boards and senior executives can use to identify the leading indicators that Finkelstein's research found to be predictors of trouble down the line. This tool provides a specific picture of the possible weaknesses and dangers companies face: "Armed with these critical insights, boards and top managers can turn their attention to the most pressing issues that need fixing, and avoid the calamities that have struck companies like General Motors, Enron, and AIG."[2]

In recent years, several authors have begun to explore bad leadership and leadership failures. Among the first to take an interest in this topic were Gary McIntosh and Samuel Rima, whose 1997 book, *Overcoming the Dark Side of Leadership*, was essentially a response to the very public moral and ethical failures of a number of prominent church and parachurch leaders in the last two decades of the twentieth century.[3] In 2000, John Maxwell wrote a popular volume entitled *Failing Forward: Turning Mistakes into Stepping Stones for Success* in which he sought to help people see their failures from a positive perspective.[4] In the decade to follow, several writers have adopted this approach. The year after Finkelstein published *Why Smart Executives Fail*, Barbara Kellerman examined issues of leadership in *Bad Leadership: What It Is, How It Happens, Why It Matters* in which she presented more than two dozen case studies of bad leadership, with a view to moving from bad to better leadership.[5] That same year, David Dotlich and Peter Cairo wrote *Why CEOs Fail: The 11 Behaviors That Can Derail Your Climb to the Top and How to Manage Them.*[6] A few years later, Hans Finzel, the former president and CEO of the international non-profit WorldVenture, which has a staff of 550 workers in 70 countries worldwide, wrote *The Top Ten Mistakes Leaders Make.*[7] In 2008, Paul Carroll and Chunka Mui published *Billion Dollar Lessons: What You Can Learn from the Most Inexcusable Business Failures of the Last 25 Years.*[8] Most recently, Donald Keough, a former president of the Coca-Cola company, wrote *The Ten Commandments for Business Failure,*[9] which is full of examples of failure, as well as advice on how to recover from mistakes and regain one's leadership footing. The study of leadership failure is a burgeoning field, and these are just a few of the books available on the subject.

This is the approach we take in *Leadership Lessons: Avoiding the Pitfalls of King Saul.* Our goal is to help readers rise from the ashes of *Saul's* failures and aspire to greatness by learning from someone else's struggles with the difficulties of leadership.

One of the unique features of this volume is that, in it, we take a sustained look at the life of a single, individual leader. This approach has a number of benefits. First, rather than arbitrarily selecting five or ten points upon which to pontificate, the selection of a key figure out of history and the examination of his life and leadership allow the problem behaviors under consideration to emerge naturally. In other words, the ten behaviors examined in this book were not arbitrarily selected nor were they invented by the authors. Instead, they emerged from Saul's own life story. They are rooted in reality. This means that, while these self-defeating behaviors are, to some extent, Saul's own character defects, they may also be, to some degree, common or universal problems.

A second benefit of tracing the foibles of one leader throughout his lifetime is that we are able to get a long-term perspective of how these problems arise and how they play themselves out if they are not addressed. Looking at the entirety of a leader's story allows us to get a real feel for how these problems can impact the overall tenure of leadership. In each chapter, we compare and contrast positive approaches with Saul's negative approaches, thereby showing specific ways we can learn from someone else's mistakes—and thereby build positive leadership.

A third benefit of studying the failures of this corrupt king is that there is something of King Saul in everyone—male or female—who is in a position of leadership. In his classic retelling of the stories of Saul, David, and Absalom, entitled *A Tale of Three Kings: A Study in Brokenness*, Gene Edwards writes that, while we may have our eyes judgmentally focused on the corrupt King Saul,

(impt)

> God has *his* eyes fastened sharply on another King Saul. Not the visible one standing up there throwing spears. . . . No, God is looking at *another* King Saul. One just as bad—or worse.
>
> God is looking at the King Saul in *you*. . . . Saul is in your bloodstream, in the marrow of your bones. He makes up the very flesh and muscle of your heart. He is mixed into your soul. He inhabits the nuclei of your atoms.

King Saul is one with you.
You are King Saul![10]

The church has always taught that humankind is hopelessly corrupt due to the Fall (Gen. 3), an idea that has been enshrined in some church traditions as the doctrine of original sin. Whether one accepts this doctrine or not, the basic idea that humankind is tainted due to the Fall is affirmed in each of the major divisions of Scripture. After the Fall, the Torah proclaims, "the wickedness of humankind was great in the earth . . . every inclination of the thoughts of their hearts was only evil continually" (Gen. 6:5 NRSV). This is a very strongly worded verse that intends to say that humankind is permeated with corruption, an idea that is repeated in the books of the prophets. For example, Jeremiah observes that "the heart is devious above all else; it is perverse—who can understand it?" (Jer. 17:9 NRSV). The idea is also enshrined in the Bible's wisdom literature. The psalmist, for example, writes:

> The LORD looks down from heaven on humankind to see if there are any who are wise, who seek after God. They have all gone astray, they are all alike perverse; there is no one who does good, no, not one. Have they no knowledge, all the evildoers who eat up my people as they eat bread, and do not call upon the LORD? (Pss. 14:2–4 NRSV)

And the Proverbs repeatedly echo the idea. Proverbs 20:9 rhetorically asks, "Who can say, 'I have made my heart clean; I am pure from my sin'?" (NRSV). The implied answer is, "No one." The point is that we are all prone to the bad leadership epitomized by King Saul. Barbara Kellerman writes that "patterns repeat themselves, and this means, among other things, that bad leadership will be replayed" according to typical scenarios.[11] She cogently argues:

> We cannot stop or slow bad leadership by changing human nature. No amount of preaching or sermonizing—no exhortations to virtuous conduct, uplifting thoughts, or wholesome habits—will obviate the fact that even though our behavior may change, our nature is constant.[12]

Christians would certainly agree that fallen people cannot change human nature. But they would also point to the Scripture's teaching about the renewal of fallen people through Jesus Christ. God, through Christ's achievement on the cross and the Spirit's work in our heart, transforms us from an old self to a new person in Christ (Eph. 4:17–30). The change is pervasive and includes our attitude (v. 23), our communication (v. 25), our emotions (v. 26), our way of life (v. 28), and our relationships with others (vv. 29–30). The apostle Paul teaches that our old self—our old "Adam"—is put to death. He therefore asks:

> What then are we to say? Should we continue in sin in order that grace may abound? By no means! How can we who died to sin go on living in it? Do you not know that all of us who have been baptized into Christ Jesus were baptized into his death? (Rom. 6:1–3 NRSV)

However, as the great Swiss Reformed theologian Karl Barth famously remarked, "Against the fact of the drowning of the old Adam is the fact that the rogue is an expert swimmer."[13] While fallen people are raised to walk in newness of life when they become Christians (Rom. 6:4ff), they do not instantly become mature in Christ. Paul describes the process in terms of brilliance and splendor:

> And we, who with unveiled faces all reflect the Lord's glory, are being transformed into his likeness with ever-increasing glory, which comes from the Lord, who is the Spirit. (2 Cor. 3:18)

They will be transformed into the image of Christ, but this is an ongoing process that will not be complete until the end of time (Rom. 8:19–30). Studying the leadership failures of King Saul is one way we can "get real" and "stay real" in the meantime.

When the nation of Israel clamored for a king, God chose Saul for them. Saul was a man who stood head and shoulders above the average Israelite. He was a man who was impressive to look upon and, apparently, adept in battle. He led the nation for forty years and made a number of important accomplishments for the nation.

Presumably his reign had many positive facets, for even David, his successor, celebrated Saul's importance in a song following his death. And yet, for all this, Saul was considered by the biblical writer to have been a failure. Although Saul had been promised that his house would reign "forever," the prophet Samuel told him that God regretted making him king. As a result of Saul's poor performance as a leader, the kingdom would be taken away from him and his house—"forever." *mind blowing*

The Pitfalls of King Saul Are Your Stepping-Stones to Success

In a gathering of several scores of leaders, we discussed how leaders learn best. I (Richard) posed a simple question, "Do you learn more from your successes or your regrets?" All agreed that leaders learn more from regrets. However, learning from an experience of regret, our own or another's, takes more than just going through the experience. Learning comes when we reflect both personally and professionally.

As you read about the failure of King Saul, you will learn best by following these guidelines for personal and professional reflection:

1. *Identify with King Saul.* You may find it tempting and even appropriate to be enraged by some of the behaviors of Saul. However, outrage does not often produce meaningful reflection. To reflect on failure, look below the surface of behavior. Ask, "What was King Saul's perspective? What were his emotions? What was his motivation?" Identify with what he saw, what he felt, and what he wanted. Ask why. You learn from regrets if you see them from the inside out.

2. *Love your enemies.* This is a guarantee: you will see the behavior of other leaders, sacred and secular, in the behavior of King Saul. You will come upon your own mirror images of situations reflected in the life of King Saul. Your own emotions will surface, feelings of anger and pain. It is appropriate and needful to experience the emotions caused by such negative and cruel behavior. However, the easiest

way to become like your enemy is to hate your enemy. The most challenging command uttered from the lips of Jesus Christ was, "Love your enemies and pray for those who persecute you, that you may be sons of your Father in heaven" (Matt. 5:44–45).

3. *Repent and rest.* The characteristics of King Saul are found not only in the leaders around you but also in you. I doubt you will throw a spear at a rival, destroy a city that hides your enemy, or seek the magic of a witch. However, uncontrolled emotions, twisted perspective, and selfish or fearful motives creep into the mind and soul of all leaders. "In repentance and rest is your salvation, in quietness and trust is your strength" (Isa. 30:15).

4. *Be accountable.* Contrary to the vast myth of American leadership, leading is not a solo sport. Leadership is a team activity. Leaders need one another to serve as a guard against poor decisions and aid in maturing in competency and confidence. Read this book with another leader or a small group of like-minded individuals. At the end of each chapter is a discussion guide that will help you reflect together on your own challenges and discover ways to help one another move forward.

5. *Challenge yourself.* The purpose of the biblical writers in giving us the history of King Saul was not to lambast the king in order that we might feel better about ourselves. The purpose of this book is not that we might lambast the bad leaders around us or beat up ourselves for our own failings. We don't need a book to teach us to deride others or ourselves; we are fully accomplished at these tasks. What we need is to reflect on a rich source of biblical material, often neglected, that guides us in learning to follow God as our King as we lead others in his name and character. At the end of each chapter is an opportunity for you to assess and analyze your own leadership and take action steps that work for you.

Colin Powell aptly shares the test of leadership failure: "The day soldiers stop bringing you their problems is the day you stop being their leader. They have either lost confidence that you can help them or concluded that you do not care."[14] The story of Saul's failure is a story of soldiers losing confidence in their king and the king losing compassion for his soldiers. Let the story be your teacher and guide as you become a better leader.

Part II

The Failures of King Saul and What We Can Learn from Them

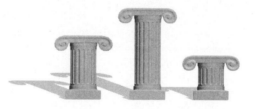

Chapter 2

Introducing King Saul

By the time the kingship came into existence in the land of Israel, the Hebrews had a long history behind them that included the stories of the patriarchs—Abraham, Isaac, and Jacob—the four-hundred-year-long period of Egyptian bondage, forty years of wandering in the wilderness, and a couple hundred years in which they had tried to occupy the land of Canaan.

Although Joshua led the Hebrews in an invasion of the land of Canaan, and they had many important initial victories, in the long run they failed to drive out the Canaanites and, instead, settled down among them. The book of Judges chronicles the Israelites' struggle to maintain their distinctive faith in God in the midst of a land full of Canaanites, Philistines, Moabites, Ammonites, and other population groups.

It was Israel's failure to occupy the land, and their continued military conflicts with the Philistines and other inhabitants of the land, that led them to ask God to give them a king. The man God chose for them was Saul, son of Kish, of the tribe of Benjamin, who towered over ordinary Israelites. Saul was a handsome man and was, evidently, skilled on the battlefield. He ruled Israel for four decades and achieved several significant undertakings on behalf of his people.

Positive Aspects of Saul's Story

Many who read the story of Saul think of Israel's first king as a tragic figure who was doomed from the start, a flawed ruler, or an outright villain. However, Saul is much more complex than that. I (Ralph) am convinced that Saul's story is a tale of a good man gone bad and that, when he was first chosen for the kingship, he exhibited some ideal character traits for that role. When the biblical author of 1 Samuel introduced Saul, I am convinced that he intended to portray him as an ideal choice for the kingship. Indeed the story of Saul contains many positive reports about his performance. We will look at these positive accounts under the rubric of three points: Saul's character, transformation, and successes.

Saul's Character

The first positive aspect of Saul's story we should note is his first appearance in the book of 1 Samuel (1 Sam. 9:1–3).[1] You'll notice the text refers twice to Saul's appearance—it tells us two times that Saul was "handsome." First, it tells us he was "handsome," and then it tells us there was "not a man among the people of Israel more handsome than he" (v. 2 NRSV).

This passage has led generations of readers to think of Saul as shallow from the beginning; the Israelites only picked him for his looks, and there was no substance to him. However, as you are probably already aware, our English Bible is a translation. The Old Testament was originally written in Hebrew, and every English translation you read is the product of someone's effort to render into English what he or she understands the Hebrew to mean.

In Hebrew, when Saul is introduced, it says he was young, and then it uses a word that has the basic meaning of "good." In 1899, H. P. Smith, professor of Biblical History and Interpretation in Amherst College, introduced Saul in his classic commentary as "goodly."[2] The Jewish Publication Society translation, published in 1915, translates it this way: Saul was "young and goodly, and there was not among the children of Israel a goodlier person than he."

We must consider that the translations that render this as "handsome" are mistaken, and that "the verse refers less to his appearance than to his character and ability."[3] And what the biblical writer is trying to tell us is that, when Saul started out, he was a good man, and a good choice for the kingship.

Saul's Transformation

The second positive aspect of Saul's story we should note is his transformation, which comes in chapter 10 of 1 Samuel (read 1 Sam. 10:1–9). Once Samuel had anointed Saul as prince over God's people, the prophet told him to expect to encounter a series of signs on his way home that would confirm that he had, indeed, been chosen as Israel's future king. One of these signs was that he would be endowed with God's Spirit, after which, Samuel said, Saul would "be changed into a different person" (1 Sam. 10:6).

This is a fascinating statement, and Samuel used the same word for *change* that the Bible uses in Exodus 7:15, where it says God "changed" Moses' rod into a snake, and in Exodus 7:20 when it says he changed the Nile River into blood. God was going to completely and constitutionally change Saul!

After Samuel told Saul all of this, Saul turned to leave in order to make the journey home. Look at 1 Samuel 10:9. It says that, when Saul turned to leave, "God gave him another heart" (NRSV). God did it—he changed him!

Saul's Successes

Now, after Saul's public confirmation and anointing as king of Israel, he had a number of important successes. First of all, he led the Israelites in a major victory over a very important enemy of the Israelites, a group called the Ammonites that were attacking Israel from the east, from across the Jordan River. This battle was so important that the entire eleventh chapter of 1 Samuel is devoted to it.

A little later, in chapter 14, another passage gives a positive account of Saul's reign. It's a summary, a thumbnail sketch, of his military leadership during his reign:

> When Saul had taken the kingship over Israel, he fought against all his enemies on every side—against Moab, against the Ammonites, against Edom, against the kings of Zobah, and against the Philistines; wherever he turned he routed them. He did valiantly, and struck down the Amalekites, and rescued Israel out of the hands of those who plundered them. (1 Sam. 14:47–48 NRSV)

Saul's successes were valuable, commemorated in 2 Samuel chapter 1 in a lamentation or funeral song that grieved over the deaths of Saul and his son Jonathan (read 2 Samuel 1:19–27). As you can see, this song expressed both national and personal grief at the loss of a man who had been an important leader in the life of the nation of Israel.

Saul's Story: A Net-Negative

Despite the positive ways Saul may have contributed to the nation of Israel, the author of 1 Samuel ultimately regarded Saul's story as one of tragedy and disappointment. The prophet Samuel told Saul that it had been Yahweh's intent to establish a Saulide dynasty (1 Sam. 13:13); but, in the end, God was full of remorse over having made him king (v. 14). Saul's failures were so pronounced that his kingdom would not be allowed to continue.

Lessons to Be Learned from Saul

There are important lessons to be learned from the story of Saul. One comes from the fact that Saul was indeed a good man. He wasn't doomed from the start; instead, he was a good or choice candidate for king, endowed with the Spirit and literally changed into another man!

He began well. He drove the Ammonites out of Israel. He made many other important victories. He spent forty years leading Israel successfully against its enemies. But something happened. Early in his reign, he began to sow the seeds of his own demise.

This is the reason we stressed Saul's good qualities at the beginning of this book. People tend to think of Saul as always having been corrupt; but Saul wasn't always corrupt. He was a good man, and Scripture teaches that good men can and do fall.

But how did it happen? How did a good man go so bad? If Saul had been endowed with the Spirit and literally changed into another man, then how in the world did he fall so hard?

The Tragic Hero

In Greek mythology, there is the concept of the "tragic hero"— someone who had a lot of extraordinary qualities, but one fatal flaw. While the hero accomplished tremendous feats, he had an "Achilles' heel" that prevented him from reaching his real potential.

Throughout history, many commentators have imagined Saul to have been a tragic hero. But, by the definition of Greek mythology, Saul was no tragic hero, for he had several serious flaws.[4] He didn't have one Achilles' heel that kept holding him back; instead, he had several flaws that eventually emerged to undermine his ability to lead the nation of Israel to greatness. This is not to say that he was doomed from the start. He could have sought the counsel of others to help him overcome his weaknesses. He could have sought to model his reign on the Torah, God's law. He could have asked Yahweh for guidance. But he did not, and he allowed his character flaws to emerge and to shape the direction of his kingship.

Learning from Saul's Mistakes

I (Ralph) have taught the book of 1 Samuel in several different congregations in different parts of the country and, each time, I have been struck by the sympathy for Saul expressed by parishioners. I think people feel sympathy for Saul because they can relate to him so well. Abraham, Moses, Joshua, and David—all characters of sterling standing before God—are held up within churches for our emulation. To some degree, however, we are not able to relate to them. Abraham talked personally with God—even argued with him. Moses was allowed to see God's "back." Joshua led Israel in the lightning blitzkrieg into the promised land. David was called "the man after God's own heart." How many of us—at least in our honest moments—really feel that we can relate to their experiences?

King Saul, however, is a man who evokes our sympathy. We feel sympathy for him because we can relate to him. We have all gone through times during which we've felt alienated from God or when we've felt that God may have been actively working against us. We've all experienced periods of melancholy. We've all resisted God's plan for our lives at times. I know I have.

And so, while Saul has never been lifted up within the church as someone from whom we can learn, he has a great deal to teach us, especially the leaders of the church. For bishops, pastors, elders, deacons—and all laity who serve in the church—Saul's leadership failures can serve as important benchmarks. For, as the old saying goes, those who are ignorant of history are doomed to repeat it.

By looking at the ways Saul failed, we can learn how to succeed as leaders.

Saul: A Man in Over His Head

The customs, traditions, and lifestyle of the Israelites faced a serious threat. A new enemy, the Philistines, invaded with iron weapons of war. "Give us a king," cried the people—people who had never had a king to rule them. The elders of the land held divided opinions over the choice of Saul as king. His was a tough position. He was a man in over his head.

Saul's experience resonates with today's leaders of business, church, and government. The present culture is changing, and the change is chaotic and confusing. There are obstacles to growth and productivity that feel like unbending iron and threaten with a sword's double edge. The expectations that organizations heap on their leaders fly in the face of reason. Leaders receive more blame than deserved and more praise than earned. Many leaders I (Richard) have spoken with in private conversations will confess, "I'm in over my head."

When overwhelmed, flaws of character and lack of competency can combine to drive a leader toward self-destructive behavior or a new self-discovery in Christ. Saul's tragic example of self-destruction serves as a warning for all leaders. His story is also an invitation to face our flaws in faith, trusting that Christ is at work in us and will work through us as we obey his voice. The experience of being overwhelmed can be a time of restoration and renewal. In the pages that follow, we will look at ten ways in which Saul failed, and we will show you how to use his failure for restoration and renewal in your own leadership, and for the advancement of God's kingdom.

Group Discussion and Personal Reflection

Group Discussion

1. To get started as a group, share your leadership story with one another. Who have been your best guides and mentors?

What positions of leadership have you held? What is your biggest current challenge as a leader?

2. Read 1 Samuel 9:1–3. The word often translated as *handsome* has the deeper meaning of goodness. Discuss until you agree on the three most important core qualities of goodness that every leader needs to bring to his or her task. Then list the qualities of character that may hinder a leader's ability to lead.

3. Read 1 Samuel 14:47–48. Getting started right is essential to leadership success. What are actions and attitudes that assist a leader in getting started right? What are actions and attitudes that hinder a leader from the beginning?

4. Read 2 Samuel 1:19–27. How would you like to be remembered as a leader?

5. This chapter recounts the story when "God gave him [Saul] another heart" (1 Sam. 10:9 NRSV). Do you remember a time when God brought a new heart to you as you faced a leadership challenge?

Personal Reflection

Assess

Answer the following three questions:

➢ To what degree do you identify with the phrase "in over my head"?

   Fully Agree 5   4   3   2   1 Don't agree

➢ Do you remember a time when you might have scored 4 or 5?

   ___ yes   ___ no

➢ Have you worked with a leader who was in over his or her head?

   ___ yes   ___ no

Analyze

Think through the following questions:

➢ What temptations come to you when you are in over your head?

➢ How does feeling overwhelmed affect your perception of the facts?

➢ How does feeling overwhelmed affect your control of emotions?

➢ How does feeling overwhelmed affect your motivation as a leader?

Act

Work out the following action steps.

___ Know your symptoms and signs that you are in over your head.

___ Know to whom you will turn when you are in over your head.

___ Cultivate a regular plan of physical activity and good diet.

___ Plan regular times to be away from work and stress.

___ Develop an interest outside of work.

Chapter 3

Saul Failed to Handle Authority Humbly

Saul, Israel's first king, began as an unknown donkey wrangler (1 Sam. 9:1—10:16). He went from total obscurity to the pinnacle of leadership. Maybe the climb was too high, too fast. He was not able to handle it, and it went to his head. Even at his anointing, we can see hints of his insecurities when, following his selection as king by the drawing of lots, he could not be found because he had "hidden himself among the baggage" (1 Sam. 10:17–27 NRSV).

The Dangers of Power

Samuel had warned the people of Israel about desiring a king. He told them that monarchies had a tendency to become oppressive. Kings usually came to rely on forced labor, including compulsory recruitment of both military recruits[1] and laborers in the field and in the foundry (1 Sam. 8:12). The palace-to-be, Samuel warned, would require large numbers of horses, and the king's chariots would need front runners (v. 11).[2] Women would not be exempt from the draft into royal service (v. 13). Even in desperate times the king would always get his share—a minimum of 10 percent of the income from field and flock (vv. 15, 17). Key words in the "regulations of the kingship" were "take" (vv. 11, 13–17) and "best" (vv. 14, 16). Samuel probably would have agreed with commentator Ronald Youngblood's assessment that "by nature royalty is parasitic rather than giving, and kings are never satisfied with the worst."[3]

Samuel's "regulations of the kingship," which would not benefit the average Israelite, were based on contemporary Canaanite society. Samuel was begging the people not to impose on themselves a

Canaanite institution alien to their own way of life.[4] If the "regulations of the kingship" attained full authority, the average Israelite would soon be little more than a peasant or a slave at the disposal of the king. Samuel said, "You yourselves will become his slaves" (1 Sam. 8:17).

Saul's Early Humility

After being anointed king, some time passed before Saul had to act in his new leadership capacity. It seems that early on in his reign, Saul retained a humble perspective about his role. First Samuel 11:5 reports that, even as king, Saul continued to personally cultivate his own fields. When messengers sought him out to report an Ammonite attack, they found him coming in from plowing. Saul made a very successful response to the Ammonite attack and liberated the people of Jabesh Gilead, who never forgot their debt to him.[5]

Even after having won a successful victory over the Ammonites, Saul still retained his humility. Seeing how he had risen to the occasion and manifested his real abilities, some of his followers suggested that he round up those who had opposed his selection as king early on, and wreak vengeance on them (1 Sam. 11:12–15). We see here how noble Saul could be, as he insisted that the divine deliverance was a cause for gratitude, not vengeful retribution (v. 13). Saul's demonstration of the leadership qualities necessary to be Israel's king was so impressive here that it led Samuel to convene an important meeting at Gilgal to "reaffirm" the kingship (v. 14). The people responded enthusiastically to this invitation (v. 15) and, in the presence of the Lord, they confirmed their earlier choice of Saul as their king by bringing sacrifices to the Lord.

Saul's "Rankism"

Unfortunately, Saul's humility seems to have been short-lived. Although we do not know how much time passed after this early success against the Ammonites, it is only a few chapters later we are told that "the LORD was grieved that he had made Saul king over Israel" (1 Sam. 15:35). From the earliest days, it was recognized that, ultimately, God himself was King[6]; he alone possessed absolute power and authority.[7] Any king of Israel would have to appreciate from the beginning that he was to rule over Israel *under* God. Israel's king was to exercise political and military power, but he was supposed to stand under the authority and judgment of God as conveyed by the prophets. In 1 Samuel 13 and the chapters that follow, we find that King Saul began to develop a problem with "rankism," a term coined by Robert W. Fuller in his book *Somebodies and Nobodies: Overcoming the Abuse of Rank*.[8] Rankism can go both ways: bad leaders can exert it, and victims can suffer under its effects. A leader who suffers from "rankism" tends to exercise autocratic, top-down leadership, and this is certainly what happened to Saul, who made unilateral decisions, rather than ones under God's authority. Saul acted autonomously, without regard for God's prophet. This would be the beginning of Saul's decline. *Cracks in Saul's character.*

Saul's first autonomous action occurred in 1 Samuel 13:1–15. On this occasion, two thousand men were under Saul's command at Micmash when the Philistines began to deploy there against Israel. Samuel had apparently instructed Saul to wait for him for seven days before going into battle (v. 8), probably so that he could consecrate the troops before they went into battle.[9] Saul waited the seven days but, while he and the army waited for the prophet to arrive, "the people began to slip away from Saul" (v. 8 NRSV). In apparent desperation, Saul disobeyed Samuel's instructions and "offered up the burnt offering" (v. 9). As soon as he had done so, however, Samuel arrived (v. 10). Samuel was furious with King Saul, and his harsh rebuke is familiar to many:

Only priests/prophet offer burnt offerings.

> Samuel said to Saul, "You have done foolishly; you have not kept the commandment of the LORD your God, which he commanded you. The LORD would have established your kingdom over Israel forever, but now your kingdom will not continue; the LORD has sought out a man after his own heart; and the LORD has appointed him to be ruler over his people, because you have not kept what the LORD commanded you." (1 Sam. 13:13–14 NRSV)

In most ancient Near Eastern cultures, kings were also high priests and were in many cases even thought of as divine.[10] In ancient Assyria, for example, the kings were designated as the chief priests of the god Ashur and a prefix appears in front of their names that suggests divinity.[11] In such cases, it would not have been a problem for the king to offer the ritual sacrifices.

In ancient Israel, however, the altar was the exclusive province of the priests.[12] When an individual presented an animal to be offered, he would slaughter the animal and butcher it himself, but then he would turn it over to a priest. The priest would place the meat on the altar and oversee the burning process. Only one Judahite king, Ahaz, is mentioned in the Old Testament as having actually manipulated blood on the altar (2 Kings 16:10–16), and the text reports that "he did what was evil in the sight of the LORD" (2 Kings 17:2 NRSV). According to the Levitical instructions for the sin offering, the king had to kill his goat and present the blood to the officiating priest, just like everybody else (Lev. 4:24–25).[13] Israelite kings were not divine and they were not to be distinguished from their subjects in how they approached God in the sacrificial system. Restricting access to the altar to the Levites showed that the king was not a god but was subject to the law, just like everyone else.

When Saul "offered up the burnt offering" (1 Sam. 13:9), he took priestly authority upon himself and thus violated the system of "checks and balances" that was built into the Torah. But how did Saul conceive of what he had done? Did he arrogantly believe he could disregard the instructions of Samuel or the commands of God? Could his disobedience have been based on a devout fear of going into battle without supplications to God having been made through the offering? Or was it simply his lack of trust in God and his need to take control into his own hands? Regardless of the answer, the prophet Samuel saw Saul's action as exceeding his rank and defying the limitations God had set on the kingship.

In a further engagement with the Philistines, Saul bound his army with an oath of abstaining from food for the entire day of the battle (1 Sam. 14:24–30). Some have said that this is an example of Saul's piety, but others have argued that he did it out of superstition rather than any real religious sensibilities.[14] However, whether his motivation was good or bad, it had a negative result—his soldiers became "faint" (v. 28) and "exhausted" (v. 31). Upon entering a forest, Saul's troops noticed a honeycomb on the ground (v. 27) and, although it was filled with honey, no one so much as tasted it because they "feared" the oath (v. 26)—that is, they respected it.[15] Jonathan, Saul's son, had not heard about the oath (v. 27), and so used the end of his staff to dip some honey from the comb. When he ate it, his eyes brightened, implying that his strength was renewed. One of Jonathan's fellow soldiers warned him about his father's oath (v. 28), explaining that the reason the troops had been so faint was because they had obeyed the command to fast. Jonathan answered that his father had "made trouble for the country" (v. 29).

Sometime later, Saul sensed that something was wrong in the army (v. 38), and he called for the leaders to come before him to determine what sin had been committed. He affirmed that whoever had sinned "must die" (v. 39). If necessary, he was even prepared to give up the life of his son Jonathan (v. 39). When it was revealed that Jonathan had violated the oath, Saul moved to kill him (v. 44). Saul's men, however, could not contain themselves in the face of this kind of gross injustice, and they reminded Saul of how cruel it would be to execute the man who had been Israel's deliverer (v. 45). Jonathan had led an attack on a Philistine garrison that had led to a total victory for the Israelites (1 Sam. 13:23—14:23). When Saul said that Jonathan must surely die for violating the oath, the people shouted, "Never! . . . not a hair of his head will fall" (14:45). Jonathan's fellow soldiers clearly felt that Saul's move to kill Jonathan was a heinous abuse of power, and their shouts were probably more than protest, but were likely a quiet threat against Saul. What they meant was, "You'll touch Jonathan over our dead bodies!"[16] The text notes that "the men rescued Jonathan, and he was not put to death" (v. 45), but this comment does not bring the passage to a conclusion. Instead, the author brings the story to a close by reporting that "Saul stopped pursuing the Philistines; and they withdrew to their own land" (v. 46). This concluding comment highlights the fact that Saul had become so absorbed with his rank that all he cared about was whether or not his people would give him complete and unquestioning obedience, even if it meant killing his own son. This episode was so distracting for Saul that he stopped pursuing the Philistines, who were able to return to their villages.

Saul further demonstrated that his "rankism" was running amuck when he refused to carry out the Lord's commands in the Amalekite war (1 Sam. 15:1–35). This occasion of disobedience on the part of Saul is a major turning point in the story which we will look at in detail in chapter 5, so we will not recount it here. Suffice it to say that Saul's disobedience was intentional and it evoked Yahweh's regret that he had made him king (v. 11).

Following these abuses of power, the king's own son and heir, Jonathan, began to shift his own loyalty away from his father to David; his friendship with David became so deep that he "loved him as his own soul" (1 Sam. 18:1–4 NRSV). Because of David's success in battle, Saul placed him in a position of leadership over the army, "and all the people, even the servants of Saul, approved" (v. 5 NRSV). David was devoted to the people, and the text reports that "all Israel and Judah loved David" (v. 16 NRSV). Even one of Saul's daughters, Michal, grew to love David (v. 20), and eventually became his wife (v. 27). As we will see in chapter 9, the word *love* means a lot more than simple friendship; it has political connotations. In the Old Testament, the word *love* refers to both personal attachment and public commitment, and it is used of Jonathan (vv. 1, 3), of all Israel and Judah (v. 16), and of the king's daughter, Michal (v. 20). The author is making the point that, because of Saul's abuse of his rank, his people gradually transferred their allegiance to another, better leader.

As Saul's popularity slipped away, his "rankism" progressively increased. He made jealous efforts to kill David, and David later became a refugee (1 Sam. 18:6–11). On another occasion, when Jonathan spoke in defense of David, the king cursed at his son and tried to kill him (1 Sam. 20:24–42). Saul lost all ability to exercise restraint in his abuse of power in the slaughter of the priests of Nob, in which he showed his contempt for a priesthood he had come to see as treacherous. After having fled the royal palace, David stopped at Nob, the site of a large contingent of priests[17] located only a couple of miles southeast of Gibeah (where Saul's palace was located) and one and a half miles northeast of Jerusalem. There, the priests gave David bread and a sword (1 Sam.

21:1–9). It just so happened that a man named Doeg, the chief of Saul's palace guard, saw him there and reported it to King Saul (1 Sam. 22:9–10), who immediately sent for the whole priestly family. Ahimelek, the priest who oversaw the shrine at Nob, urged Saul not to "accuse" him or his father's family (v. 15), but Saul would not listen. He ordered the execution of the priests at Nob for having harbored David, and eighty-five were killed that day. Saul and his chief of the palace guard, however, were not satisfied with the killing of the eighty-five priests—which in and of itself qualified as a massacre—and they extended the slaughter by putting the entire town "to the sword" (v. 19).

Saul had come full circle. Having first appeared in the text as an unknown donkey wrangler, he continued to work his own land even after having been crowned king. But once Saul began to exercise his royal prerogatives, he began to abuse his rank. And these abuses became more and more severe until, far from working to advance the causes of Yahweh, Saul turned on an entire town of Yahweh's priests and people and destroyed them.

Authority Is Essential and Dangerous for Leaders

Power is essential for leadership. In simple terms, leadership is getting work done through other people. A more sophisticated definition of leadership includes a battery of concepts including influence, process, relationship, and goals.[18] Each element of leadership involves a gathering, deploying, and targeting of an organization's energy. To move the power of an organization, the leader must have and exert power.

It is in the exertion of power that leaders, especially young and new leaders like Saul, may run afoul. Power looks different from a distance than it feels when worn as a crown. Let me suggest a common path of demise, a path we can trace through Saul's journey.

First, a young leader is often promoted into a leadership position due to his or her skill as an expert in sales, teaching, technology, and so forth. A top salesman is promoted to sales manager. A high quality teacher advances to the position of principal. A first-rate project manager is given leadership of the division. Or, a tall, good-looking farm boy who can clear a field, fight a foe, and find lost donkeys is anointed king (1 Sam. 9–10). Here is the challenge: the competencies required to be an expert may not align with the competencies required to be the leader. Closing sales and leading a sales force are different tasks. The result is that the new leader immediately moves from a position of competent expert to novice leader. Self-image and self-confidence are challenged.

Second, a leader receives legitimate authority when promoted to a new rank. Someone put his or her reputation on the line to see that the young and new leader received advancement. In the case of Saul, it was Samuel (1 Sam. 9:24). And in the case of Saul—as is the case with almost everyone who advances to a new position—not everyone was pleased to hear the news; there are always trouble-makers (1 Sam. 10:27). For the leader, two issues come to light: 1) the leader, to some degree, is beholden to those who helped him or her advance; and 2) the leader must hold the tension between conflicting groups and agendas. Welcome to the playing field of realistic leadership and legitimate power. Negotiate carefully lest you lose your soul.

Third, a leader soon learns (or already knows) that the only way to get things done is to influence others to get things done. This requires the development and maintenance of professional working relationships. This can be a great shock to the leader. Once inside the role, he primarily realizes his lack of power and control. Leaders are given more credit than they are due and shoulder more blame than they deserve. The leader's inner child cries out, "It's not fair!" Correct, it is not, but that's the way it is. Will the leader deal with the feelings of injustice and impotence by manipulation, leveraging friendship for personal power, duplicity, and other Machiavellian tools? Saul descended on this path of twisted and vicious leadership behavior (1 Sam. 18). Working out the uncomfortable combination of authority and relationships is a significant "heart challenge" for the leader.

Fourth, a leader learns there are ways to exert power that sidestep the difficult challenge of developing professional relationships of mutual trust and respect: for example, reward and punish, or marginalize and intimidate. We see the terrible outcomes of resorting to these methods of leadership by tracing the difficult and temptation-filled path of Saul, a leader who could not adjust to new self-understanding and self-awareness, who could not negotiate hard choices and conflicting interests, and who was unable to live with the balancing act of positional authority and professional relationships. Such a leader either drops out of leadership or drops into a pattern of leadership by "rankism," which Robert Fuller defines as "abusive, discriminatory, or exploitative behavior towards people because of their rank in a particular hierarchy."[19]

Self-Awareness and Soul Work Are Required for Leaders

To combat the dangerous and subtle influences that come along with positions of authority, leaders may implement two strategies: 1) lead the organization toward a culture of professional trust and respect, and 2) do soul work in order to rise to the challenge. However, the goal of changing the culture is dead on arrival unless and until the leader engages in the necessary and personal soul work. Therefore, the question confronts us: What is the leader's soul work?

First, leaders must deal with the perspective, emotions, and motives that challenge their self-understanding and confidence. When facing a new assignment or a major change, it is not simply the organization that is shaken but the leader as well. As a leader, you may experience a sense of loss of control and feelings of inability or even helplessness. You can deal with these feelings or bury them. If you bury them, your personal and professional life suffer. When you do not deal with the harsh emotions of leadership, the organization suffers. Instead of burying your feelings: 1) trace them back to their origins as much as possible, 2) talk them out with a trusted mentor or advisor, and 3) turn them over to God with trust and confidence.

Second, the soul work of a leader requires learning to accept ambiguity and uncertainty. You do not know all you would like to know before you must make a decision. Your own opinion may be unclear and divided. You receive mixed messages and evasive responses from others. The situation becomes personal. Not everyone likes you or your decision. Others measure your choice with shifting scales that are often unjust. An old mountain woman revealed the secret of her inner strength: "When there is trouble all around me, I make sure it doesn't get in me." In leadership, things never really settle down. The calm signals a new storm. Dealing with the storm of ambiguity and uncertainty requires the inner work of searching for greater purpose rather than simply solving problems. You will be tempted to calm the storm by applying the easiest solution. You need inner strength to envision a larger and better purpose.

Finally, it is essential to the soul work of a leader to sort out relationships in ways that are genuine and appropriate. Much of the work of leadership is motivating, influencing, and persuading others. It is all about relationships. Leaders deal with toxic people, professional people, authentic people, broken people, eager people, lethargic people, etc. The challenge of relationships is complicated by the fact that relationships change, at times without warning. The facts are clear: the hard part of leadership involves the soft skills. Dealing with people is wearisome. The soul work of relationships can be stated clearly: To manage relationships, you must manage your inner life. You will invest hours analyzing the emotions, perspectives, and motivations of others. Your work must also include self-analysis and awareness. Face your own inner life and bring it under the good judgment, compassion, and cleansing of God.

As a leader, you need 1) a pattern of spiritual practice that provides perspective, 2) a plan of self-care that rejuvenates your energy, and 3) a few deep and trusted friends outside your work with whom you can be free of the role of leader. I (Richard) have worked with many leaders in business and the church as they develop their own patterns of prayer, personal care, and supportive relationships. This is a deeply personal process. However, the process itself is simply assessment and action. What are you doing now? What can you do to improve? Let me provide a few examples. I know one leader who will not take his first bite of food in the morning until he has fed his soul. The leader of a large organization keeps her date at the gym religiously. Across the years, I have found that a group of close friends outside the work setting is essential for a balanced life. If you want a place to begin, practice Psalm 46:10, "Be still, and know that I am God."

The Number One Leadership Hang-up

In his recent book on leadership, *The Top Ten Mistakes Leaders Make*, Dr. Hans Finzel suggests that "the number one leadership hang-up" is the "top-down attitude," which he defines simply as "top-down autocratic arrogance."[20] He writes:

> You would think people would have learned by now. Yet it still keeps cropping up, that age old problem of domineering, autocratic, top-down leadership. Of all the sins of poor leadership, none is greater and none is still committed more often, generation after generation.[21]

The autocratic leader follows a military model of leadership, barking orders to those he perceives as "weak underlings." I (Ralph) pastored a church for a number of years that was governed by a board of elders. Although all of the elders were supposed to have equal input and authority, one was regarded as the unofficial "chief." He had a very strong personality. He frequently expressed, "It's my way, or the highway." Dr. Finzel suggests that, if you have this approach, "it will spread to everything your leadership hands touch."[22] In the case of this elder, it was certainly true. In the years I knew him, he went through a series of wives who would not tolerate his autocratic approach to marriage!

In his book *Somebodies and Nobodies: Overcoming the Abuse of Rank*, Robert Fuller writes about the tendency toward autocratic, top-down leadership and the problems it creates. As we noted earlier, Fuller coins the term "rankism," by which he refers to the tendency to see yourself as either superior or inferior to someone else. Rankism produces far-reaching and adverse effects in all relationships. Fuller explains:

> . . . interpersonal abuse in the context of a difference of rank is antithetical to reciprocity, mutuality, and equality. It is meant to demean, to exploit, to wound, to harm, and to damage—and it does. No wonder that under assault we are wary and withdrawn, not open-minded and generous. Even when not deliberately malicious, rank abuse can still warp our interactions.[23]

Indeed, most of us have experienced this "rankism." "Sooner or later," Fuller writes, "everyone gets taken for a nobody. Sooner or later, most of us treat someone else as a nobody. It always hurts to be 'dissed,' no matter what your status."[24] The far-reaching effects of rankism pervade every aspect of life: "Rankism erodes the will to learn, distorts personal relationships, taxes economic productivity, and stokes ethnic hatred. It is the cause of dysfunctionality, and sometimes even violence, in families, schools, and the workplace."[25]

It is important to note that power or rank differences are not, in and of themselves, to blame. These differences are as natural and necessary as differences in color or gender. "Difficulties arise only when these differences are used as an excuse to abuse, humiliate, exploit, and subjugate" other people.[26] Unfortunately, while racists and sexists are now "on notice," and can no longer blatantly mistreat others, "rankists" often go largely unchallenged. There seem to be many reasons that rankism continues to be tolerated in organizations today, including the fact that it is traditional. It has simply been the most commonly practiced form of leadership. In addition, it is much easier to simply tell people what to do than to work on implementing leadership techniques that require personal growth. Finally, autocratic leadership comes naturally, and it simply reflects the depravity of humankind.[27] For these and other reasons rankism is oftentimes tolerated or overlooked in the workplace, and those who get their feelings hurt are told to "toughen up," that they need to be "thick-skinned" to work in their respective field, or some other such sage advice that diverts blame from the abuser onto the abused.

This mistreatment of others, however, is often something like a time bomb ticking in the midst of our institutions, organizations, and even in the larger society. People cannot receive maltreatment indefinitely without adverse effects eventually manifesting themselves. Fuller explains the ripple effect of rankism:

> The consequences range from school shootings to revanchism, even to genocide. The twentieth century has seen many demagogues who have promised to restore the pride and dignity of a people that felt nobodied. Hitler enjoyed the support of Germans

humiliated by punitive reparations in the aftermath of World War I. The national impotence imposed on the German nation (the Fatherland) by the victors reverberated through every German family, as well. In opting for Hitler, many Germans were not only voting to restore rank to the Fatherland, but also to overcome the sense of inadequacy they had experienced as the heads of German families. Similarly, President Milosevic of Yugoslavia traded on the wounded pride of Serbs in the 1990s. Once war begins, people will become apologists for crimes they would otherwise condemn to get even with those they believe have nobodied them.[28]

Group Discussion and Personal Reflection

Group Discussion

Part 1. From Relationships to Rankism

Saul began his career with solid relationships that founded his authority as king. He moved into rankism, touting his position as his authority. Review the chapter and trace the steps that led to the rankism of King Saul. How did Saul's perception of events, his handling of emotions, and his motives change to depend on rankism?

Part 2. Alternatives to Rankism

Dr. Finzel suggests several alternatives to "top-down" authority.[29] When is each one appropriate and when might it be inappropriate? Discuss which one best fits your style of leadership. Also, discuss which one is most unlike you.

a. *Participatory Leadership*—the practice of empowering subordinates to participate in decision-making. This practice came out of the Human Relations movement of the 1920s. Participatory leadership consists of inviting employees to share in decision making by gathering their ideas and opinions, and integrating their suggestions into the decision.[30]
   • In what circumstances would this approach be effective?
   • In what circumstances would this approach be ineffective?

b. *Facilitator Style*—the practice of Management by Wandering Around (MBWA) became popular in the 1980s. The leader is 1) a listener as a way of "being in touch," getting firsthand experience, and demonstrating care for subordinates and 2) a teacher and coach in the face-to-face transmission of values. These two roles support the leader as a facilitator; the leader provides direct help as a servant to subordinates and a protector from bureaucrats.[31]

- In what circumstances would this approach be effective?
- In what circumstances would this approach be ineffective?

c. *Democratic Leadership*—in a democratic group, the rank-and-file make decisions by vote. Making choices that directly affect them may be more highly motivating to employees. One form of a more democratic process is to involve employees in suggesting alternatives and envisioning consequences, while the final choice is left to a smaller group or the leader.[32]

- In what circumstances would this approach be effective?
- In what circumstances would this approach be ineffective?

d. *Servant Leadership*—Robert Greenleaf coined the phrase and defined it: "The servant-leader is servant first . . . it begins with the natural feeling that one wants to serve, to serve first. Then, conscious choice brings one to aspire to lead. That person is sharply different from the one who is leader first. The difference manifests itself in the care taken by the servant-first to make sure that other people's highest priority needs are being served. The best test, and difficult to administer, is: Do those served grow as people?"[33]

- In what circumstances would this approach be effective?
- In what circumstances would this approach be ineffective?

Personal Reflection

Assess

➤ I am a humble leader.

Always True   7   6   5   4   3   2   1   Never True

➤ I practice rankism as a leader.

> Always True 7 6 5 4 3 2 1 Never True

➤ I respect and trust my subordinates.

> Always True 7 6 5 4 3 2 1 Never True

➤ My subordinates respect and trust me.

> Always True 7 6 5 4 3 2 1 Never True

Analyze

➤ What tempts me to rely on rankism rather than work at building strong, professional relationships with my subordinates?

➤ What do I need to do right now to improve the professional relationship I have with my subordinates?

Act

___ Select and implement a style of shared leadership for a specific decision or duration of time. (Choose from the list above.)

___ Name a situation that tempts you to rely on rankism rather than to maintain a humble heart as a leader.

___ Read and pray Romans 12:3–5, *For by the grace given me I say to every one of you: Do not think of yourself more highly than you ought, but rather think of yourself with sober judgment, in accordance with the measure of faith God has given you. Just as each of us has one body with many members, and these members do not all have the same function, so in Christ we who are many form one body, and each member belongs to all the others.*

Chapter 4

Saul Failed to Break Out of His Tendency to Isolate Himself

Niccolo Machiavelli, the political philosopher who described the evil deeds that leaders do, also provided a wise word that King Saul certainly could have used:

> A good and wise prince, desirous of maintaining their charac-
> ter, and to avoid giving the opportunity to his sons to become
> oppressive, will never build fortresses, so that they may place
> their reliance upon the good will of their subjects, and not upon
> the strength of citadels.[1]

It is no wonder that leaders are tempted to build citadels of isolation. Leading places you in a dangerous position. As a leader, it is your task to challenge values, the way things are done, and the comfort zones of others. Leadership comes with critiques and critics. The temptation to isolate yourself is compounded when you experience loss and setbacks (also part of leadership). Surrounding yourself with yea-sayers, morale boosters, and pleasant distractions is appealing. It is also dangerous.

When you lose contact with people and seek security in isolation, it is almost certain that trouble is brewing. Take for example the Swedish study[2] on the need for social and emotional contact as a lesson for leaders. A total of 752 men born in 1933 in the city of Göteborg were offered a medical exam. Descriptions of each man's life stress was collected and catalogued.

Seven years later, the men were contacted again, and forty-one of the men had died. The men who had reported intense emotional stress (common in leadership) had a death rate three times greater than those who said that their lives were calm and peaceful. The emotional distress was due to financial trouble, insecurity at work, being forced out of a job, being the object of legal action (all too common in leadership today), or going through a divorce. These men had high blood pressure, concentrations of triglycerides in the blood, or high cholesterol levels. That's the bad news.

Here is the good news. For men who said they had a dependable web of intimacy—wife, close friends, and such—there was no relationship whatever between high stress levels and death rate. People to turn to, talk with, and offer solace, help, and counsel protected them from the harshness and ordeals of life. For the man or woman who leads, have an ear to hear. Leaders need good counsel, honest talk, and respectful critique.

Saul Escapes into Isolation

In chapter 1, we saw how Saul deteriorated to a point at which he lost all ability to exercise restraint in his abuse of power and slaughtered eighty-five priests at a sanctuary in Nob (1 Sam. 22:18–19). However, one priest, a man named Abiathar, escaped. He fled to David, who was living in exile in the wilderness. David had already acquired the loyalty of a prophet named Gad, but he welcomed Abiathar into his camp, and the man of God performed priestly functions for David for the rest of his life.[3]

The contrast between David and Saul could not be more pronounced. David was the recipient of the guidance and protection of God via Gad and Abiathar, while Saul, on the other hand, who was enthroned in Gibeah, remained isolated in paranoia and jealousy. Barbara Green notes that, though Saul was scrambling to find out where David was hiding, every action he took alienated him from those who might have given him information.

> . . . The slaughter does not undo the failure to which it reacts. Saul has compounded his isolation from God by closing down priestly inquiry and allowing a lone survivor to escape into the camp of David. Saul's action here, whatever else must be said about it, is counterproductive. What he most needs—information—he drives off; what he most fears—disloyalty—he invites. Saul becomes ever more isolated in his quest to get the information he needs.[4]

Saul's approach to securing his throne and protecting it from those who might be disloyal to him was self-defeating. Because he sought to maintain an autocratic rule, he pushed away those who might have been loyal to him. In essence, through his oppressive, top-down rule, Saul sabotaged his own leadership.

Saul's self-defeating behaviors caused him to be more and more isolated. Instead of trying to break out of his isolation, Saul fostered it. Adopting a posture of defensiveness, he chose a seat with his back to the wall, which the text says became his "usual place" (1 Sam. 20:25 NLT).

King Saul's forty years of autocratic, top-down leadership, his failure to consult with his spiritual counselors (priests and prophets), his refusal to heed the advice of those closest to him, and his insistence that he alone would make the decisions for the nation ultimately drove all those who had been loyal to him away from him.

Leaders cannot lead with their backs to the wall, afraid of anyone and everyone. The Bible has a great deal of clear teaching on the fact that successful leaders are those who surround themselves with "an abundance of counselors" (Prov. 11:14 NRSV). This idea, which we will look at further below, is taught repeatedly and illustrated with examples, showing how a leader can capitalize on the wisdom of his or her associates to create scenarios in which everyone wins.

Roots of Saul's Tendency Toward Isolation

There were many factors that contributed to Saul's tendency toward isolation. These factors contributed to Saul's initial leadership problems, but they also perpetuated them throughout his reign.

Fear of Being Challenged

One of Saul's problems was that he was not willing to be personally challenged by those closest to him. Henry and Richard Blackaby note that "being criticized, second-guessed, and having one's motives questioned are unpleasant but inevitable aspects of leadership."[5] And, according to the Scriptures, the only way we can be certain our map of reality is valid is to expose it to the criticism of other "mapmakers." Otherwise, we live in a closed system, only exposed to our own ideas, unable to grow. Many proverbs teach about the value of openness:

- "Iron sharpens iron, and one person sharpens the wits of another" (Prov. 27:17 NRSV). Constructive criticism between friends develops character.

- "Well meant are the wounds a friend inflicts, but profuse are the kisses of an enemy" (Prov. 27:6 NRSV). In other words, reproof given in love is better than insincere expressions of affection. The wounds of a friend can be trusted because they're meant to correct. But an enemy's kisses are deceptive, even though they may be many. Think of the kiss of Judas.

- Proverbs 25:12 says, "Like an earring of gold or an ornament of fine gold is a wise man's rebuke to a listening ear." A wise rebuke that is properly received is of lasting value. The rebuke is compared to ornamental jewelry—like jewelry that decorates a person's appearance, these rebukes are pleasing and complimentary. The rebuke is received by a "listening ear," which means the person is obedient to the rebuke.

- "In an abundance of counselors there is safety" (Prov. 11:14 NRSV).

- "In abundance of counselors there is victory" (Prov. 24:6 NRSV).

- "Do not be wise in your own eyes" (Prov. 3:7 NRSV).

- "Whoever walks with the wise becomes wise" (Prov. 13:20 NRSV).

- "But with many advisers they succeed" (Prov. 15:22 NRSV).

Contrary to popular American thought, the book of Proverbs teaches that wisdom is found in healthy relationships rather than individual insight. Leadership wisdom is a team sport. Team members spar with one another, challenge each other's weaknesses, and build on each other's strengths. In the same way, a wise leader needs, creates, and nurtures trusted advisers.

The same is true in life and leadership, and Proverbs teaches that wise people will seek out criticism. They will seek out counsel and feedback on what they are doing in their lives.

Rebuke a wise man and he will love you.
Instruct a wise man and he will be wiser still;
>   teach a righteous man and he will add to his learning.
The fear of the LORD is the beginning of wisdom,
>   and knowledge of the Holy One is understanding.
For through me your days will be many,
>   and years will be added to your life. (Prov. 9:8b–11)

The wise person will love the one who is trying to correct him. In the final analysis, those who fear the Lord, add to their learning, and receive discipline will look forward to a long and productive life.

Organizations and their leaders, therefore, must be open to those who would ask hard questions of us, challenge our preconceptions, and reevaluate the way we do things. In regard to the church, James Thompson writes:

> I am convinced that a healthy church will have vigorous discussion—even debate—as it meets the challenge of change. Vigorous debate, if it is conducted without rancor and within the context of a search for truth, may help us clarify the important issues of our time. The ultimate question that will frame the discussion will involve the goal which Paul sought for his church: "That the aim of our charge is love that issues from a pure heart and a good conscience and sincere faith" (1 Tim. 1:5).[6]

The natural tendency—whether among leaders or followers—is to avoid those who might challenge our thinking. But just because something is natural does not mean that it is good. It is natural for babies to go to the bathroom in their pants, or to never brush their teeth! And yet, adults try to teach them to do the unnatural until the unnatural becomes second nature.

Leaders must embrace the challenging of their conceptions, seeing this as God's design for growth.

Fear of Being Honest and Open

Saul's inability to receive counsel from those close to him seems to have come from deep-rooted insecurities. He seems to have had a fundamental difficulty being honest and open, both with himself and with others. The Proverbs devote much attention to the human difficulty of being honest with ourselves and others. Proverbs 13:7 says, "One man pretends to be rich, yet has nothing; another pretends to be poor, yet has great wealth." While this proverb may seem enigmatic, it is simply saying that people may not be what they seem to be. Some who are poor pretend to be rich, maybe to save face. Others who are rich may pretend to be poor, maybe to conceal wealth and avoid responsibility. The proverb seems to instruct that people should be honest and unpretentious. Acting is not the way to real relationship.

Proverbs 21:29 talks about the genuineness that righteous people try to implement in their own lives:

> A wicked man puts up a bold front,
>> but an upright man gives thought to his ways.

The wicked man, the person who engages in unhealthy or destructive behavior, "puts up a bold front." He is not able to be himself with other people—he puts up a front or builds a wall, as it were. John Powell explains some of the rationale for this unhealthy behavior:

> Rather than expose a self which we imagine to be inadequate or ugly, we instinctively build walls . . . . To the extent that we experience scars of anxiety, guilt and inferiority feelings, we are tempted to wear masks, to act roles. We do not trust or accept ourselves in order to be ourselves. These walls and masks are measures of self-defense, and we will live behind our walls and wear our masks as long as they are needed.[7]

Robert Frost wrote a wonderful poem called "Mending Walls" that is an analogy for the wall-building we do in our own lives and relationships. He writes:

> Something is there that doesn't love a wall,
> That sends the frozen ground-swell under it,
> And spills the upper boulders in the sun;

And makes gaps even two can pass abreast.
. . . No one has seen them made or heard them made,
But at Spring mending-time we find them there.[8]

As he reflects on the human tendency towards wall-building, Frost urges himself that next time,

Before I built a wall I'd ask to know,
What I was walling in or walling out.[9]

Who are you, as a leader, walling in or walling out when you put up fronts? The book of Proverbs teaches that the wicked man or woman—the person who is not yet guided by righteousness— throws up walls with no thought as to how it will affect his or her relationships. The upright person, on the other hand, gives thought to his or her ways. That is, he thinks about how his pretensions will affect his relationships, and so he seeks to be honest in those relationships. John Powell warns us about building these walls or putting up these facades, explaining:

> While it may seem to be a safer life behind these facades, it is also a lonely life. We cease to be authentic, and as persons we starve to death. The deepest sadness of the mask is, however, that we have cut ourselves off from all genuine and authentic contact with the real world and with other human beings who hold our potential maturity and fulfillment in their hands. When we resort to acting our roles or wearing masks there is no possibility of human and personal growth. We are simply not being ourselves, and we cannot emerge in an atmosphere of growth. When the curtain drops after our performance we will remain the same immature person that we were when the curtain went up at the beginning of the act.[10]

Unfortunately, Saul is an example of a leader who, when the curtain dropped after his performance, found himself totally isolated from friends, family, trusted advisors, and even God. The upright person who wants to be a successful leader will live in genuine relationship with other people by seeking to tear down walls, lower his guard, and let go of his pretensions in relationships.

The Dangerous Retreat into Isolation

In practical terms, how does a leader retreat into isolation? The leader creates organizational or psychological structures that provide insulation from the burdensome task of leading. Organizationally, the leader might create levels of bureaucrats and gatekeepers that isolate the leader from people. Or, the leader might organize extended, frequent, and irresponsible time away from the organization. Psychologically, the leader may use emotional outbursts and intimidation to keep people at a distance, display a lack of engagement or passion that frustrates others, or retreat into survival mentality and protectionism. However, how a leader isolates him- or herself is not as significant as the key events that produce the temptation to retreat into a citadel.

Isolation begins when you, the leader, deny the threats and problems that are settling in around you. The two paths to isolation are arrogance and despair. Arrogance and despair may look like opposites, but they have this in common: they deny, avoid, and refuse to deal with the issues. Leaders in isolation refuse to deal with the truth about their situation and the truth about themselves.

Every leader experiences loss, setbacks, criticism, and attacks. You become isolated when you refuse to talk about it, when you stop communicating. You are moving into dangerous territory when you catch yourself doing these things: you avoid dealing with the issue, you retreat into secrecy and seclusion, or you start looking for scapegoats to blame for every problem. If you are doing one or more of these things, then indeed, like King Saul, you are on the verge of making self-destruction a lifetime habit. Here are the signs[11] of a leader who is retreating into isolation:

1. You stop talking about the difficult issues and problems.
2. You increase your criticism and blame of others in order to avoid dealing with yourself.
3. You lose respect for other people and believe that you are surrounded by incompetence and laziness.
4. You start to sequester yourself because you are avoiding the people and situations that might make you face yourself.

5. Your focus becomes self-centered with self-interest and survival as your primary goals.

6. You start to hoard your assets, play favorites, and set up a "me—them" mentality.

7. You are paralyzed by fear and find that you are not taking any action to change the situation.

8. You lower your goals, give up on your dreams, and look for satisfaction in other places (often in unhealthy places and ways).

9. Your negativity infects everyone else at work and at home.

It is possible to step out of isolation and back into the center of things. However, there is a difficult issue you should be aware of as you leave your fortress of isolation. There are some people who supported you in your isolation because they gained influence or rewards by keeping you away from other people. These folks feel like trusted allies. However, they may turn against you when you step back into the world of listening to and leading through a wider range of people.

Stepping out of isolation requires that you enact three principles in your own life:

1. Face facts. It takes straight talk about problems and expectations. Find the courage to take responsibility for the problems. Be accountable.

2. Work with others. Learn from others, team with others, and find positive energy in working with others. Be collaborative and seek wise counsel.

3. Take positive action. Scuttle the victim mentality. Focus on what you can do to make a positive difference. Focus on what you can do rather than what you cannot do.

King Saul was never able to pry himself out of his protective isolation. It ended badly. You can choose another path. The way out of isolation is dialogue. You must open up, talk, listen, and be authentic. Here is a bit of wisdom:

Listen to advice and accept instruction,
    and in the end you will be wise. (Prov. 19:20)

Through reengaging with a wider group of people, you shoulder the more responsible duties of a leader, which are personal accountability, professional collaboration, and positive initiative.

Group Discussion and Personal Reflection

Group Discussion

1. Review the chapter and find the ideas or concepts you found a) most helpful, and b) most troubling. Why were these ideas helpful or troubling to you?

2. Recall a time in your life when you struggled with the temptation to isolate yourself as a leader. What happened? What did you learn from it?

3. The chapter is filled with proverbs. Find two proverbs cited in the chapter that are particularly poignant for you at this time.

4. Saul went into isolation because of a fear of being challenged and a fear of being honest and open. What other reasons might have driven Saul (or might drive other leaders) into isolation?

5. Leaders must avoid isolation. However, leaders need solitude from time to time. What is the difference between isolation and solitude? How can you protect yourself from using the need for solitude as a cover-up for escaping into isolation?

Personal Reflection

Assess

Rate each statement as it applies to your past tendency to isolate and your current isolating behavior.

5 = regularly 4 = often 3 = occasionally 2 = seldom 1 = never

Past	Today	
_____	_____	I stop talking about the difficult issues and problems.
_____	_____	I increase my criticism and blame of others in order to avoid dealing with myself.
_____	_____	I lose respect for other people and believe that I am surrounded by incompetence and laziness.
_____	_____	I sequester myself to avoid the people and situations that might make me face myself.
_____	_____	My focus becomes self-centered with self-interest and survival as my primary goals.
_____	_____	I hoard my assets, play favorites, and set up a "me—them" mentality.
_____	_____	I am paralyzed by fear and find that I am not taking any action to change the situation.
_____	_____	I lower my goals, give up on my dreams, and look for satisfaction in other places (often in unhealthy places and ways).
_____	_____	My negativity infects everyone else at work and at home.
_____	_____	TOTAL

Analyze

1. What does your score tell you about yourself?
2. What has caused you to seek isolation in the past?
3. How do you meet your need for solitude without moving into isolation?

Act

___ *Personal Accountability*—create your accountability system for staying engaged and inclusive in seeking the counsel and advice of critics and admirers.

___ *Professional Collaboration*—list three people you need to counsel with at this time and initiate a meeting with each one.

___ *Positive Action*—list and implement two actions that will increase your engagement with groups that you have a tendency to avoid or ignore.

Chapter 5

Saul Failed to Think
Before He Spoke

If you have been in leadership long, you know how important your words are. Leaders—especially those who speak publicly—are held accountable for each and every word. Speaking impulsively is one of the greatest pitfalls of leadership, especially for those new to leadership. The author of the book of Proverbs wrote, "Do you see someone who is hasty in speech? There is more hope for a fool than for anyone like that" (Prov. 29:20 NRSV). It appears King Saul often spoke rashly, without thinking through the effects his words might have, thereby alienating friends, family, and supporters. By speaking impulsively, Saul sabotaged his own leadership.

Saul's Rash Speech and Actions

Saul began his reign with what seemed to be a great deal of humility and only slid into self-defeating patterns over time. His speech exhibited the same sort of gradual decline. Initially, in fact, Saul showed great forethought in the way he responded to the efforts of his supporters who encouraged him to vengeful actions early in his reign. The battle into which Saul led his troops was against the Ammonites, who had invaded Jabesh Gilead, an Israelite town east of the Jordan River, and Saul secured a smashing victory (1 Sam. 11:1–15). After having begun to fight early in the morning, the Israelites fought "until the heat of the day; and those who survived were scattered, so that no two of them were left together" (v. 11 NRSV). When Saul's victory had been secured, his supporters suggested this would be a good opportunity to put to death any and all those Israelites who had initially opposed his selection as king of Israel. There had been a number of people who had insultingly

55

asked, "How can this man save us?" (1 Sam. 10:27 NRSV). The text says that these "worthless fellows" "despised" Saul and "brought him no present." When the people, following his victory over the Ammonites, urged Saul to have them put to death, he responded to this invitation to exercise vengeance with carefully and wisely chosen words: "No one shall be put to death this day, for today the LORD has brought deliverance to Israel" (v. 13 NRSV).

The words of Saul in this instance are very significant for several reasons. Saul was Israel's first king and, as such, he had been anointed by the prophet Samuel for the role. The term *anointed one* would come to have tremendous significance in later Judaism and in Christianity in its untranslated form, *Messiah*. Saul had been chosen to be Yahweh's anointed one, and the Spirit of God had been poured out upon him when he heard that the Ammonites had invaded Jabesh Gilead, but his role as king had not yet been confirmed in battle. His spectacular victory over the Ammonites provided that confirmation and, when the fighting was over, those who had initially opposed him found themselves in mortal danger. Since Saul was the Lord's anointed, then by questioning his ability to save, they were implicitly slandering Yahweh.[1] As king, Saul had a right to carry out judgment against them.

Saul's response, however, demonstrates "not only his magnanimity, but also his genuine piety."[2] This becomes clear when one glances back over the entire episode, which began with the inhabitants of Jabesh Gilead expressing their need to have someone "rescue" them (1 Sam 11:3). Once Saul had mustered his troops, he sent word to the inhabitants of the oppressed city that "tomorrow, by the time the sun is hot, you shall have deliverance" (v. 9 NRSV). And then, once the battle had been won, he announced, "No one shall be put to death this day, for today the LORD has brought deliverance to Israel" (v. 13 NRSV). Even though Saul had led the battle against the Ammonites, he insisted that it was Yahweh who had really brought the day's victory and that he himself did not have any special prowess. This incident is very significant because it shows how Saul carefully chose his words to shape the people's perception of him and his leadership in relation to God and his role as Israel's true king and deliverer. Saul's words pointed the people to a generous understanding of leadership, and they identified

Yahweh as the basis for such generosity. Saul's generous words of forgiveness demonstrated that he possessed the leadership qualities that were necessary for serving as Israel's king, and prompted Samuel to call the meeting at Gilgal (v. 14) at which Saul was confirmed as king.

As discussed in chapter 3, in a later battle with the Philistines, Saul foolishly bound his troops to an oath of abstaining from food for the entire day of the battle (1 Sam. 14:24–30). Whatever his motivation in making the oath, he did not think about the effects it would have during a time when his soldiers would need their strength. So, whether his motivation was good or bad, it had negative results—his soldiers became "faint" (v. 28) and "exhausted" (v. 31). Not only that, but it almost resulted in the death of his son, who violated the oath out of ignorance (v. 27). The foolishness of Saul's rash oath was so clear that even his troops ignored his order for them to execute Jonathan (v. 45).

On another occasion, later in his reign, we see Saul explode in foul-mouthed rage. After Saul had set himself against his son-in-law, David, and determined to kill him, the young harp player convinced Jonathan to see how Saul would react if he, David, were to skip a special religious feast that was about to occur (1 Sam. 20:1–5). David told Jonathan that, when Saul asked about David's absence, he should tell him that David needed to go to his own hometown for a family sacrifice in order to test his reaction (v. 6). The next day, David skipped the festival, as planned. When David did not appear on the first day of the festival, Saul assumed he surely had a good excuse (such as ritual uncleanness). But when his seat was empty on the second day, Saul naturally wanted to know why. When Jonathan offered Saul the fabricated reason for David's absence, Saul became violently angry, just as David had feared (v. 7). King Saul exploded in what Old Testament commentator Hans Wilhelm Hertzberg called "foul-mouthed anger,"[3] which the NIV renders: "You son of a perverse and rebellious woman!" (v. 30). Some of the more recent translations capture the explicit insult intended in the original, such as the New Living Translation's "You stupid son of a whore!" and the New Jerusalem Bible's "Son of a rebellious slut!" However it is translated, this is clearly "the standard insult-your-enemy's-mother curse found in many cultures."[4]

We do not include these translations to be crass, but to make the point that Saul was out of control here in terms of his speech.

Saul went on to lambast Jonathan's friendship with David, shouting that this was "to your own shame, and to the shame of your mother's nakedness" (v. 30 NRSV). In the original language, the word *nakedness* is sometimes a euphemism for *genitals*. Saul is literally saying that Jonathan is a shame to his mother's genitals. This may be a way of saying that Jonathan was a mistake from the start,[5] or that Jonathan may not be his son,[6] or that he was a shame from the moment of his birth.[7] Regardless of exactly what Saul meant by his lewd outburst, our point is that such rash and uncontrolled speech must have had a powerful and indelible impact on Jonathan.

The Importance of Communication

Communication is so important. All social relationships in our lives depend on it: marriage, friendships, church relationships, and even business relationships. So many things can affect what we communicate when we talk or write: our facial expression, our tone of voice, whether or not we make eye contact, and especially the words we use. I (Ralph) once heard a story that illustrated how confusion about the meaning of a single word can affect an entire conversation. An English schoolteacher was looking for rooms in Switzerland. She called on the local schoolmaster to help her find a suitable apartment. A room was found, and she went back to London to get her things. She remembered that she had not noticed a bathroom or, as they call it in England, a "W.C.," or "Water Closet." She wrote to the schoolmaster and asked if there was a W.C. in or near the apartment. The Swedish schoolmaster was not familiar with this English expression, was puzzled by the W.C., and never dreamed that she was talking about a bathroom. He finally sought advice from a local minister. They decided that by W.C. she must be referring to a Wayside Chapel. So, a few days later the lady got the following letter from the schoolmaster:

Dear Madam:
   The W.C. is located 9 miles from the house, in the heart of a beautiful grove of trees. It will seat 150 people at a time, and is open on Tuesdays, Thursdays, and Sundays.

Some people bring their lunch and make a day of it. On Thursdays there is an organ accompaniment. The acoustics are very good. It may interest you to know that my daughter met her husband at the W.C. We are now in the process of taking donations to purchase plush seats. We feel that this is a long-felt need.

My wife, being rather delicate, hasn't been able to attend regularly. It's been six months since she last went. Naturally, it pains her to not be able to go more often.

I will close now with the desire to accommodate you in every way possible, and will be very happy to save you a seat either down front or near the door, as you prefer.

We can certainly see here the importance of communication—or miscommunication!

A friend and colleague, a professor of communication, asked me (Richard) to substitute for him in his Communication Foundation class. I know the art of communication, but I am not a scholar in the academic discipline of communication theory. What could I offer? "Tell them your process for creating a speech: how you find ideas, how you determine a purpose, how you size up the audience, how you organize your thoughts, etc.," he requested.

I agreed, but I wanted to learn something from him in return. I told him I would teach the class, but I asked him for one thing first: "Summarize your understanding of communication theory in a way that even I can understand it and remember it."

He gave me an answer. I share it with you. Communication takes place at three levels. You can think of it as bowling, ping-pong, and chess.

- *Bowling* is one-way communication. It is a useful form of communication for getting an idea on the table, for presenting a program, or for giving a report. In one-way communication, you answer the question, "What is this about?" Sadly and ineffectively, some leaders think this is leadership communication. It is a part, but only a small part.

- *Ping-pong* is two-way communication. This is a simple Q&A or a top-down conversation when the leader clears up misunderstandings, sharpens the discussion, or provides individualized reasoning and motivation. The leader answers the question, "What does this mean?" For leaders, playing a good game of communication ping-pong requires listening skills. You must stop thinking about what you are going to say next and listen to what someone is saying to you. This is a larger part of communication for leaders. Yet, there is more.

- *Chess* is a negotiating process of communication. A chess player makes a move. The other player then makes a move. They negotiate positions and outcomes. In leadership, much communication is chess. For the leader, this requires self-control. When is it best to bite your tongue? When is it best to lay your cards on the table? In the chess match of communication, everyone is dealing with the question, "What does this mean for me?" This is the level of motivation and influence.

There are two more steps in the communication challenge for leaders. They come after the games of communication—bowling, ping-pong, and chess. These steps take place when the leader is out of the room. People ask each other, "What do you think about this?" They compare notes, discuss the issues, and make value decisions. Finally, individually or in small groups, people come to a final question, "What part of this will I accept?" The way people answer to this question is what the leader must deal with in order to lead effectively.

Often leaders are frustrated with the communication process for two reasons: 1) it takes longer than the leader wishes, and 2) some of it is beyond the control of the leader. This frustration can lead to pent-up emotions, suspicion, and disgust. Saul exploded. He lost his "cool." Under the pressure of frustration, the temptation for leaders is to force the issue, give directives louder and longer, or intimidate and coerce.

Chris Argyris, a leadership expert on faculty at Harvard, outlines two types of communication styles. He calls them Theory 1 and Theory 2.[8] Theory 1 is the most tempting for leaders to use in their efforts to communicate. This approach to communication has the following characteristics:

- Strive to stay in control of the situation and outcome.
- Minimize losing and maximize winning.

- Stifle all expressions of negative feeling from others.
- Seek to look rational while you are doing all this.

There is another approach to communication, Theory 2. This theory is not the opposite of Theory 1 but follows another strategy.

- Strive to maintain mutual trust and respect.
- Work with valid information.
- Provide free and informed choice.
- Ask for internal commitment.

You can see the difference between the two models. However, the challenge is that for leaders, when under frustration, pressure, and conflict, it is tempting to retreat to Theory 1. Moreover, when a leader operates out of Theory 1, it seems that things are going well. There is no negative talk (that winds its way to the leader's ear). The leader's agenda is moving forward (at least people make it look that way). The leader feels in control (since what is out of control is out of sight). Finally, the leader looks rational and competent (in his or her own eyes).

Communicating within the scope of Theory 2 is difficult. It requires more than reason. It takes emotional wisdom. Emotional foolishness is the source of outbursts, tirades, and harmful communication. Emotional wisdom calls for self-control and awareness of the emotional state of others. Let me explain this difference using the academic language of the great professor, Chris Argyris:

> To the extent that individuals dedicate themselves to the value of rationality and "getting the job done," they will tend to be aware of and emphasize the rational, intellective aspects of the interactions that exist in an organization and suppress the interpersonal and emotional aspects, especially those that do not seem to be relevant to achieving the task. . . . As the interpersonal and emotional aspects of behavior become suppressed, we may hypothesize that an organizational norm will tend to arise that coerces individuals to hide their feelings. . . . Under these conditions, we may hypothesize that the individuals will find it very difficult to develop competence in dealing with feelings

and interpersonal relationships. . . . As the degree of openness decreases, the capacity to experiment will tend to decrease, and the fear to take risks will tend to increase.[9]

Here is the bottom line: communication is rational and emotional. Leaders must deal with the rational and emotional dynamics of good communication. To do so, leaders must face and control their own rational and emotional capacities. Good communication is born out of emotional wisdom.

Biblical Wisdom for Taming the Tongue

The book of Proverbs teaches us how important speech is for our relationships. Proverbs 14:3 says:

> A fool's talk brings a rod to his back,
>   but the lips of the wise protect them.

This proverb teaches that what people say has a great bearing on how they are received. The fool's conversation brings punishment, while the speech of the righteous brings safety. What a person says can bring either healing or harm, as Proverbs 15:4 teaches:

> The tongue that brings healing is a tree of life,
>   but a deceitful tongue crushes the spirit.

The image of the "tree of life" brings to mind Genesis 1 and the tree in the midst of the garden of Eden. Healing, truthful words, the writer is telling his readers, are a source of vitality to others. Speech can even affect the larger society, above and beyond our personal relationships. Proverbs 11:11 explains:

> Through the blessing of the upright a city is exalted,
>   but by the mouth of the wicked it is destroyed.

Words can have powerful social effects. The "blessing of the upright" here consists of beneficent words and deeds that bring enrichment to a community. But the words of the wicked have a disastrous effect on society, endangering, weakening, and ruining it with demoralizing, slanderous, and malicious criticism.

The book of Proverbs sees speech as falling into two broad categories—positive speech and negative speech. There are plenty of examples of negative speech in the Proverbs.

Negative Speech

1. Gossiping

In Proverbs 16:28 readers are told:

A perverse man stirs up dissension,
     and a gossip separates close friends.

Slanderers and gossips cause divisions. This kind of person will destroy close friendships by what he says. In another place, we are told that wicked people actually find destructive speech appealing!

A wicked man listens to evil lips;
     a liar pays attention to a malicious tongue. (Prov. 17:4)

Wicked people are drawn to destructive speech; they are attracted by it. The two lines of this particular proverb show that those who listen to malicious talk are, in fact, malicious themselves.

Leaders should easily see the value in this simple wisdom. Gossip can spread quickly throughout an organization, stirring up dissension and driving a wedge between people. When leaders become aware that gossip is circulating, they should do what they can to put the quietus on it. This may require talking with those who are involved in spreading the gossip. In general, leaders should set an example of refusing to criticize, condemn, or complain.

2. Starting Arguments

Some kinds of speech invite trouble. Proverbs 18:6 indicates:

A fool's lips bring him strife,
     and his mouth invites a beating.

Foolish people get themselves into trouble by what they say. The fool's speech brings him into controversies and, since he is wrong, he is punished. The original context of this proverb may have been a legal one, but it could certainly apply to all kinds of situations and relationships today. It is referring to someone who always sticks her foot in her mouth, offending people, causing controversy, running relationships "onto the rocks." It is almost as if she likes to start arguments. This is a negative kind of speech.

It seems that, for whatever reason, some people just like to argue. If a leader sees that he has this tendency of starting arguments, then he needs to work on eliminating this habit. Les Giblin, author of the classic *Skill With People*, proposed that the art of being agreeable is one of the most important steps one can take in human relations.[10] He suggests that the art of being agreeable has six parts: (1) learn to agree with people; (2) tell people when you agree with them; (3) do not tell people when you disagree with them unless it is absolutely necessary; (4) admit it when you are wrong; (5) refrain from arguing; and (6) handle those who want to argue by simply refusing to fight with them. Giblin's advice, originally written in 1968, may sound trite to some, but it is sound advice. Arguing is probably the poorest technique known in human relations, and nobody wins arguments or friends by arguing. Even when you are right, don't argue. It will only achieve negative results.

3. Undeserved Criticism with Its Lasting Effects

There is another kind of speech that the Proverbs call the "undeserved curse," which we might bring into colloquial English as "undeserved criticism." Proverbs vividly portrays this kind of speech as having ongoing, destructive effects.

> Like a fluttering sparrow or a darting swallow,
>   an undeserved curse does not come to rest. (Prov. 26:2)

The "undeserved curse" is simply an unkind word, some kind of negative statement or criticism. What this proverb is saying is that, although one might think critical words are not that significant, they cannot simply be taken back and forgotten once they have been spoken. "Like a fluttering sparrow or a darting swallow," this kind of negative speech does not simply "come to rest." Rather, it continues to hover in the air between the speaker and the one unduly criticized, just as a bird that cannot find roost.

This verse expresses the fact that words do not simply convey sound, but they actually transmit meaning. And since they transmit meaning, they have a powerful effect on reality.[11] Once they have been spoken, they cannot be unspoken; they have already been spoken and have had their effect. When Saul called his son Jonathan a "son of a perverse, rebellious woman" and said that his behavior was to his own shame and "to the shame of your mother's nakedness" (1 Sam. 20:30 NRSV), these words could not simply be taken back. They must have reinforced a deep-seated sense in Jonathan's mind and heart that Saul was no longer fit to be king and that, even though he was heir to the throne, a Saulide dynasty was not in the nation's best interests.

As a pastor, I (Ralph) have often been in meetings or counseling sessions in which two or more people have been arguing, and one will say something harsh that hurts another's feelings. The one who made this harsh statement will then often say, "Oh, just forget that I said that. I didn't mean it." But, as this proverb teaches, wounding words cannot be so easily forgotten. They have been spoken, and the effects of those words will remain for some time. We had better be careful what we say, the writer is saying, because our words have powerful, lasting effects. This advice is especially applicable to leaders, who are often in the position of addressing both individuals and groups. We must watch our words!

Positive Speech

The book of Proverbs gives a lot of attention to positive speech and relationship patterns as well. Proverbs 16:7 sums up well what the proverbs have to teach us about positive speech and relationships:

> When a man's ways are pleasing to the LORD,
>> he makes even his enemies live at peace with him.

This proverb teaches that a lifestyle pleasing to God disarms social hostility. Although speech certainly plays a part here, it is really the man's lifestyle that disarms the enemies. What is really being said here is that the righteous are able to get along with people, even their enemies. There are several types of speech—or ways of communicating—that foster positive human relations.

1. Small talk.

The pastorate often attracts introverts, especially in denominations that require an advanced degree for ordination. Men and women attracted to graduate study in theology and ministry are often those who are drawn to study, and who get excited by the idea of spending hours alone in the library or office. They may be happier alone with a book than with other people. When they enter the pastorate, these men and women struggle with having to greet visitors and socialize with strangers at city functions, weddings, funerals, community services, and maybe even potlucks at their own congregation. I cannot tell you how many times I have visited congregations while traveling and have entered the building, worshiped in the midst of the congregation, and left the building without being spoken to, not only by the pastor but by anyone at all. Our tendency is to talk with those with whom we already have a relationship and with whom we are comfortable.

Whether we are an introvert or an extrovert, we have all faced uncomfortable situations when we have had to go into a room full of strangers and have not known what to say to anyone. Many of us have grabbed a cup of coffee or punch in such situations, and found an isolated wall to lean against, away from the crowd, hence the term *wallflower.* And technology certainly has not helped in this area. Wallflowers see instant messaging and e-mail as a handy escape hatch from having to interact with others.

I (Ralph) am an introvert by nature, and I struggled with this early on in the pastorate. I made convenient excuses to not call on visitors, avoided public involvement, and spent hours in my office studying and preparing Sunday school lessons and sermons. I thought I was bad until my wife told me about an experience when she had to stop by another church on business. She was walking down a hallway, trying to find an office, when a pastor (identified by his collar) turned the corner at the other end of the hall and began walking toward her. She was relieved, thinking the pastor would greet her and ask her if he could help her. As the pastor approached, however, he did not make eye contact, and he continued walking until he had passed her and turned the next corner. This pastor was apparently so shy that he could not even welcome people who had come into his own church building looking for help. Not surprisingly, he was ultimately dismissed by his congregation and eventually left ministry altogether.

I was fortunate to have a mentor, Mike Beatty, a Georgia businessman and politician, who told me, "Kell (my middle name), you'll never make it in ministry or any other kind of leadership unless you learn to talk to people." Mike explained to me that not only are people skills necessary to successfully interact with people, but they are necessitated by biblical teaching, which values welcoming strangers (Matt. 25:43) and extending hospitality and kindness to them (Rom. 12:13; 1 Tim. 5:10; Heb. 13:2). He gave me three books that changed my life forever, and to which I attribute any success I have had: Frank Bettger's sales classic *How I Raised Myself from Failure to Success in Selling*, Dale Carnegie's *How to Win Friends and Influence People*, and Les Giblin's *How to Have Confidence and Power in Dealing with People*. These books helped me begin to develop the skills I needed to feel comfortable interacting with people.

Each of these books makes the case for the vital importance of small talk, which is the kind of conversation that happens between two people who don't know each other. Keith Ferrazzi, the founder and CEO of Ferrazzi Greenlight, insists that "small talk . . . is the most important talk we do."[12] The ability to make conversation with anyone in any situation is an essential quality of leadership. Every leader regularly finds him- or herself face-to-face with supervisors, colleagues, secretaries, customers, or parishioners. Every leader finds him- or herself in front of an audience, or at a dinner, or in a cab, where he or she needs to know how to talk with people.

But how do you do it? Les Giblin suggests that, when you talk with people, pick out the most interesting subject in the world to them to talk about. And what is the most interesting subject in the world to virtually every person you will encounter? The answer is, themselves![13] This may sound cynical, or like it is pandering to people's self-interests. However, we each live in a world of one, surrounded by others. Our whole experience in life revolves around our self. Self-centeredness and altruism are both developed in the context of the self. It makes sense, then, that when we talk to others, we should start by talking with them about themselves and their interests. I once heard the acronym FORM, which stands for family, occupation, recreation, and message, as a tool for starting conversations. It's easy to get people talking when you ask them about their family or about their occupation, progress to the subject of their recreational interests and, finally, the message that you would like to convey to them.

How do you keep a conversation going? The advice in Dale Carnegie's classic, which was first published in 1936, is as timeless as ever: become genuinely interested in other people; be a good listener; encourage others to talk about themselves; let the other person do a great deal of the talking; don't criticize, condemn, or complain; smile; talk in terms of the other person's interests; give honest and sincere appreciation.[14] By practicing these basics skills of conversation, you will realize the wisdom of Proverbs,[15] which teach that "a man has joy by the answer of his mouth, and a word spoken in due season, how good it is!" (Prov. 15:23 NKJV).

2. Avoiding strife

In reviewing some of the characteristics of negative speech and relationship patterns, we see that the fool likes to argue. He wants to get people going. He does not think ahead to the possibility that other people might get their feelings hurt. The wise man, on the other hand, the book of Proverbs suggests, avoids strife:

> It is to a man's honor to avoid strife,
>   but every fool is quick to quarrel. (Prov. 20:3)

Honorable people, this proverb tells us, find ways to avoid strife. It is certainly true that we cannot always avoid strife entirely, but we should avoid unnecessary confrontations. The honorable person stops short of an argument. This is the kind of person who has the capacity of preserving a working relationship with even the most difficult people.

People do get into conflict sometimes, however. And when that happens, there is another kind of speech that can diffuse the argument.

3. Conciliatory speech

Proverbs 15:1 explains:

> A gentle answer turns away wrath,
>> but a harsh word stirs up anger.

When we are in an argument, the way we answer the other person will have an effect on whether the argument gets worse or whether it gets better. The proverb is talking about not just gentle or soft speech but conciliatory speech. Conciliatory speech is the kind of answer that will bring an argument to an end and restore good temper and reasonableness. Another proverb teaches:

> A hot-tempered man stirs up dissension,
>> but a patient man calms a quarrel. (Prov. 15:18)

It takes great patience and calmness to maintain peaceful relationships. There is a kind of person who thrives on arguing and who is always looking to find a way to turn every difference or disagreement into a bitter contest. And then there is his opposite, one who will do everything in his power to minimize contention and to get along. One proverb that relates to this theme is often misunderstood. It reads:

> If your enemy is hungry, give him food to eat;
>> if he is thirsty, give him water to drink.
> In doing this, you will heap burning coals on his head,
>> and the LORD will reward you. (Prov. 25:21–22)

This has sometimes been misconstrued as teaching that, if you want to get revenge, you can somehow satisfy that vengeance through kindness. This makes kindness into some kind of sarcasm. The real meaning of the proverb has to do with conciliatory speech and behavior. If we will treat our enemies with kindness, the proverb teaches, we will bring them remorse. The imagery of "burning coals" represents pangs of conscience, which we will bring about much more quickly through kindness than by criticism. If we want someone to change their negative behavior, we are much more likely to help him do it not by criticizing but by reaching out in love.

This is how Jesus responded on one occasion when a woman who had been caught in adultery was brought to him. Jesus was teaching in the temple courts when the scribes and Pharisees brought a woman to him who had been caught in adultery (John 8:1–11). They made her stand before him, and reminded him that the law of Moses required that someone caught in adultery was to be punished by stoning, and they asked what he thought should be done. Jesus caused the authorities to disband by calling their attention to their own past actions, and once they had departed, he asked her, "Woman, where are they? Has no one condemned you?" (v. 10). She answered, "No one, sir" (v. 11). Jesus replied, "Neither do I condemn you. . . . Go now and leave your life of sin" (v. 11). Instead of speaking "fire and brimstone" to the woman, he freely acquitted her and urged her to make his pardon the beginning of a new life. Kindness will usually evoke a more positive response than criticism.

4. Making amends

When we have hurt someone, we should make amends. Proverbs 14:9 teaches:

> Fools mock at making amends for sin,
>   but goodwill is found among the upright.

This proverb tells us that folly offends people, but wisdom makes amends with people. What is really being said here is that the righteous have the humility and willingness, and therefore the power, to mend relationships. The average person will lie, deny, or make an alibi when she has done something wrong. Leaders cannot afford to do this, not only because it is wrong, but also because when they do it they will lose their people's trust. When you are wrong, you should say so out loud: "I was wrong" or "I made a mistake." It takes courage to do this. People will admire you for it, and you will have earned their trust.

5. Praising and edifying

The expression of favor from a leader is encouraging to his people. Proverbs 16:15 says:

> When a king's face brightens, it means life;
>> his favor is like a rain cloud in spring.

The proverb teaches that it is beneficial to have a king who is pleased with his subjects. The favor is like a "rain cloud." A rain cloud is a blessing, in that rain is necessary for a successful harvest.

The same principle applies for contemporary leaders. When their "face brightens"—that is, when they show that they are pleased with their people—then their people are more productive. The leader's encouragement facilitates productivity.

This principle is incredibly important, but so often unpracticed. It seems that it is very easy for conversations to drift toward the negative—but who wants to be around negative people? If people tend to avoid their friends who are chronically negative, then how will a leader's negative speech impact his or her organization? Negatively! So, focus on the positive. Speak the positive. Be lavish and sincere in compliments. Build up rather than tear down.

6. Learning to listen

One of the most positive kinds of speech really is not speech at all, but it is keeping our mouths shut and learning to listen. Proverbs 18:13 reads:

> He who answers before listening—
>> that is his folly and his shame.

Poor listening is a sign that we do not care much about what the other person is saying, or that we are too self-absorbed to really listen. If we really want to understand a person, we need to listen to what he is saying to us. Proverbs 10:14 reiterates the importance of listening. It says:

> Wise men store up knowledge,
>> but the mouth of a fool invites ruin.

What we are being told here is that a wise man or woman listens. A wise leader silently stores up knowledge instead of foolishly talking prematurely.

People tend to be uncomfortable with silence, however, and naturally resist listening. We tend to fill up empty spaces in conversation with words and, even when the person we are talking with attempts to talk, we will often interrupt her, talk over her, or find other ways not to listen. In her book *Listening Ministry: Rethinking Pastoral Leadership*, Susan Hedahl, Herman G. Stuempfle Chair of Proclamation of the Word at Lutheran Theological Seminary, explains why:

> Resistance to listening is . . . at heart a spiritual issue: truthful listening is more demanding [than not listening], calls forth the listener's vulnerabilities, and may result in changes the listener will resist when confronted with new possibilities.[16]

Listening, however, is of supreme importance. Those we love and those we lead long to be listened to. Taylor Caldwell speaks of the desire to be listened to as "the most desperate need" of men and women today. She explains:

> The most desperate need of men today is not a new vaccine for any disease, or a new religion, or a new "way of life." Man does not need to go to the moon or other solar systems. He does not require bigger and better bombs and missiles. He will not die if he does not get "better housing" or more vitamins. He will not expire of frustration if he is unable to buy the brightest and newest gadgets, or if all his children cannot go to college. His basic needs are few, and it takes little to acquire them, in spite of the advertisers. He can survive on a small amount of bread and in the meanest shelter. He always did.
>
> His real need, his most terrible need, is for someone to listen to him, not as a "patient," but as a human soul. He needs to tell someone of what he thinks, of the bewilderment he encounters when he tries to discover why he was born, how he must live, and where his destiny lies.[17]

Caldwell explores this need to be listened to in her book *The Listener*, in which she tells the story of a building, nestled in a wooded park, bequeathed to a city by an elderly philanthropist named John Godfrey. Stenciled on an arch over the tall bronze doors of the building were the words, "The Man who Listens." A pamphlet explained:

> This building was built for the reason that Mr. Godfrey believed that few listened these days to anyone. He believed that it was desperately necessary for men to listen to each other, as they had listened to meistersingers, priests, poets, and philosophers in the past. He believed that time had taken on a kind of "fragmentation," and that though there was more leisure than ever before in the world there was less time, less solidity, less meaning, few roots, and no real security. Therefore, more despair and loneliness.
>
> And so he built this "sanctuary," as some call it, where someone will listen to anyone who comes. There is no set time. A visitor may take up to ten minutes, or an hour, or even two hours. The building is open twenty-four hours a day. It is maintained by the Stella Godfrey Memorial Fund, established by Mr. Godfrey, her husband.[18]

The book is made up of short stories of normal people who share their conflicted thoughts with a listener hidden behind a curtain, whose identity is not revealed until the final chapter.[19]

This haunting story makes a powerful case that the desire to be listened to may indeed be "the most desperate need" people have in modern times. Listening draws people out. It makes them feel valued. If you intend to lead, listen to your people!

One Leader Who Alienated Himself, Another Who Ingratiated Himself

In AD 405, a man named Jerome translated the entire Bible from Hebrew and Greek into Latin, the vernacular of his day. Although achieving such a grand feat in translating the Bible, he was described as a man who loved to argue simply for the sake of arguing. Despite his brilliance, it seems that Jerome may have been something of a "jerk," whose communication style made many people uncomfortable.[20]

One might think someone that smart—who achieved in twenty-three years what few would do in a lifetime—would be very successful. In regard to Jerome, however, the opposite was true. Following his masterful translation, Jerome was passed over in the quest for a bishop of Rome—likely due to his irascibility. He finally retreated into seclusion, in Bethlehem, though he never wavered from his tendency to engage in bitter conflict and his seeming love for being known as the "unconstrained controversialist."[21]

No one could dispute that Jerome was a brilliant translator. In that respect, he was a leader and an influencer. However, like Saul, he failed to connect with the people with whom he worked. Consequently, his impact as a well-rounded leader was limited.

"To connect is to touch others' hearts in such a way that they want to follow you; they want to be with you. Jerome lacked the ability to connect."[22]

In contrast to Jerome's tendency to alienate others, one thinks of Benjamin Franklin, a man who ultimately endeared himself to thousands. Franklin came from humble beginnings, having arrived in Philadelphia as a grubby, seventeen-year-old runaway. But by the end of his eighty-four-year-long life, he had become known internationally as America's greatest diplomat. Franklin was not necessarily brilliant, but he was immensely practical and always interested in self-improvement. Early on he became interested in finding ways of cultivating self-improvement, and he would often write these up as articles for the newspaper.

Franklin was, by nature, gregarious, with "an eagerness to impress."[23] He became concerned that these tendencies would limit his associations to "trifling company." So, early on, he concluded that good relations were cultivated "rather by the use of the ear than of the tongue," and he began to focus on being a good listener. In his articles on self-improvement, he often wrote of the value of asking questions in conversation, using curiosity "to avoid contradicting people in a manner that could give offense."[24] In an article on conversation, Franklin explained the importance of deferring—or at least of giving the appearance of deferring—to others. He explained:

> Would you win the hearts of others, you must not seem to vie with them, but to admire them. Give them every opportunity of displaying their own qualifications, and when you have indulged their vanity, they will praise you in turn and prefer you above others . . . Such is the vanity of mankind that minding what others say is a much surer way of pleasing them than talking well ourselves.[25]

Franklin went on to list some of the most common conversational mistakes, one of which, he said, is talking too much.

Over the course of his life, Franklin came to be known as a great communicator. His recent biographer, Walter Isaacson, summarizes thus:

> He used silence wisely, employed an indirect style of persuasion, and feigned modesty and naïveté in disputes. "When another asserted something that I thought an error, I denied myself the pleasure of contradicting him." Instead, he would agree in parts and suggest his differences only indirectly. . . . This velvet-tongued and sweetly passive style of circumspect argument would make him seem sage to some, insinuating and manipulative to others, but inflammatory to almost nobody. The method would also become, often with a nod to Franklin, a staple in modern management guides and self-improvement books.[26]

Franklin's approach to communication won him success as a printer, as a public citizen, and, eventually, as a politician in Philadelphia, and as a courtier in Paris. During the American Revolution it became clear that America may not survive without the recognition and aid of France and its navy and, because Franklin had been successful in cultivating relationships there, Congress charged him with securing France's support. In pursuing negotiations with France, Franklin "would display a dexterity that would make him the greatest American diplomat of all times."[27] The treaties were signed in 1778.

Jerome and Franklin were in different parts of the world, in different eras, pursuing different tasks. What determined one's failure and the other's success, however, was the very same factor: communication. One failed to see its value in cultivating human relationships, the other understood that it was the key not only to human relations but also to solving critical problems of national importance! Make positive, successful communication the hallmark by which your leadership is recognized.

Group Discussion and Personal Reflection

Group Discussion

1. I (Richard) once suggested to a room full of leaders, "Every communication breakdown is the responsibility (not necessarily the fault) of the leader." In what ways is this statement true? When might the statement not be true?

2. Leaders are held to a higher standard in communication and a higher level of fault in miscommunication. Why is this so? Should it be? How can leaders live up to the higher communication expectations?

3. The chapter is filled with wonderful proverbs to teach lessons of communication. Select two or three proverbs from the chapter that you can relate to a story from your own life. Share the proverbs you selected and the stories behind them.

4. Look back into the chapter at Theory 1 and Theory 2. When have you seen Theory 1 in action? When have you experienced Theory 2 in action?

Communication Theory 1:

- Strive to stay in control of the situation and outcome.
- Minimize losing and maximize winning.
- Stifle all expressions of negative feeling from others.
- Seek to look rational while you are doing all this.

Communication Theory 2:

- Strive to maintain mutual trust and respect.
- Work with valid information.
- Provide free and informed choice.
- Ask for internal commitment.

5. As you read the stories of Jerome and Franklin, which one did you find most meaningful and helpful? Why?

Personal Reflection

Assess

It is difficult to assess your own communication. Therefore, for this assessment, consult with three to five trusted individuals and ask them two questions:

➢ What are my best communication skills?

➢ What can I do to improve my communication skills?

Analyze

➢ What did you learn from your conversations with trusted individuals about your communication skills?

Act

___ Read Dale Carnegie & Associates' *How to Win Friends & Influence People in the Digital Age* (New York: Simon and Schuster, 2011).

In addition to reading Dale Carnegie's book, consider the five keys for having successful conversations, adapted from the classic business book by Les Giblin, *How to Have Confidence and Power in Dealing with People* (New Jersey: Prentice-Hall, 1959):

___ *Become an expert at striking up a conversation.* If you cannot think of what to talk about, remember the acronym FORM. It stands for Family, Occupation, Recreation, and Message.

___ *Make a "U-Turn" in the conversation.* "You" is everyone's favorite word. Do not talk about yourself in a conversation and, if the conversation comes around to you, make a "U-Turn" by asking them more about themselves.

___ *Avoid the deadly conversational sin—talking about yourself!* Don't refuse to talk about yourself to the point of being bizarre. Answer questions about yourself, but then, when you can, make the "U-Turn." Keep the spotlight on the other person.

___ *Use the magic of agreement.* People like those who agree with them, and dislike those who do not. When we agree with others, they feel that we are like them, and we establish rapport. So, when possible, agree with people, and help them to like you more easily.

___ *Use "happy talk."* As we said earlier in the chapter, no one wants to be around a chronically negative person. Giblin quotes from a song from the movie *South Pacific*, which says: "Nobody likes a Gloomy Gus. Nobody likes to sit and listen to a prophet of doom. People don't like to hear bad news." Those who fall into the habit of always talking pessimistically will find their friends and associates avoiding them. If you have problems you need to discuss, go to a pastor or a counselor. When you are trying to lead, however, be upbeat and positive. Use praise!

Chapter 6

Saul Failed to Act
When the Time Was Right

Much of Saul's reign was during wartime situations. The Philistines were Israel's main enemy, and 1 Samuel 13 and 15 tell us about some of Saul's early successes against them. Chapter 15 gives details about a victory over a smaller enemy, the Amalekites. Other victorious campaigns are mentioned, but they are not described in any detail.

> When Saul had taken the kingship over Israel, he fought against all his enemies on every side—against Moab, against the Ammonites, against Edom, against the kings of Zobah, and against the Philistines; wherever he turned he routed them. He did valiantly, and struck down the Amalekites, and rescued Israel out of the hands of those who plundered them. (1 Sam. 14:47–48 NRSV)

From one point of view, these chapters describe a very successful start to Saul's reign, in which he constantly delivered the Israelites from their enemies (1 Sam. 14:47). And yet, these chapters end on a grim and unhappy note: "The LORD was grieved that he had made Saul king over Israel" (1 Sam. 15:35). The events recorded in chapters 13–15 were occasions not only of warfare against foreign enemies but also of personal conflicts between Saul and other Israelites. In chapter 14, Saul might have killed his own son, and he ended up quarreling with his own troops. Even more seriously, in both chapters 13 and 15, we find Saul caused great offense to Samuel, the prophet of God. So, despite all the good signs up to this point, Saul quickly proved that though he could win battles, he was not the right man to lead Israel. The basic reason given is that Saul refused to submit to God's instructions mediated through Samuel the prophet. The message is clear: God would not bless a king of Israel who set himself above the prophets whom God established. And so we can see the events in chapters 13–15 as a power struggle, God siding with the prophet against the king.[1]

As Saul struggled for autonomous leadership, he was unsure when to take action. He sometimes hesitated and, therefore, lost opportunities. This is the area of failure we will focus on in this chapter.

Saul's Long Record of Failure

It is not clear at what point during his reign Saul began to decline. After Saul's initial victory over the Ammonites, the Bible records a sort of "farewell address" from Samuel (1 Sam. 12), and then it begins to recount the story of Saul's unlawful sacrifice. At the beginning of this story, we are given a muddled chronological reference about the length of Saul's reign. The King James Version tried to make the best of a bad situation by translating the Hebrew of 1 Samuel 13:1 this way: "Saul reigned one year; and when he had reigned two years over Israel. . . ." The New International Version says, "Saul was thirty years old when he became king, and he reigned over Israel forty-two years." Finally, the Revised Standard Version says, "Saul was . . . years old when he began to reign; and he reigned . . . and two years over Israel."

The Revised Standard Version follows the Hebrew faithfully, which actually reads that same way: "Saul was . . . years old when he began to reign; and he reigned . . . two years over Israel." It seems clear that a number was lost in the first and second gaps. The New International Version has restored them based on information from other passages. Acts 13:21, for example, reports that Saul reigned "forty years," and the first-century Jewish historian Josephus tells us that Saul ruled "eighteen years while Samuel was alive, and two [and twenty] years after his death."[2] While it is not clear why the numbers were left out,[3] it is clear that Saul had a long record of failure. The instance that follows is simply one occasion of failure in Saul's apparently lengthy reign.

Saul's Hesitation—Jonathan's Initiative

Saul's failure—brought about by his own hesitation—can best be seen when it is contrasted with Jonathan's own initiative.

Saul Sends Men Home

The people had "chosen" a king to lead them into battle,[4] and now the king granted their wish: Saul "chose" three thousand Israelite men to serve as his standing army.[5] Two thousand were under Saul's command at Micmash, while one thousand were at Gibeah under the command of his son, Jonathan. Apparently Saul felt confident in the size of his military units, because he sent the rest of the men home (1 Sam. 13:2–7).

Jonathan Takes Initiative

The smaller unit under Jonathan started a war against the Philistines by attacking their outpost at Geba in Benjamin (1 Sam. 13:3). Saul, ultimately responsible for the attack (v. 4), and realizing that the main Philistine army had heard about it, had second thoughts about his own troop strength. He therefore had the ram's horn trumpet blown throughout Israel to summon additional men.

Israel had now become a "stench to the Philistines" (v. 4), which is another way of saying that Philistia would muster its troops to fight Israel—and so it did (v. 5). The Philistines were feared far and wide for their wooden chariots armed with iron fittings at vulnerable and strategic points. And besides being able to put three thousand two-man chariots into the field, the enemy had summoned troops "as numerous as the sand on the seashore" (v. 5). This was, of course, an exaggeration, but it serves to emphasize the magnitude of the Philistine threat.

Saul Takes a Census

This Philistine deployment at Micmash caused mass desertions in the Israelite army. Some Israelites hid in whatever out-of-the-way places they could find (1 Sam. 13:6). Others fled eastward across the Jordan River (v. 7). After a serious fiasco with Samuel (vv. 8–14), which we will look at in a separate chapter, Saul took a census of his fighting men to assess their numerical strength (v. 15). In spite of his original two thousand men,[6] and the general call to arms to supplement those original numbers (vv. 3–4), the huge defections had reduced his troops to "about six hundred" (v. 15 NRSV). The combined forces of Saul and Jonathan at Gibeah, therefore, numbered only in the hundreds,[7] while those of the Philistines at Micmash, just four miles to the northeast, numbered in the thousands (1 Sam. 13:5).

Jonathan Again Takes Initiative

A "detachment" of Philistines had left their main camp at Micmash (1 Sam. 13:16) and had gone out to defend a pass leading to it. And, in this case, it was Saul's son Jonathan, rather than Saul himself, who took the initiative against the enemy. Without telling his father, Jonathan suggested to his armor-bearer that they attack the recently established Philistine outpost.

Saul Takes His Ease

Meanwhile, Saul's modest army of six hundred men was with him near Gibeah, his hometown. Saul himself was sitting "under the pomegranate tree" (1 Sam. 14:2 NRSV) in a situation of timidity and relative ease, even luxury, since the pomegranate was a highly prized fruit.[8] This certainly contrasts him with Jonathan, who was out on the front, willing to sacrifice his very life for Israel. Saul was left reclining under the pomegranate tree.

Jonathan Secures Victory

Jonathan and his armor-bearer attacked the Philistine garrison and began the slaughter. Although they were outnumbered about ten to one, Jonathan and his armor-bearer dispatched "some twenty men in an area about half an acre" (1 Sam. 14:14). The text is simply telling us that the Philistines were killed in a brief period of time and in a short distance. Confusion struck the Philistine troops (v. 15) whatever their location: in the camp at Micmash (1 Sam. 13:16), out in the field, at the various outposts, with one or another of the three raiding parties (1 Sam. 13:17–18). This panic was the kind that God promised to send against Israel's enemies when the people trusted him (Deut. 7:23).

Saul Takes Another Census

Curious about what was causing the Philistine threat, and maybe thinking about the possibility of turning it into a total rout, Saul decided once again to take a census of his troops (1 Sam. 14:17). After the census, he considered consulting God but, when he heard the increasing frenzy in the Philistine camp, he told the priest to stop the ritual proceedings (v. 19). Instead, he gathered his men and marched into battle (v. 20)—presumably without the benefit of priestly blessing of any kind, since he had interrupted the priest's work. As Saul engaged the battle, the Philistines had become filled with "total confusion," and brother was wielding sword against brother (v. 20).[9] Saul, Jonathan, and the Israelite army were soon joined by two other groups of reinforcements. Some were Hebrews who had previously deserted and had been hiding out in the hill country (v. 22; 1 Sam. 13:6).

Saul's Hesitation Meant Lost Opportunity

The reduction of Saul's troops to six hundred men is a literary way of telling us that he had an opportunity to become another Gideon. For seven years, in the days of the judges, the Israelites were oppressed by eastern peoples, Midianites and Amalekites, who would destroy the produce of the land, leaving no sustenance in the land (Judg. 6:1–4). The text says that when these eastern tribes would come into the land of Israel, they were "as thick as locusts" (NRSV), and that "neither they nor their camels could be counted" (v. 5 NRSV).

God raised up Gideon to be a judge, a deliverer, and he was able to muster an army of thirty-two thousand troops to fight the invaders. However, Yahweh said that the army was too large and that, if they won, "Israel would only take the credit away from me, saying, 'My own hand has delivered me'" (Judg. 7:2 NRSV). Gideon was instructed to cull out troops until he had reduced the size of the army to a mere three hundred men (7:5–7), so that it would be clear that Yahweh, and not the Israelite warriors, had won the victory.

Saul had the opportunity to be another Gideon by achieving victory with only a small contingent of courageous followers.

However, when this opportunity arrived, Saul hesitated to take action. By his hesitation, he missed the opportunity to replicate Gideon's great victory, and it was left up to his son, Jonathan, to trust the Lord and initiate the battle. Barbara Green concludes that, "On a cultic/military occasion Saul cannot lead well. He had dismissed and regathered his men; the battle commences not at Saul's command but when Jonathan strikes."[10]

The Courage to Take Action

Leadership is about getting things done. "Good intentions" do not count in leadership. At the end of the day, are the Philistines dead? Is the enemy vanquished? Are sales numbers up? Did the bills get paid? Is the new building complete? Have test scores improved? Did membership increase? Leaders are measured by results. Results demand action. Action is born of courage. It is a hard thing to know when to act and when to wait. Saul failed at both. He failed to wait for Samuel to appear and make the sacrifice before the battle (1 Sam. 13:9). He failed to act against the enemy, and his son Jonathan initiated the action (1 Sam. 14:1). The challenge for leaders is to combine courage and wisdom. When this alignment is missing, failure is almost always inevitable. Samuel said it concisely, "You acted foolishly" (1 Sam. 13:13).

In sane and reasonable moments of confidence and quiet, we know that courage and wisdom need each other. Courage without wisdom is foolhardy. Wisdom without the courage to act is ineffective. Either way, when the votes are counted, the leader has lost. In Saul's case, it was both and neither. He displayed neither courage nor wisdom; he acted foolishly.

Why is it difficult for leaders to act with wisdom and courage? In a word: *fear*. Fear is the archenemy of good leadership. Other motives, such as greed, resentment, or envy, can take down a leader. However, in my (Richard's) personal experience, the greatest culprit, the personal demon that has destroyed more leaders than any other, is fear.

Fear attacks courage. As has been noted by many writers, there is no courage except in the presence of fear. Courage is the willingness to act in a way that faces the challenge. At a conference in Washington D.C., Winston Churchill observed, "Courage is what it takes to stand up and speak; courage is also what it takes to sit down and listen."[11] It takes courage to act and courage to refrain from acting. Fear attacks courage with an alternate plan: fight, flight, or freeze. There is fear behind the foolish action of attacking without the facts or support needed. Fear drives a leader off the playing field into any and every alternative distraction that avoids facing the true crisis. Furthermore, fear unchecked has the power to freeze all action, also called the "deer in the headlights" syndrome.

Fear strangles wisdom. Many years ago, as a young man, I (Richard) paid twenty-five dollars (a huge amount for me at that time) to hear Norman Vincent Peale speak at a large auditorium in Kansas City. My seat was near the ceiling in the back. However, when Dr. Peale spoke I hung on each word. In his presentation, he described the power of fear. He reported that the word came from an old Saxon word with the root meaning "to choke." He took his hands and put them around his throat and squeaked out the words, "This is what fear does to your thinking." When afraid, leaders make poor decisions.

Fear will get the best of any leader who succumbs to its seductive power. When you face a crisis and fear attacks your courage and wisdom, ask yourself the following questions:

1. *What can you control?* The temptation is to focus on what you cannot control, what everyone else seems to control, or what is out of control. Ultimately, you only have control over yourself, your attitude, and behavior.

2. *Where can you turn for help?* Leaders often feel alone, especially when fear attacks. Be careful. You need someone who will allow you to sound off in safety. If you speak your fear you will find that it is not as great as you imagined. If you write it down, you can capture it on paper. Many of the psalms express distress and, in doing so, come to a new point of courage and calm (Pss. 16, 34, 46, 56, 112).

3. *What positive contribution can you make?* You may not be able to do all you want, but you can do something that makes

a positive contribution. In the face of fear, respond with grace and dignity. It is tempting to get even, settle the score, or give some payback. How do you want people to think about you and remember you? Do the right thing. You are better at dealing with fear when you know that you have acted with integrity.

4. *What can you create out of this situation?* Answering the first three questions will ease your fear to the point that you will be able to step back and take a wider, longer view of the situation. Every breakthrough comes of something that broke! In the brokenness of the situation you face, what is the possibility? This requires that you fulfill your primary duty as the leader, keeping your eye on the horizon rather than the bottom line. Yes, it takes both, of course. However, fight your fear by looking at the far side of the valley, to the phoenix that will rise from the ashes, to the greater good that will come out of the challenge and difficulty of the moment.

The Wisdom to Act

Leaders make decisions. In fact, the quality of a leader's decisions is the measure of a leader's success. Harry Truman dropped the atomic bomb. Roberto Goizueta launched New Coke. John Kennedy handled the Cuban missile crisis. A manager shifts everyone's office, reassigns sales territories, adjusts the compensation formula, or combines responsibilities. A minister moves a Sunday school class, adds a new ritual to the worship service, changes the date of a children's event, or repurposes a midweek program. As a leader, your decisions, by definition, affect the lives of others,[12] sometimes a single individual, and at other times the whole organization. Your decisions, your judgment calls, determine your legacy as a leader.

Leaders make decisions in three important areas: people, strategy, and crisis.[13] Personnel issues are the most difficult and call for the greatest consideration. Good team members can sometimes turn a leader's poor decision into a positive outcome, as was the case of Jonathan's initiative and Saul's hesitation. Strategic plans require constant attention, monitoring, and reconsideration. Plans are a combination of goals and contingencies. The third area of leadership decisions, crisis, is more rapid and demanding today than at any time in living memory. Crisis requires decisiveness and confidence. In addition, leaders also make decisions about decisions. They decide how decisions will be made. They decide who to include and exclude in the decision-making process. They even decide if a decision needs to be made. Jean Paul Sarte, the French existentialist, had it right: "It is only in our decisions that we are important."[14]

Here is the difficulty: the leader often must make decisions in a fog of ambiguity. It may seem as though you never have all the information you would like. You never have all the time you would like. You can't anticipate all the consequences. You may not have perfect confidence in your choice. At the battle of Micmash (1 Sam. 13–14), Saul experienced the haze of decision ambiguity that resulted in hesitation and poor judgment. Indecisiveness is fatal for a leader. Even a decision to delay a decision is better than no decision. However, as in Saul's case, postponing a decision in the hope that *events* will deal with the problem makes you a hostage to the future.

The fatal result of hesitation is illustrated in the story of American Civil War General Gustavus W. Smith.[15] When the Union army advanced on Richmond, Virginia, General Johnson, charged with protecting the Southern capital and President Jefferson Davis, was seriously wounded. The next in command, Gustavus Smith, was given a field promotion. Immediately, President Davis asked Smith to detail his plans to save the capital. Smith asked for time to think. Davis was displeased. The next day, Davis returned and asked again for the battle plan. Smith said he didn't have a plan and asked Davis if he had any ideas about what to do. President Davis said, "Yes." He fired Smith on the spot and brought in Robert E. Lee. Indecisiveness is fatal for leaders.

How does a leader work through the fog of ambiguity and make better decisions? First, clarify your own intentions in the situation. You need to know yourself, your purpose, and your intended outcomes. When conflicting intentions muddle the mind of the leader, the troops receive conflicting messages with blurred meaning. In their book *Judgment: How Winning Leaders Make Great Calls*, Noel Tichy and Warren Bennis[16] advise that judgment is improved when the leader evaluates and capitalizes on the following:

1. A clear knowledge of yourself. Clarify your values and goals before you make a decision and determine that you are willing to learn.

2. An in-depth knowledge of your network of influencers. Regard those who surround you daily and help you implement your plans and achieve your goals.

3. A realistic knowledge of your organization. Consider what is possible and whether the team and organization is equipped with required competency and capacity.

4. A wider knowledge of the context. Respect stakeholders of every variety and engage the support of those who have a vested interest in the organization.

This framework will help you make better decisions about people, strategy, and crisis. However, there is one more issue involved in making good judgment calls—experience. The wisdom exhibited in good leadership judgment is not picked up solely in the library or the bookstore. Leadership wisdom comes from experience.

Often you hear that a certain leader "has forty years of experience." Consider the statement carefully. It is possible that the leader has only ten years of experience, but has it four times over. This seems to have been the case with King Saul. His early years gave him great experience for cultivating wisdom as a leader. However, it appears that he did not know how to turn his experience into wisdom. He did not learn from his successes or regrets.

How does a leader turn experience into wisdom? Reflection is essential for nurturing maturity and wisdom. I (Richard) open my leadership classes by asking wide-eyed students why they have not brought to class the large and assigned textbook. Befuddled, they look at one another and the stack of recently purchased books listed in the syllabus. After a moment of dramatic confusion, I make my point, "I am talking about the big book on leadership, the expensive one, the book of your own experience. That is the book you must bring to class each day. That is the book you must learn to read."

What can you learn from your experience? What can you learn about advancing what is best in you? What can you learn about the limits and boundaries you need? What can you learn about handling people issues, implementing strategy, and crisis management? What can you learn about dealing with your team, the limits and potential of your organization, and the context of your challenges and opportunities? You will need to struggle with your regrets and embrace the lesson from them. You will need to look past the celebration of success and sift out the lessons to be guarded. Take courage and endure. Be steadfast, and you will discover rich veins of gold and precious gems of personal wisdom.

When you distill the wisdom of your own experience into practical use, you cultivate discernment. You have better judgment. You are better able to anticipate and predict outcomes and consequences. You have increased insight into the dynamics of a challenge or problem. Discernment is figuring out a smart way to do the right thing. It is determining a wise way to do what's best. Discernment is applying what you have learned from your experience.

I (Richard) remember only one time in thirty years of board meetings when I raised my voice in anger.[17] The momentary loss of self-control cost me dearly. When I reviewed the experience to see what I could learn, I came to two conclusions. First, I had accepted and put into action someone else's advice that did not fit me. Now, I am better able to test the advice and expectations of others. On occasion, I must decline advice and disappoint someone by not meeting his or her expectations. Inevitably, I cannot make everyone happy, but come to think of it, using advice that doesn't fit me makes people unhappy anyway, including me.

The second lesson I dug out of the "raised voice" incident is that there is a smart way to do the right thing. I "raised my voice" over a core value. I was upset over a situation in which I had done the right thing and what others were doing was wrong. So I stood up and spoke up (with my raised voice) for a just end. Therefore, I was foolish in the way I did the right thing. Just as important as doing the right thing is doing the right thing in a smart way. This is discernment in action.

Two decades later, I sat in a meeting with a group of colleagues. We were dealing with a complex situation. A number of people were involved. Vested interests were at stake. Emotions were high. The decision would have practical effects. But, at the core, it was a clear question of right and wrong. At that point, I was lost in thought. My mind was spinning. After an uneasy silence, a colleague questioned me, "Are we going to do the right thing?"

His question broke my concentration. I looked up. The group was waiting for my decision. I smiled. You see, I was past the decision. I was thinking about the ramifications of the decision. I said to the team, "We are going to do the right thing. I was thinking about a *wise* way to do the right thing."

Take this story for example: A young college graduate entered her first year of teaching in the classroom. It was a class of first graders. The young teacher focused intently on the math lesson she had prepared. She presented her problem, "Johnny had ten apples. He gave his friend five apples. How many apples did Johnny have left?"

A hand in the first row shot for the ceiling. The little boy could not contain himself: "Teacher, teacher, me, me!"

"Yes, Jason. How many apples did Johnny have left?"

Jason replied, "Why did he give his apples to his friend?"

In our "adult world" of stress, expectations, and quick decisions, we often focus on "how" and ignore "why." We want to know how to get the job done, meet the demand, and solve the problem. We grab for a quick answer and move to the next issue. In doing so, we must be careful not to neglect the more important question, "Why?"

When you look for the best answer, don't start with "How?" Begin with "Why is this important?" Then ask, "What do I want to create?" If you stop and ask yourself these two questions, your discernment, leadership wisdom, and good judgment will increase.

Group Discussion and Personal Reflection

Group Discussion

1. Upon review of the chapter, what do you think caused Saul to make a series of such bad decisions? How did his perspective on the situation, his emotions about it, and his personal motivations influence his bad judgment?

2. Read Matthew 7:24–29 as well as the quote below from John Chrysostom. What words in the Scripture passage best describe your current leadership challenge?

More than sixteen hundred years ago, John Chrysostom (c. 347–407) wrote a homily on this passage. You would think he was describing the challenge of decision making for today's leader:

> By "rain" here, and "floods," and "winds," He is expressing metaphorically the calamities and affliction that befall men [or "leaders"]; such as false accusations, plots, bereavements, deaths, loss of friends, vexations from strangers, and all the ills in our life that anyone could mention.[18]

3. What makes leadership decisions difficult? What are the dynamics, pressures, and ambiguities that surround many leadership decisions? What difficult decision are you dealing with at this time?

Chrysostom goes on to describe how to overcome the challenges and make wise decisions:

> But to none of these does such a soul give way; and the cause is, it is founded on the rock. He calls the steadfastness of his doctrine a rock; because in truth His commands are stronger than any rock, setting one above all the waves of human affairs. For he who keeps these things strictly, will not have the advantage of men only when they are vexing him, but even of the very devils plotting against him.

4. What is your decision-making process as a leader?

5. Share a piece of leadership wisdom you have learned from personal experience.

Personal Reflection

Assess

When making a significant leadership decision:

➤ I clarify my values and goals.

Always 5 4 3 2 1 Never

➤ I consult with the members of my team.

Always 5 4 3 2 1 Never

➤ I communicate with the whole organization.

Always 5 4 3 2 1 Never

➤ I consider all the stakeholders.

Always 5 4 3 2 1 Never

Analyze

Leadership decisions involve people, strategy, and crisis. Many leadership decisions involve a combination of all three.

1. Consider a difficult decision you've made in the past. What was the process you used to make the decision?

2. Consider a difficult decision you are facing now. What is the process you will use to make the decision?

Act

____ Recognize when a decision needs to be made.

____ Realize why you may be hesitant to make the decision.

____ Accept the ambiguity that comes with leadership decisions.

____ Ask, "Why is this decision important?"

____ Ask, "What do I want to create out of this situation?"

Chapter 7

Saul Failed to Lead the People, but Let Them Lead Him Instead

Another area in which Saul failed was in leading the people. Rather than maintaining and developing a positive influence over the people as their leader, Saul caved in to their negative influence. The events we will consider in this chapter take place mostly in 1 Samuel 15, in which the writer tells a detailed story to confirm Saul's unsuitability to rule Israel, and to confirm Yahweh's rejection of him. Through the prophet Samuel, Saul was given some explicit orders. He carried them out, in part, but he saw no harm in disregarding the rest of them when the people pressured him to do so.

Difficult Marching Orders

The story opens when Saul received difficult marching orders from the prophet Samuel:

> Samuel said to Saul, "The LORD sent me to anoint you king over his people Israel; now therefore listen to the words of the LORD. Thus says the LORD of hosts, 'I will punish the Amalekites for what they did in opposing the Israelites when they came up out of Egypt. Now go and attack Amalek, and utterly destroy all that they have; do not spare them, but kill both man and woman, child and infant, ox and sheep, camel and donkey.'" (1 Sam. 15:1–3 NRSV)

The Amalekites were a Bedouin tribe from the deep south. They had been Israel's chief enemy during the wilderness wanderings under Moses. They tried to deny Israel entry into the promised land. When the Israelites were struggling through the desert toward Canaan, the Amalekites picked off the weak, sick, and elderly at the end of the line of marchers and brutally murdered these stragglers. At that time, Moses said: "Remember what the Amalekites did to you along the way when you came out of Egypt. When you were weary and worn out, they met you on your journey and cut off all who were lagging behind; they had no fear of God" (Deut. 25:17–18). The Amalekites had some cities, but they were, for the most part, nomads, brutally raiding and plundering farms and livestock, especially on the southern borders of Israel. So their very existence was a permanent threat to Israel, and stern measures were essential and justified.[1] The Amalekites were, in the judgment of the Samuel writer, a wicked people (1 Sam. 15:18), and the Israelites had been told that "when the LORD your God has given you rest from all your enemies on every hand, in the land that the LORD your God is giving you as an inheritance to possess, you shall blot out the remembrance of Amalek from under heaven; do not forget" (Deut. 25:19 NRSV).

One of the chief objections to the notion that the God of the Old Testament is a God of love and mercy is the divine command to exterminate all the men, women, and children belonging to the seven Canaanite nations (Deut. 7:1–2). How could God approve of blanket destruction, of the genocide of an entire nation of people?

In both Moses' instructions to the Israelites and Samuel's instructions to Saul, a distinctive Old Testament concept known as *herem* is present. *Herem* means "curse," "that which is under the ban," or "that which is devoted to destruction." The root idea of the term is "separation": to set aside or separate something for destruction. God dedicated the Canaanite nations to destruction because they violently and steadfastly opposed his work over a long period of time. This "dedication to destruction" was not used very often in the Old Testament. It was reserved for the spoils of southern Canaan,[2] Jericho,[3] Ai,[4] Makkedah,[5] and Hazor.[6]

In addition, God did not impose the ban flippantly. Abraham was told that his descendents could not enter the promised land for four hundred years. The reason for so long a delay, Genesis 15:13–16 explains, was that "the sin of the Amorites [the Canaanites] [had] not yet reached its full measure." And so, God waited for centuries while the Amalekites and other Canaanite groups slowly filled up their own cups of condemnation by their sinful behavior.

God never acted hastily against them: his grace and mercy waited to see if they would repent and turn from their headlong dive into self-destruction.

The Canaanite nations were cut off to prevent the corruption of Israel and the rest of the world (Deut. 20:16–18). When a nation starts burning their children as gifts to the gods[7] and practicing sodomy, bestiality, and all sorts of loathsome vices,[8] the day of God's grace has begun to run out. One is reminded of a surgeon who does not hesitate to amputate a gangrenous limb, even if he cannot help cutting off some healthy tissue in the process. God had to do the same. This is not the same as doing evil so that good may come; rather, it is the cancer that could infect all of society and eventually destroy anything good that is left.[9] The Amalekites, in their refusal to fear God,[10] sowed the seeds of their own destruction. God is patient and slow to anger, "abounding in love and faithfulness (Ex. 34:6)"; nevertheless, he "does not leave the guilty unpunished" (v. 7).[11]

Saul's Preparations

Saul made preparations for the battle against the Amalekites (1 Sam. 15:4–6). He did so by calling two hundred thousand foot soldiers from Israel and ten thousand men from Judah (v. 4). Before Saul's main attack against the Amalekites, he urged the Kenites living in or near Amalekite territory to move out, at least temporarily, to avoid being killed in the crossfire. Saul's concern for the welfare of the Kenites was in recognition of the fact that they had showed kindness to the Israelite spies centuries earlier.[12]

The Battle and Samuel's Reprimand

Saul engaged the Amalekites and secured a smashing victory. However, he failed to carry out the specific instructions God had given him in regard to the ban. The Bible reports:

> Saul defeated the Amalekites, from Havilah as far as Shur, which is east of Egypt. He took King Agag of the Amalekites alive, but utterly destroyed all the people with the edge of the sword. Saul

and the people spared Agag, and the best of the sheep and of the cattle and of the fatlings, and the lambs, and all that was valuable, and would not utterly destroy them; all that was despised and worthless they utterly destroyed. (1 Sam. 15:7–9 NRSV)

The description of the total destruction of "all" the people (v. 8) is clearly a hyperbole, since the Amalekites as a whole survived to fight Israel again in the future.[13] In any event, Saul spared Agag. Besides sparing the king, Saul and his troops also set aside the best of the enemy's animals while destroying those that were worthless and weak (v. 9). When Saul was reproved by Samuel for not slaughtering even the best animals, he gave the excuse that his "soldiers" intended to sacrifice them to the Lord (vv. 14–15, 19). Verse 24, however, shows that he knew perfectly well what he was doing, and that he did it because he was afraid of his men. Saul lied to Samuel about it twice over, pretending that he thought he had obeyed orders.[14] In the end, he was forced to admit the truth and confess that he had sinned and intentionally violated the Lord's command.

In fact, the NIV translation of verse 9 clearly says Saul and his men were "unwilling" to destroy the Amalekites. This is a verb specifically linked elsewhere with the sin of rebellion,[15] such as when the Israelites refused to enter the promised land. Deuteronomy 1:26–27 reports:

But you were *unwilling* to go up. You rebelled against the command of the LORD your God; you grumbled in your tents and said, "It is because the LORD hates us that he has brought us out of the land of Egypt, to hand us over to the Amorites to destroy us." (NRSV, emphasis mine)

One can see that "unwilling," as it is used in the Deuteronomy passage, is associated with the Israelites' stubborn refusal to have faith, to follow after God in faith.

Following Saul's disobedience, the Lord communicated to Samuel that he regretted having made Saul king (1 Sam. 15:11). Samuel spent the rest of the night crying out to the Lord. Samuel rose early and set out to meet Saul, but was told that the king had gone to Carmel, where he was setting up a monument to himself. Military leaders often erected large, upright stones with inscriptions on them to tell those who passed by about their military exploits and victories. Verse 12 specifies that Saul set it up "for himself" or "to himself"; this probably means that he did not give any credit for his victories to the Lord.

When Samuel arrived at Gilgal, Saul—either genuinely or pretending ignorance—greeted him in the traditional way and then told him that he had carried out the Lord's instructions (v. 13). But Samuel would not be denied, and he asked why he heard the bleating of sheep and the lowing of cattle in the background (v. 14).

Saul answered in verse 15 that his soldiers spared them for sacrifice. Saul's meek report failed on two counts. First, whether he actually had commendable motives or not, Saul was told to destroy every living thing and, therefore, he should not have spared even the best of the animals. Secondly, even if his soldiers were primarily responsible for saving the animals, Saul was their leader, and he should not have tried to shift the blame to them. In the midst of Saul's feeble self-defense, Samuel heartily rebuked him:

> Then Samuel said to Saul, "Stop! I will tell you what the LORD said to me last night." [Saul] replied, "Speak." Samuel said, "Though you are little in your own eyes, are you not the head of the tribes of Israel? The LORD anointed you king over Israel. And the LORD sent you on a mission, and said, 'Go, utterly destroy the sinners, the Amalekites, and fight against them until they are consumed.' Why then did you not obey the voice of the LORD? Why did you swoop down on the spoil, and do what was evil in the sight of the LORD?" (1 Sam. 15:16–19 NRSV)

Saul had no better defense against Samuel's accusations than to simply repeat what he had already said in verse 13:

> Saul said to Samuel, "I have obeyed the voice of the LORD, I have gone on the mission on which the LORD sent me, I have brought Agag the king of Amalek, and I have utterly destroyed the Amalekites. But from the spoil the people took sheep and cattle, the best of the things devoted to destruction, to sacrifice to the LORD your God in Gilgal." (vv. 20–21 NRSV)

Saul stressed his *own* obedience (v. 20), and he also tried to justify the actions of his troops (v. 21) by attributing to them the worthy intention of sacrificing the animals they had spared to the Lord.

Samuel's response to Saul's defense reveals much about Saul:

> And Samuel said, "Has the LORD as great delight in burnt offering and sacrifices, as in obedience to the voice of the LORD? Surely, to obey is better than sacrifice, and to heed than the fat of rams. For rebellion is no less a sin than divination, and stubbornness is like iniquity and idolatry. Because you have rejected the word of the LORD, he has also rejected you from being king." (vv. 22–23 NRSV)

God does approve of sacrificing, but he does not want to have it at the expense of full obedience to his Word or as a substitute for a personal relationship of love and trust with him.[16] Saul seemed to think that a sacrifice would somehow either mask or make up for his disobedience.

When Saul was first reproved by Samuel for not slaughtering even the best of the animals (vv. 14, 19), he gave the excuse that his soldiers intended to sacrifice them to the Lord. But when we get to verse 24 we discover that Saul knew perfectly well what he was doing when he violated the Lord's command:

> Saul said to Samuel, "I have sinned; for I have transgressed the commandment of the LORD and your words, because I feared the people and obeyed their voice." (NRSV)

Saul violated the Lord's command because he "feared the people and obeyed their voice." Literally, he "listened" to their voice. As the anointed one, Saul's primary duty was to listen to the voice of the Lord. He failed because, instead of listening to the Lord, he listened to his constituents.[17]

When Samuel turned to leave, Saul reached out in desperation and seized the hem of Samuel's robe (v. 27). When the robe tore, Samuel used it to make his point: "The LORD has torn the kingdom of Israel from you this very day" (v. 28 NRSV). The chapter ends with the mournful statement that "the LORD was grieved that he had made Saul king" (v. 35).

Saul's Sins

At the outset of Saul's reign, he had been given significant tasks as Israel's leader. Barbara Green identifies three particular tasks he had been charged with.[18]

1. Saul was to rule over and fight for his people (1 Sam. 8:5–7, 19–20).
2. He was to save them from the Philistines and to "restrain" them in some sense (1 Sam. 9:15–17).
3. And, he was to immerse himself in the Law of Deuteronomy, making it the foundation of his leadership of the people (Deut. 17:18–20).

Saul failed miserably at all these charges. Rather than ruling over the people, he seems to have been ruled by concerns about his acceptability to them. Rather than restraining the people, he was swept along by them. And rather than being absorbed with the requirements of the Law, he was absorbed with poll numbers. Green summarizes:

> Saul concedes: "I have sinned." But his next words seem fatal to me, since his acknowledgement slides immediately into blame of the people. Saul's alibi underlines that he violated his monarchic charge *as fundamentally as possible*, by *obeying people instead of God*, by caving in to rather than restraining the people. (emphasis mine)[19]

Why We Go Along with the Crowd

Carried Along

Leaders go along with the crowd because they get swept up in the crowd. Leaders are surrounded by voices, causes, problems, concerns, and options that all vie for attention and action. Ronald Heifetz, head of the Kennedy leadership center on the campus of Harvard University, suggests that leadership takes place on a dance floor. Imagine several bands, each playing a different song to a unique beat, surrounding you. Each band competes for your attention. Each wants you to dance to their rhythm.

Saul found himself in a battle of the bands for his attention and approval. On one side stood Samuel, who gave Saul a clear directive from the Lord. On the other were the troops who expected to receive the plunder of their victory. Saul listened to the wrong song and danced to the wrong beat. He got swept away in the music. Heifetz observes:

> Working amidst the cacophony of a multiple-band dance floor, one needs a sanctuary to restore one's sense of purpose, put issues in perspective, and regain courage and heart. When serving as the repository of many conflicting aspirations, a person can lose himself in the role by failing to distinguish his inner voice from the voices that clamor for attention from the outside. Partners can help greatly, as can a run, a quiet walk, or a prayer to break the spell cast by the frenzy on the floor. We need sanctuaries.
>
> To exercise leadership, one has to expect to get swept up in the music. One has to plan for it and develop scheduled opportunities that anticipate the need to regain perspective. Just as leadership demands a strategy of mobilizing people, it also requires a strategy of deploying and restoring one's own spiritual resources.[20]

The key issue is to hear, trust, and respond to the right voice, the right music. Saul's example is so blatant, yet telling. He knew the command of God, yet turned to the desire of the troops. You and I can identify with Saul. In a previous encounter, he did not allow the troops to take plunder, and that was disastrous (1 Sam. 14:24–35). He had asked for a decision from God, and the troops stood against the decision (1 Sam. 14:38–45). Saul did not know his own core values and beliefs as a leader. When this happens, the result is that the loudest band wins the battle.

Like Saul, it is very easy for us to succumb to popular thinking, give in to peer pressure, and to "go along with the crowd." Why is that? While there are surely many reasons for this all-too-human tendency, let's focus on three reasons.

1. Group-think

Leaders go along with the crowd because they get caught in the simple rut of what psychologist Denis Waitley calls "group-think." Waitley writes, "Group-think is powerful in all professions, organizations, industries, and societies. It's the idea that 'this is how we do things around here, so fall in step and march to the cadence.'"[21] Group-think is an ethos created within organizations and peer groups that places great stock in the weight of the past and puts up great resistance to change, new ideas, and even the introduction of improvements.[22]

Group-think begins early in life. You can likely remember feeling the strong need to conform to the standards of your peer group when you were a teenager. Dr. Waitley explains:

> Teenagers have a strong need to conform to the standards of their group. While they may feel that their special way of grooming is an act of independence, on the contrary, their styles and activities adhere very strictly to the peer code. Those who refuse to be responsible and honest for their own deeds, looking to others for behavior cues, have not reached maturity. Unfortunately, many adults spend their entire lives at this level of maturity.[23]

Dr. Benno Muller-Hill, a professor in the genetics department of the University of Cologne, told a story about an experience he had in high school that cogently illustrates the power of group-think. Muller-Hill's physics teacher had set up a telescope in order to show his students a planet and its moons. While Muller-Hill waited last in a line of forty students, the first young person stepped up to the telescope, looked through it, and, when the teacher asked whether he could see anything, said that no, his nearsightedness was obscuring his view. Once the teacher had shown the boy how to adjust the focus, the boy reported that he could make out the planet and moons. One after another, the other thirty-eight students went to the telescope, looked through it, and claimed that they could see the planet and its moons. Finally, when the student just in front of Muller-Hill went to the telescope, he reported that he could not see anything. The teacher, calling the student an idiot, repeated that he had to adjust the lens. When the student claimed that he still could not see anything, the teacher looked through the telescope himself and was shocked to find the lens cap still on the telescope. None of the students had been able to see anything at all![24]

Group-think does not just affect young people. It affects adults, often entire communities and/or societies. Waitley tells about a South American tribe whose members had been dying prematurely for generations.[25] Scientists discovered that the cause of this was a rare disease carried by an insect that lived in the walls of their adobe huts. The natives had several options. They could destroy the insects with a pesticide. They could destroy their homes completely, eliminating the insects in the process. Another option was simply to relocate to a place where that particular insect did not live. Lastly, they could remain where they were, do nothing, and continue to die at young ages. What do you think they chose? The natives chose the last option. The majority of the tribe members did not want to change, and so they all remained where they were, continuing to succumb to this disease.

Group-think can prevent individuals from achieving their own dreams and goals. It can infect organizations. And it can even affect the behavior of entire societies.

2. Fear of going it alone

impt. Caving in to fear is a second reason that leaders go along with the crowd. Often, even if we have a good idea, we go along with group-think because of the fear of ridicule from our family, friends, or colleagues. We worry about what others will think if we go out on a limb, sell everything we have, and start that business we have always dreamed of owning. We fear criticism that may come if we uproot and move across the country to pursue that Ph.D. program we have always dreamed of doing. We fear possible negative reactions that may come from colleagues if we present the hypothesis we've been nurturing that challenges accepted notions.

In the era of Shaka Zulu,[26] the great African warrior who forged a nation from disparate tribes, a story is told of a tribal chief who, at the decisive moment of battle, could not be found on the field of contest. He was found in the thicket. "The chief is in the thicket" became a Zulu proverb for a leader who is unwilling to face a difficult challenge. What are the fears that send the leader to the thicket? Fear often dances in the leader's head as nagging, threatening questions:

What if I don't know enough?

What if I make a mistake?

What if they don't respect me?

What if I am wrong?

What if they turn against me?

What if I am humiliated?

What if I disappoint everyone?

There are leaders whose primary leadership trait is *fear*. Before decisions are made, they engage in countless discussions of whether the decision is acceptable, who might be offended by the decision, where criticism might come from, or how the choice is out of step with the majority. Fear means lots of second-guessing, revisiting an issue, dragging feet, and anxiety about moving forward. Here is the hard truth: it is impossible to lead the people if you are afraid of the people.

3. The path of least resistance

All people tend to move away from what causes fear. Since taking a course of action that might bring criticism, attack, or scorn is painful, we tend to choose courses of action that bring either acceptance or little reaction from our peers. Just as water seeks out the lowest places, so the natural tendency of all people is to seek out the least controversial course of action. It is always more comfortable to take the path of least resistance, the third reason leaders go along with the crowd.

You remember the children's nursery rhyme:

Row, row, row your boat
Gently down the stream
Merrily, merrily, merrily, merrily,
Life is but a dream.

Leadership rarely, if ever, floats downstream. The essence of leadership is to move against the current, to lead upstream. The challenge of leadership is to persuade, influence, and motivate the rowers to pull with you against the current. There will be critics; row on! There will be attacks; keep rowing! There will be scorn; "never, never, never give up," as Winston Churchill put it. Your confidence, your competence, your commitment, as well as your compassion for those who row with you will turn the tide of thinking away from what is easy to what is best.

Swimming Against the Tide

A famous example of swimming against the tide is that of John Shea, an audiologist of world repute who pioneered an innovative approach to a particular kind of ear surgery. John had graduated from Harvard Medical School, after which a stint in the Korean War interrupted his studies. He completed his education in Europe, where he encountered otosclerosis, which is a form of arthritis that assails the bones within the middle ear that conduct sound.

Dr. Shea sought to find a cure for this condition, and he pored over old medical journals, dissected the ears of hundreds of cadavers in the basement autopsy room of the Vienna Hospital, and worked eighteen hours a day on his quest. Dr. Shea would sit in the Vienna University's unheated library, studying in his overcoat, searching for the hidden cure to otosclerosis. One snowy night he discovered the answer: a procedure called "stapedectomy," which had been tried briefly—but then abandoned—in the early 1900s.

The procedure had quickly fallen out of use because its success was only sporadic. Dr. Shea thought he knew why. In otosclerosis patients, the small stapes bone would become rigid and unable to conduct sound. The stapedectomal procedure that had been previously practiced but then abandoned was one in which the stapes bone was simply removed. The expectation was that the eardrum would then grow in such a way that it would be able to conduct sound. This oftentimes did not happen, however.

Dr. Shea hypothesized that the old procedure could be successful by simply remaking the sound-conducting mechanism by creating an artificial stapes. He returned to the United States and designed an artificial stapes out of Teflon. He performed the new stapedectomal procedure successfully, and so decided to present his findings at an international conference of ear surgeons. Prior to the conference, a trusted friend of his late father's advised him not to make the presentation, explaining that to do so would be professional suicide—tarnishing not only his own career but that of his late father, who had been a well-respected doctor. John insisted that he knew he was right, and that he felt he owed it to others to reveal what he had discovered.

Dr. Shea went through with his presentation, and was professionally ostracized for the next several years. Very few of Dr. Shea's colleagues accepted his innovation; most simply dismissed it out of hand. Eventually, the doctor was vindicated, and the procedure gained wide acceptance. Years later, Dr. Shea reminisced about those difficult times:

> "The people who oppose you most," he said, "are those who represent the establishment your innovation will overthrow. The people who criticized what I'd done were doing another operation called a fenestration, which created a window in another part of the ear. That operation was difficult. Only a small number of surgeons could do it well, and it gave only fair results. The stapedectomy threatened them. Their pride was involved because here was somebody coming along and making them look silly— and of course they were making a lot of money from it."[27]

Almost any time an innovation challenges the status quo, it will attract criticism and scorn. Innovative leaders must be prepared for this, and be prepared to take the heat for what they know is right.

Practical Advice for Swimming Upstream

Neil Armstrong reflected on the challenge of landing on the moon, saying, "I think we're going to the moon because it's in the nature of a human being to face challenges. It's by the nature of his deep inner soul . . . we're required to do these things just as salmon swim upstream."

Here is practical advice to help you swim upstream, against the popular current of peer pressure.

1. *Break out of the rut of group-think.* John Mason, founder and president of Insight International, writes that "nothing significant has ever been accomplished without controversy or criticism," so "don't let your life depend on the permission and opinion of others."[28] A leader must be willing to question the acceptance of popular thinking, rather than just following automatically. John Maxwell, founder of EQUIP and the John Maxwell Company, writes, "If you want to succeed, you need to think about what's best, not what's popular."[29] Any old dead fish can float downstream, but a leader must be willing to swim upstream—against the current.

2. *Reevaluate whom you associate with.* We become like those we spend time with. Are you spending your time associating with people who reinforce your dreams and goals, who edify you, and who are high achievers? Or are you spending time with people who are always shooting down your ideas, who de-edify you, and who are low achievers? While friendships are important, there may be times when it is necessary to restrict whom you associate with. Remember that "eagles fly alone; crows fly in groups."[30]

3. *Change what you feed your mind.* The body manifests what the mind harbors. Whatever you are feeding your mind is what will manifest itself in your life. Just as a steady diet of junk food will cause the body to be sluggish, clunky, and generally unhealthy, so a steady diet of mental junk food will inhibit the mind's ability to work in positive, healthy, and creative ways. Leaders are readers—but *what* they read is important. Steamy romance novels, pulp fiction, and comic books—while they may give an occasional respite from stress—should not be your staples. Instead, set up a regular program of audios, books, and seminars that give you an ongoing program of personal and professional growth.

4. *Turn off the TV.* Television has become a national addiction and, while most people may think of it as a fairly benign habit, it has had tremendously important effects on our society. By the time children reach the age of five today, they have typically watched over three thousand hours of television. Dr. Waitley calls television "the model for losers." He writes:

We all hope that the bombardment of nightly television situation comedies and violent cops and robbers shows, ranging from
incest to homosexuality, has no effect on our own lives and the
lives of our children. How dumb can we get? If 60-second com-
mercials cost more than $100,000 for one minute of prime time
just to try to give us a subliminal hint to buy a product or service,
can you imagine the impact of 48 minutes of situation comedies
and hour after hour of deviant behavior in the name of entertainment served to our children who watch day after day in a
semi-stupor? . . . If a commercial can get you to buy a new toy,
you can believe that the rest of the show can get you to buy a
losing lifestyle as a normal way of life.[31]

Jane Healy's important book *Endangered Minds* uncovered
several shocking facts regarding the implications of the volume of television input on our nation's children, most notably
that children who watch a lot of television actually have smaller
brains.[32] Television's impact extends far beyond its impact on our
children, however, to a larger societal impact. Neil Postman has
written:

When a population becomes distracted by trivia, when cultural
life is redefined as a perpetual round of entertainments, when
serious public conversation becomes a form of baby-talk, when,
in short, a people become an audience and their public business
a vaudeville act, then a nation finds itself at risk; culture-death is
a clear possibility.[33]

Waitley explains how this far-reaching effect takes place:

By concentrating on what is wrong with society, we find ourselves unable to spend much time thinking about what we are
doing right or what we can do right. We become very depressed,
we lose our real incentives and excitement about life and see
society as an historical pattern of losing, from Mayan and Grecian
times, to the Roman Empire, up to the present. We spend much of
our time gleefully predicting the coming of the end.[34]

Rather than spending time doing things that are tension relieving, find something to do that is goal achieving.

> There's more benefit from turning off the television than refusing to fill your mind with mental junk food. When you turn off television, you must create something else to do. Overcoming boredom is one of the greatest impetuses you can ever experience for your creativity. Your mind engages once again in the world around you. You become a participant, not a spectator. Try it tonight! After momentary pangs of withdrawal, you'll probably like the feeling you have after spending an evening doing something other than sitting passively in front of a big box with moving colors and disruptive sound effects.[35]

Instead of watching TV, listen to audio-recorded lectures or enroll at a night class at the nearest community college. Read a book. Start a reading group. Go for a walk with your spouse. Play games with your children. Write letters. Write a book. Paint a picture. Start a side-business.

5. *Be willing to go it alone.* When you refuse to follow the crowd, you will often encounter resistance. But remember that God rarely uses a person whose main concern is what others are thinking. "Every great idea and dream must be established within you and you alone. There will come times when only you will believe it is going to happen. Can you stand alone? Can you believe when it looks as if no one else does?"[36]

6. *Take a stand.* The pitfall of King Saul discussed in this chapter was his tendency to go along with the crowd and to blame his troops, and his unwillingness to take a stand and lead. It is tempting to thoughtlessly go with the flow. It takes inner strength to resist being passively swept along downstream by what others would have you do, think, and believe. As we have sought to show, this usually involves a conscious decision to look for, explore, and possibly take a different path. Henry Kissinger, Secretary of State during the turbulent years of the Vietnam conflict, made a potent remark, "A leader does not deserve the name unless he is occasionally willing to stand alone."

Group Discussion and Personal Reflection

Group Discussion

Not to Lead

For each statement below, discuss three questions: 1) How does this statement relate to the story of King Saul told in this chapter? 2) How have you seen this statement demonstrated in the life of a leader you know? 3) How have you seen this statement demonstrated in your own life?

➤ You cannot lead the people if you are afraid of the people.

➤ You cannot lead the people if you blame the people.

➤ You cannot lead the people if you are in a survival mode.

➤ You cannot lead the people if you ignore the people.

To Lead or Be Led

Discuss the difference between leading the people and being led by the people.

➤ To be led by the people means . . .

➤ To lead the people means . . .

Lead the People

Both King Saul and Moses faced difficult times and hard choices when leading the people. You have studied the story of King Saul. Now discover how Moses found the strength to lead the people in a time of crisis. Read Exodus 33:12–17 and discuss how a leader can find the inner strength and courage to lead rather than be led by the people.

> Moses said to the LORD, "You have been telling me, 'Lead these people,' but you have not let me know whom you will send with me. You have said, 'I know you by name and you have found favor with me.' If you are pleased with me, teach me your ways so I may know you and continue to find favor with you. Remember that this nation is your people."

The LORD replied, "My Presence will go with you, and I will give you rest."

Then Moses said to him, "If your Presence does not go with us, do not send us up from here. How will anyone know that you are pleased with me and with your people unless you go with us? What else will distinguish me and your people from all the other people on the face of the earth?"

And the LORD said to Moses, "I will do the very thing you have asked, because I am pleased with you and I know you by name."

Personal Reflection

Assess

➤ I tend to ignore the people when I make my decisions.

      Fully Agree 5   4   3   2   1 Completely Disagree

➤ I am in a survival mode in my leadership assignment.

      Fully Agree 5   4   3   2   1 Completely Disagree

➤ I am inclined to blame the people for problems and crisis.

      Fully Agree 5   4   3   2   1 Completely Disagree

➤ I am secretly afraid of what the people might do or say.

      Fully Agree 5   4   3   2   1 Completely Disagree

Analyze

Complete the following sentences:

➤ I am more confident and competent in leading the people when I . . .

➤ I am more likely to pander and indulge the people when I . . .

Act

It is not easy to swim against the current. Perhaps the advice of W. C. Fields presents the challenge clearly: "Remember, a dead fish can float downstream, but it takes a live one to swim upstream."

Choose actions steps that would be most appropriate for you:

___ Read more quality books and articles that focus on your goals.

___ Watch less television that is mindless and repetitive.

___ Invest time with people who inspire you to take on challenges.

___ Think about what's important enough for you to go it alone.

___ Clarify what is popular and what is best.

___ Prepare for criticism with a clear mind and a unified purpose.

Chapter 8

Saul Failed to Promote
or Make Necessary Changes

To be human is to change. From conception to birth, birth to maturity, maturity to death, the journey of each human being is a journey of change. The story of humanity is a story of change from one form of society to another, one geographic center to the next, and one advancement to another. Yet, human beings receive and resist change. We take it on with an admixture of anticipation and apprehension. William A. Pasmore, author of *Creating Strategic Change* and professor of organizational behavior at Case Western Reserve University, describes the enchantment, excitement, and frightfulness of change:

> The unfolding interplay among all [the factors surrounding change] . . . makes the process of change mysterious if not miraculous, as dynamic an achievement as any mankind could hope to accomplish. The process is beautiful to behold, enchanting in its shifts between subtlety and storminess, no more predictable in its course than the cutting of a river through granite. With its origins in our spirit and our primal acquaintance with it, change in human systems remains as thrilling to experience as the wind of a thunderstorm sweeping across an open lake. Slightly apprehensive, forever expectant, we approach change in organizations with our heads and our hearts fully straining toward the goal like a horse pulling a heavy carriage. We will succeed; we will make the organization better; we will arrive at the moment of fulfillment in which we can look back upon our work and rest, at least momentarily, with pride.[1]

One of the areas over which churches and other organizations are in constant tension is change. While the axiom that "the only thing truly constant is change" is true, it is also true that change is one of the things to which people are most resistant. Leaders must be very sensitive to this when seeking to promote change in their organization, and choose their battles wisely. When a leader pushes change that is perceived as change for change's sake alone, he or she may encounter resistance when truly important changes need to be made. Leaders should, therefore, use discernment, or "pick their battles," when it comes to deciding what changes do or do not need to be made. When it is determined what changes need to be made, a leader must then have the courage to implement those changes for the good of the organization. Saul failed to do this.

The Rule of Saul—Little Positive Change for the Nation

After Saul was anointed king, he established only a simple government. It seems likely that he did this intentionally. The people had never had a centralized government, and it would not be easy, therefore, to impose rigid controls on them. And, while some taxes would be necessary to maintain a centralized government, time and education would be necessary before people would accept them. So, the government was initially simple and inexpensive. When we first encounter Saul in Scripture after he was made king, we find him coming in from the fields, where he had been working just like everyone else.

Saul did ultimately establish a capital at Gibeah, which was his own hometown. He built a fairly simple palace, which really served as more of a fortress. While we do not have full information on the subject, it does not seem that any special privilege was given to the capital city in the land of Israel. Saul did not create any kind of elaborate court. The biblical record gives us the name of only one officer—Abner—and he was the cousin of Saul (1 Sam. 14:50). The Bible does tell us that monthly meetings were held at the time of the new moon, which probably included problem solving and strategic planning (1 Sam. 20:24–27).

Throughout Saul's reign, it seems he instituted few policies that brought about any substantial or positive changes for the nation. Saul did not do away with the old tribal borders, for example. Prior to the founding of the monarchy, the "nation" was really nothing more than a loose federation of separate tribes. Centralization could have resulted in either the eradication or alteration of the old tribal borders in an effort to achieve unity among the disparate tribes. While the tribes were no longer to think of themselves as separate following the founding of the monarchy, Saul did not promote any change in this regard. While orders that defied the traditions of Israel might possibly have stirred rebellion, Saul did not even suggest or encourage these kinds of changes. Old Testament scholar Leon Wood, former professor of Old Testament Studies and dean of the Grand Rapids Baptist Seminary, observed:

> Likely the people were pleased that Saul instituted this manner of rule. They had the satisfaction of a king like other nations, and yet they did not suffer irritating interference in their private lives. Radical new laws, systems, or institutions had not been imposed, and taxes had not been greatly increased.[2]

The people of Israel were pleased by the minimal change Saul instituted with his reign. They felt good, knowing that a chief ruler was in power to ensure their security after years of oppression by foreign nations. The people felt that the nation of Israel was guaranteed a degree of stability now that it had a standing army. We could say that, to some degree, Saul was wise in the way he began his reign, because he sought to bring about change gradually. It seems prudent to bring about changes slowly. Drastic and sudden changes could have incited the people to rebellion.

In some ways, Saul's reign is very dissimilar to that of an actual "king," and some scholars have argued that he would more accurately be described as a "chief." Indeed, the people of Israel had been led by "judges" for many years, and this may account for Saul's reluctance to institute monarchical policies throughout his reign. In terms of a final assessment of Saul, Dr. Wood gives him low marks:

> Saul's manner of continuing the rule, however, did not show the same good judgment; for even though reasons existed for not starting with strong government, before many years had passed he should have begun to institute policies and measures toward

unification. If the tribes were to be welded into a nation, these were needed. But no evidence exists that Saul ever tried to effect them.[3]

While Saul started well—not imposing drastic changes—he ended poorly. In the long run, he failed to implement or even promote positive and necessary changes.

Resistance to Change

Resistance to change seems to be a universal characteristic, crossing all classes and cultures. Well-meaning and well-educated people often resist making positive and necessary changes, even after they have been presented with the facts as to why those changes are positive and necessary. Scientific and medical advancements have been delayed for generations because of refusal to let go of old ideas. Diseases have continued to plague societies because of a refusal to believe that a cure has been discovered. In his powerful book *Developing the Leader Within You*, John Maxwell suggests fourteen reasons why people are so resistant to change.[4]

1. The change isn't self-initiated.
2. Routine is disrupted.
3. Change creates fear of the unknown.
4. The purpose of the change is unclear.
5. Change creates fear of failure.
6. The rewards for change don't match the effort change requires.
7. People are too satisfied with the way things are.
8. Change won't happen when people engage in negative thinking.
9. The followers lack respect for the leader.
10. The leader is susceptible to feelings of personal criticism.
11. Change may mean personal loss.
12. Change requires additional commitment.

13. Narrow-mindedness thwarts acceptance of new ideas.

14. Tradition resists change.

I (Ralph) think there are two main ideas that pervade all fourteen of Dr. Maxwell's reasons that people resist change. Both of these can be seen clearly in the context of the church.

The first is the comfort of the predictable. Our world is changing at a breakneck speed, and many people like to know that their church is the one place they can go and know what is going on. The second main idea is that when people have a personal investment in what they know, in what they are familiar with, or in what they helped build or develop, they will resist change. When changes are proposed, people will oftentimes, therefore, become protective of their church and "the way we have always done it." When it comes to their church, believers can become defensive—or even hostile!—about seemingly mundane matters: about where a certain picture should be placed; about whether a decrepit bookshelf should be disposed of; about whether the "new" hymnal should be purchased; about whether Sunday school should change its time in order to add a coffee social before the 11:00 a.m. service to try to make the church more welcoming. The idea of canceling a service that is poorly attended, adding a new, "contemporary" service, or even changing the time of the traditional service can all be extremely threatening to some church members. The point is that, while these matters may seem mundane to those who are not rooted in the traditions of the congregation, they become crucially important to those who hold the church's routines near and dear.

There are certainly many reasons people resist change. Ultimately, however, "people don't resist change, per se. They resist loss."[5] Loss comes in many forms. James O'Toole lists more than thirty hypotheses for why people resist change.[6] I have reproduced a portion of his list below. As you read the list, consider the sense of loss hidden in the resistance to change.

- Change is not a natural condition.
- The burden of proof is on the change.
- It takes energy to change course.

- The time isn't right.
- Fear of the unknown.
- Change may be good for others, but not me.
- We don't think we are up to the challenge.
- We are overwhelmed by too many changes.
- Change doesn't really make any lasting improvement.
- We don't know how to change.
- We suspect the motives of the people who are asking us to change.
- We fear the unintended consequences of change.
- We can't see the value of making this change.
- We don't want to admit we were wrong.
- Why suffer now for good that may come later?

I (Richard) see that beneath all the explanations for resistance to change, one theme emerges: people resist loss. People resist the loss of esteem, comfort, perspective, relationships, tradition, values, habits, positions, power, etc.

While for most people change represents loss, it does not negate the fact that change is a necessity. It is inevitable. Just as in a biological context an organism must respond to changes in its environment or the organism will die, in order to survive and thrive, organizations must deal with the changes that are thrust upon them. And while the need to change often comes from outside the organization—from a change in markets, clients, members, delivery systems, economic realities, products, services, expectations, generations, neighborhoods, technology, government, or requirements—leaders are the ones responsible for initiating and implementing those changes.

Therefore, leaders look dangerous to followers. The leader questions mission, values, strategy, routines, personnel, and policy. The leader's questions feel like a threat. Relationships, comfort, goals, compensation, and, especially in the church, spiritual meaning are put at risk. People respond to threat with defense. In business, team spirit devolves into personal agendas and ugly office politics. In the church, people defend their "church home" using all the tools available to beat back the threat to the survival of the "church family." It is no wonder that leaders, if they are mature and experienced, think deep and long before advancing a profound change in the organization. Here are the questions to ask before implementing a change:

- For the business leader: "Is this change required to advance the mission of the organization?"
- For the church leader: "Is this change required to remain faithful to God's calling on the church?"
- For all leaders: "Am I the one to lead the change? Am I willing to pay the price to lead the change?"

The Risks of Refusing to Change

While there are some changes that may need to be resisted, there are others that should be embraced. And the refusal to change can sometimes bring with it terrible costs. Hiroo Onoda, a former Imperial Japanese Army Intelligence officer who fought in World War II, wrote an autobiography entitled *No Surrender: My Thirty-Year War*, in which he recounted his own refusal to change and the terrible price it cost him. Stationed on the island of Lubang in the South China Sea on December 26, 1944, Lieutenant Onoda led his soldiers into the mountains in the course of a battle just prior to the war's end. Almost two and a half months after the war came to an end, Onoda and his partners began to find leaflets on the island which read, "The war ended on August 15. Come down from the mountains!" Neither Onoda nor his fellow soldiers believed this.

Like the other Japanese soldiers of his day, Onoda had been trained to have unflagging loyalty to and faith in his country. Explaining the orders he received when assigned to Lubang, Onoda writes:

> [My superior said,] "It may take three years, it may take five, but whatever happens, we'll come back for you. Until then, so long as you have one soldier, you are to continue to lead him. You may

have to live on coconuts. If that's the case, live on coconuts!" . . .
I was doubly impressed with the responsibility I bore. I said to
myself, "I'll do it! Even if I don't have coconuts, even if I have
to eat grass and weeds, I'll do it! These are my orders, and I will
carry them out . . . I will fight till that day comes."[7]

Although patrols combed the island from May until August, leaving leaflets with orders to surrender given by Onoda's own general as well as his chief of staff, Onoda and his two fellow soldiers would simply relocate to another part of the island, remaining in hiding.

Over the years, the Japanese launched repeated efforts to bring Onoda out of the jungle, flying helicopters overhead with family members shouting his name through loudspeakers, dropping leaflets with messages from the military and from family members. They also dropped newspapers which explained the end of the war along with current events which had followed since the war's end. But Onoda was so convinced in his own mind that the war was still going on that he twisted those messages around. The rescue missions were interpreted to be nothing more than enemy hoaxes, with traitors cleverly disguised as family members in order to coax him into showing himself. Magazines and newspapers that were dropped were interpreted to be elaborate hoaxes invented by the enemy to try to draw him out of the jungle. Again, he writes:

By that time [my partner and I] had developed so many fixed
ideas that we were unable to understand anything that did not
conform with them. If there was anything that did not fit in with
them we interpreted it to mean what we wanted it to mean.[8]

It was thirty years later, in 1974, before he finally emerged from the mountains of Lubang. He emerged in response to an attempt to contact him. Although tempted to dismiss this contact in the same way he had done for thirty years, he tentatively concluded that he could not hide forever. He said, "If you doubt everything, you end up not being able to do anything." Having lived in isolation for so long, it occurred to Onoda that he had cherished the way he had come to see his role in the "ongoing war," and that he was actually afraid of leaving those perceptions. He writes,

> What was to happen now? Major Taniguchi had said that I could
> go back to Japan immediately, but the idea of going back and
> trying to live among ordinary people frightened me. I could not
> quite imagine it. . . . For the first time, I began to feel the weight
> of those thirty years. . . . Why had I fought for thirty years? Who
> had I been fighting for? What was the cause?[9]

Hiroo Onoda refused to question his long held assumptions and,
as a result, he remained in the wilderness for thirty years, only to
discover that he had needlessly sacrificed many precious years of
his life. All too often, individuals, congregations, and other organizations suffer because of the refusal to consider the need for
adjustments in their perspectives.

Working Toward Change

What Kind of Change?

If we are going to begin working toward change, we must
first understand it. There are two types of change. First, there is
problem-solving change carried out by the leader on behalf of the
followers. For example, if I break my arm, I ask the doctor to set the
arm, give me a shot for pain, and expect others to help me recover.
Except for a mild intrusion, my lifestyle remains intact or soon will
be restored. This kind of change is acceptable. We want a leader to
fix things, take care of problems, and maintain our comfort zone. In
Saul's day, the people cried out for such a king, one who would rid
them of their enemy and return them to the comfort of their daily
lives. This type of change is primarily a management issue. We like
this type of change. However, there is another type of change.

A second type of change is a culture change. This requires a
change from followers. To continue the medical analogy, if I go to
the doctor and discover that I have a heart problem, I want the doctor to fix it and return me to my comfortable life. However, if the
doctor says I must change my comfortable life with exercise and a
new diet, I want a second opinion. I want another doctor.

We don't like change that demands a shift away from comfort
into something different. We don't like change that demands that

we must change. Samuel envisioned this type of change when the people demanded a king (1 Sam. 8, 12). This type of change requires leadership.

Adjusting to the monarchy wasn't Israel's first experience with culture change. Prior to Moses, Joshua, and the judges, the Israelites were slaves in Egypt. After leaving Egypt, they learned to let go of their culture of slavery and become free people in the land God promised. Culture change is not easy. Plenty of kicking and screaming accompanied this process (Num. 13). As leader of the Israelites during this time of culture change, Moses would not give up or give in. The people needed to change in order to receive the promise of God's new land. In contrast, when the monarchy was established with the anointing of Saul as the first king of Israel, Saul did not ask the people to change. He did not even seem to envision a new promise from God for God's people.

Leaders avoid the challenge of leading change because it is so difficult. A popular leader can fall in the polls when the people are required to change, to sacrifice, or to give up comfort. Yet the need for change is the same as the need for leadership. Leaders produce change. I (Richard) attended a week-long seminar on deep change, guided by Robert Quinn and Jeff DeGraff at the Ross Business School of the University of Michigan, Ann Arbor. One participant, a leader in a major corporation, made this observation: "If the leader knows there is a need for change, but is unwilling to lead the change, hasn't the leader crossed an ethical line?"

Why Do People Change?

It has been said that people change for only two reasons—either they are in crisis or they are in love. Some speculate that the two situations are the same. While we may smile at this simplistic conclusion, the underlying principle is sound. Business thinking refers to the first reason for change, crisis, as the burning platform. The leader emphasizes the need for immediate and radical change because of impending disaster. The second motive for change could be more aptly described as a burning passion. Inspiration, vision, purpose, and a greater good for people are also powerful and passionate motivations. In order to do the painful and scary work involved in culture change, people must believe in a leader and a cause. People need a leader to communicate a compelling vision.

In his book *The Dance of Change*, Peter Senge, director of the Center for Organizational Learning at the MIT Sloan School of Management, weds the two motives for change into a single description of the leader's task: to hold the creative tension, the energy generated between a vision of the future and the truth about today's reality.[10] This task represents a shift in the emphasis of leadership. Rather than a leader attempting to get the people to do what the leader wants them to do, the leader helps the people solve the problem of change.[11] Good leadership requires the skill of delivering disturbing news, raising difficult questions, and pointing to a compelling future in a way people can absorb (and not kill the messenger).

Creating a Climate for Change

People don't change because it is a good idea. Change is not the result of intellectual reasoning and clear thinking. Change only comes through struggle. If people are going to change, they need a safe place and a safe way to struggle with the change, the emotions, the fears, the hopes, the hard truth, and the fresh vision. Here are several suggestions that help create a climate for successful change:

- People need to identify with compelling reasons for change. It takes more than discussing reasons to change, it requires embracing the reasons for change. The mind has reasons, but the heart has reasons also.
- People need a vision for change. They need more than a vision statement, a growth chart, or an architect's rendition, however helpful these may be. The vision that a leader projects for the future must be clearly better than the present.
- People need some early wins. The long picture is essential, but people also need quick wins. They need to see something happen promptly that is the result of their effort to make the change.

- People need a team they trust. Leaders put together coalitions, teams, and partners. People need a team to lead the change, a team that understands, relates, and represents them.

- People need something big. Big change influences deep thinking, core values, new patterns, and setting aside old ways that hinder the fulfillment of the vision.

- People need to insert their own ideas. We don't resist our own ideas. People need and deserve the opportunity to add their ideas to the structure of the new future.

What is the leader's task in creating the change climate? The leader must struggle with the change. Change in the organization will demand that you, the leader, change. You will suffer loss. If you refuse to see the loss you must embrace, you will not understand the change you are leading. Often, to the people, change looks like all gain for the leader. However, to lead change, you must struggle with and for your people. Saul never did this and nothing much changed. However, David knew how to struggle with the people. David took the Israelites into a new future, into God's future.

Change in the Church

One of the areas in which Christian leaders most grapple with change is the church. The church is, by its very nature, a place where traditions are preserved and passed down. The apostle Paul commended the Corinthians for maintaining "the traditions just as I handed them on to you" (1 Cor. 11:2 NRSV). Later, he urged the Thessalonians to "stand firm and hold fast to the traditions that you were taught by us, either by word of mouth or by our letter" (2 Thess. 2:15 NRSV). The church has preserved many traditions for thousands of years, many of which are still practiced in congregations today. Many people find comfort in the traditions of the church. In a world that sometimes seems to be changing at a breakneck pace, they appreciate the church as a place that is unchanging. They can go to church and know what to expect. It is predictable.

The reality, however, is that there is a degree of change that is inherent within church, and some religious traditions have and will continue to change from generation to generation. The reason for this fact is that we live our religious lives in changing contexts, or what we might call different "ages." Social scientists have identified three distinct ages by which they define the stages of history: the agricultural age, the industrial age, and the information age. These ages cover periods of time during which families, occupations, and society in general had in common some key qualities. The *agricultural age* is a blanket term describing most of known history up until about 1860, and it is named for the occupation which employed almost everyone during that time. People worked and conducted their lives among extended families in the context of a small, rural town.

Society transitioned into the *industrial age* in about 1860, an era that continued until approximately 1956. Industrialization was a process that changed the face of America. Prior to industrialization, 95 percent of all U.S. workers found their occupation in the farming industry. Industrialization created factories in the cities, and we began to see the demise of rural America. Today, less than 4 percent of Americans pursue agricultural occupations. Within forty years of the time industrialization began, 40 percent of the workforce had moved into factories, a number that continued to increase until the information age. Families were nuclear during this period, making their homes in the cities.

The beginning of the *information age* came in 1956 and, of course, continues into present times. The information age is named thus because it is characterized by the rapid increase in availability of information. During the last several decades, Americans have experienced the access to and manipulation of more information than previous generations experienced in their entire lifetimes, and the information continues to double every five years. In an often cited article, readers learn that between the years 1946 and 1960 the number of computers grew from one to ten thousand. In the next twenty years that number skyrocketed to ten million. And by the year 2000 there were over eighty million computers in the United States alone.[12]

Change, in other words, is the order of the day. Whether we lived and ministered in congregations in the agricultural age, the industrial age, or the information age, change has always been part and parcel of the human experience. Most churchgoers today do not consider their church's traditions to be innovations. Rather, they view them as the stable, time-tested practices of the body of Christ. But the truth of the matter is that in one age or another, many of the things we do as churches were probably innovations at one time. In evaluating the changing models of ministry throughout the ages, authors Glen Martin and Gary McIntosh consider common worship times as one such example.[13]

The 11:00 a.m. worship services we are so accustomed to are traditions established in relatively modern times. During the agricultural age, churches needed to allow farmers time to bring their morning chores to a close prior to hitching the horse and wagon together and driving into town, so 11:00 a.m. services met that need. Changes in lifestyles indicate that variations in these times might be in order for today's worshipers.

In a similar vein, evening services originated in the industrial age with the invention of electric lights. Following the introduction of electric lights into the marketplace, not every business or home was able to have these lights installed immediately. By installing electric lights in their buildings, therefore, some innovative church leaders discovered that they could attract crowds to nighttime services. Evening services were an innovation designed to take advantage of changing technology in order to win people to the Lord.

There are certainly other traditional elements of worship that were, at one time, innovations, but that have become antiquated with the passing of time. Many traditional hymns that are still sung in many churches today were newly written during the agricultural age (or shortly thereafter), and are based on agricultural metaphors, such as "Bringing in the Sheaves" (1874) or "The Church in the Wildwood" (1857). In nineteenth-century American churches, these hymns reflected the experience of 95 percent of the populace, who lived and worked in an agricultural setting. Many other popular hymns from the same era were based on nautical metaphors, such as "Let the Lower Lights Be Burning" (1871), "Jesus, Savior, Pilot Me" (1871), "Throw Out the Lifeline" (1888), "The Harbor Bell" (1891), and "I've Anchored in Jesus" (1901). Again, in the nineteenth and early twentieth century, when transportation and trade were often conducted by boat, these songs made sense. In twenty-first-century America, however, where less than 4 percent of the population is employed in agriculture and the majority of the population lives in an urban setting, agricultural and nautical metaphors reflect lifestyles and surroundings that few people relate to or even understand, and yet many congregations continue to use hymnals that are full of such songs. Rubel Shelly and Randy Harris, in their book *The Second Incarnation: Empowering the Church for the Twenty-First Century,* surveyed over six hundred songs contained in hymnals in use in congregations associated with their denomination, and they found that only one of them had a clearly urban setting.[14] Obviously, when these songs were first written, they were written by and for people for whom these images and ideas were meaningful. The present generation, however, lives and works primarily in large, urban centers, surrounded not by agricultural or ocean environments, but by concrete, steel, and urban sprawl.

Our preaching ministries also represent traditional approaches. Long, expository sermons have been a feature of many American churches for much of the nation's history. While the tradition of explaining the Scriptures can be traced back to the earliest days of the church, it became especially prominent in the period of the Protestant Reformation (1500–1648), because the Reformers saw Scripture as supreme over tradition and the sacraments. Reformation leaders placed a tremendous emphasis on expository preaching, and produced many collections of sermons and commentaries. In the post-Reformation period, Puritan preachers would not hesitate to preach for several hours at a time, and this approach continued in early American history. In an age without Internet, television, or other electronic devices, people would attend talks, lectures, and even debates for entertainment. The culture was literate in the sense that texts predominated as the means for disseminating information. Today's culture is primarily nonliterate, in the sense that present-day culture is dominated by visual images that come primarily in short segments. Long, expository sermons presented in a formal style may not be as effective today as they were in previous ages.

It seems indisputable that many models of worship and ministry used in the modern, information age were developed in prior ages, and they have become the focal point of conflict in contemporary churches. Martin and McIntosh conclude:

> The models of ministry developed in the agricultural and industrial ages are colliding head-on with the information age. . . . Our nation has changed; people have changed; and we must develop new models of ministry relevant for today's society if we are to fulfill Christ's commission to "make disciples."[15]

Gregg Allison, professor of Christian Theology at The Southern Baptist Theological Seminary, suggests that "the most serious challenge to the traditional worship service in evangelical churches came from the introduction of innovative elements such as contemporary Christian music."[16]

He notes that the origin and growth of parachurch movements, the church growth movement, and the integration of contemporary Christian music into the mainstream music market all worked together to compel congregations to design "contemporary" services and led to what has come to be known as the "worship wars." Many advocates of "contemporary worship," particularly in evangelical churches, have argued that the best way to be modern is to do away with the choir, traditional hymns, and any kind of liturgy, and put a worship band and spontaneous acts of praise in their place. Marva Dawn, a theologian with Christians Equipped for Ministry and author of *Reaching Out without Dumbing Down*, argues that this response is prejudiced. She critiques churches that seek to be contemporary by pandering to our society's voyeuristic obsession with media, individual choice, anti-intellectualism, and other ills, on the basis that the form of a church's worship is the key to its being contemporary.[17]

I (Ralph) am not convinced that the *form* of a church's worship is the key to being "contemporary." The pastor may wear a coat and tie, or he may wear blue jeans and a T-shirt. The service may include a choir, or it may feature a praise band. The worship may be liturgical or non-liturgical. But *form*, in and of itself, is not the key.

Charles Denison, an associate for new church development in the Presbyterian Church USA, proposes two keys to being truly contemporary. If churches really want to reach their generation, they must be (1) missional and (2) indigenous.[18] Adopting a missional mind-set means realizing that we live in a post-Christian culture that is no longer familiar with the stories, ideas, and language of what has become a Christian subculture. In previous times, it may have been safe to presume a certain level of familiarity with the Bible and its stories and teachings. This is no longer the case, and biblical literacy is at an all-time low. We must realize that we are missionaries in our own culture.

Once we have decided that we want to reach this post-Christian culture with the gospel, we must then distill the gospel to its cross-cultural core, and then re-enculturate it into the new culture.[19] In other words, we must communicate it in a way that is understandable to the indigenous population. This does not automatically mean that a pastor should wear jeans and a T-shirt to lead worship, or that the worship service should have a loud praise band instead of a pipe organ and a liturgy. Being indigenous means learning about and adapting to the culture. Denison uses the example of a missionary or missions team who attempts to go into a foreign culture with no useful knowledge of that culture.

> They have not studied the language, so they are unable to communicate effectively. They are ignorant of the traditions these people hold sacred, so they make deeply offensive mistakes without ever realizing their indiscretions. They are not only attempting to introduce the objective claims of Christ to a new people group, they are forcing their potential converts to embrace new styles of music, dress, relationships, and, in fact, a new culture if they are to convert to Christianity. The culture of the missionaries, as they inadvertently transplant it, has become a huge barrier to the message of Christ.[20]

In the same way that missionaries going into a foreign culture must avoid allowing their own culture to become a barrier to conveying the gospel, so must modern missionaries avoid the same problem in contemporary America. We must seek to be indigenous, and depending on our audience, this may look different in assorted contexts. Jeans and a T-shirt may be fine in a congregation made up of younger college students, but it may not work in a church of older urban professionals. A Geneva robe would probably not go over too well in a congregation seeking to reach out to bikers, while it may be a necessity in a church designed to appeal to those who place a high value on academic qualifications.

Liturgy, too, must be adapted to the culture. Even the Roman Catholic Church, which sees liturgy as sacred and necessary, recognized in Vatican II that while some parts of the liturgy are theological and must always be retained, other parts of it are cultural and may be adapted. In his report on the *Constitution on the Sacred Liturgy*, Austin Flannery explains:

> For the liturgy is made up of unchangeable elements divinely instituted, and of elements subject to change. These latter not only *may* be changed, but *should be changed with the passage of time*, if they have suffered from the intrusion of anything out of harmony with the inner nature of the liturgy or have become less suitable.[21]

Liturgy can be updated to reflect new cultural situations and address the needs of indigenous worshipers. In terms of music, new songs need to be written that will speak to this generation. In terms of preaching, telling interesting stories that people can relate to—which, incidentally, seems to have been Jesus' most common style of teaching—may be more effective than a formal, lecture-style sermon. Other forms of teaching might include a dramatic reading, or even a dramatic monologue based on biblical passages. Five- or ten-minute dramatic segments may make a more lasting impression on a contemporary audience than a forty-five-minute sermon. Denison suggests:

> Emerging worship will draw from many ancient components: from chant to candlelight, from silence to Eucharistic feasts. Many evangelical movements seem to be discovering these components as if for the first time [but] these are all part of our historic birthright. We can fearlessly cull the finest from all our traditions to move ahead with confidence and relevance.[22]

Aside from the issue of the form(s) worship might take *inside* the church, there are also factors *outside* the church that are having a phenomenal impact on the way the church is manifested in America.[23] Some of these factors include generational differences that are currently at work in America. The generations born between 1965 and 1979 (Generation X), 1980 and 2000 (the Millennial Generation, also known as Generation Y), and 2000 and 2020 (Generation Z) embrace God in personal, rather than institutional, ways. Generation X was behind the national average for church attendance and appears to have been one of the least Sunday-schooled generations in the last half century. They are cynical and distrustful of institutions. These trends appear to have continued among Millennials (Generation Y),[24] with the result that, depending on the survey used, about 16 to 20 percent of Americans may now be described as "nones" or "unaffiliated." These are survey respondents who, when asked what church or denomination they are affiliated with, check the box that reads either "none of the above" or "unaffiliated."[25]

LifeWay Research recently conducted a survey of twelve hundred Millennials in the United States, and Thom Rainer and Jess Rainer, in addition to conducting interviews with many of the survey respondents, have synthesized much of the findings of the survey in their new book, *The Millennials: Connecting to America's Largest Generation.*[26] Rainer and Rainer explain that Millennials tend to have a syncretistic belief system and to generally be less interested in religious or spiritual matters than previous generations. Six percent of the survey respondents identified their religious preference as atheism, 8 percent agnosticism, and 14 percent said that they had no religious preference at all.[27] These three categories total 28 percent. Furthermore, about 65 percent of Millennials report that they attend church either rarely or never.[28] The Millennials as a whole are largely anti-institutional with regard to the church and have decided that American churches are irrelevant.[29] Rainer and Rainer conclude:

> The church's challenge is not overcoming an adversarial attitude from the Millennials. The true challenge is overcoming apathy. Christianity is not the belief of the vast majority of this generation. And they believe the American church to be one of the least relevant institutions in society.[30]

Statistics on the American church have been dismal for about the last half century, and the attitude of Millennials toward the church have caused many observers to wonder if there is any hope for the survival of the church.

However, while many in this generation represent a truly post-Christian mind-set, there is also reason for optimism. One is that, strangely enough, the Millennials as a whole are a theistic group. More than 72 percent agree that God is a real being and not just an idea.[31] A second reason for optimism is that those Millennials who *are* Christians are fervent about their faith. While this is cause for optimism, it is bad news for churches that are only interested in "business as usual." Maybe it is a reaction to the self-centeredness of the Boomer Generation (1946–1964), but Millennials abhor churches that focus inwardly—on things like facilities mainte- nance and denominational politics. Millennials are a passionate generation that wants to make a contribution, and they are not attracted to a lukewarm church with a lukewarm faith.

Rainer and Rainer argue that, if today's churches are going to attract Millennials, they must become radically committed to the community, go deep in biblical teaching, love the nations, direct revenue outwardly, and demonstrate transparency, humility, and integrity.[32] Since Millennials are a very social generation, simply inviting them to church may be a powerful way to reach them.[33] If churches make the radical changes necessary to reach the Millen- nial generation, American churches could experience a dynamic renewal.

Another external factor that has had a powerful impact on the church in recent decades is the emergence of the Internet and the burgeoning of social media. In the late 1990s, a new breed of Chris- tian communities began to emerge that only met in cyberspace. By the year 2000, some researchers concluded that up to 12 percent of adults were already substituting the Internet for their current church experience, and 16 percent of teens were expected to do so within five years. Ronald Cervero speculated that by the year 2010, 10 to 20 percent of the population would probably rely solely on the Internet for their spirituality.[34] By the early 2000s, a number of Internet-only churches had been launched, such as Totalchurch. com, St. John's Internet Church, the Connecticut-based Virtual

Church, and others. Many of these cyber-churches received up to 14,000 visitors per day, and 70 percent of Totalchurch's members did not attend a local church but relied completely on the online services. David Yonggi Cho, pastor of the 750,000-member Yoido Full Gospel Church in Seoul, South Korea, told younger converts, "Don't come to church, just stay home and get your teaching through the Internet."[35] He explained that the next logical step in ministry was "to go into total cyberspace ministry because it is a real waste of money to build larger church buildings."[36]

It does not seem likely, however, that cyber-churches will completely replace physical churches, because people want to find community in relationships, and also because it is impossible to be baptized or participate in holy Communion over the Internet. At one time cyber-churches did experience an initial surge in popularity, but this appears to have stabilized and even declined.[37] "Brick-and-mortar" churches will probably always continue to exist, and cyber-churches and congregational or denominational Web sites will likely serve to enhance rather than replace them.[38] Even Cho, as zealous as he was for online communities, conceded that "we need both ministries together: a strong . . . church and a powerful Internet service."

The Internet has been praised by many as an opportunity for a centralized institution like the church to decentralize, which is "the greatest structural impact of the Net."[39] Trend watchers have given some grave warnings to churches slow to adopt the new technologies:

> . . . None can survive by following a "We've always done it this way" approach. To insist on preserving the familiar for its own sake is to make all but certain that the . . . church . . . will quickly lose strength and eventually will die.[40]

It must certainly be true that, as computers become more affordable, churches that use them creatively are more likely to survive than those that insist on doing communication, ministry, and education in the same old ways. If churches are going to survive and thrive in the new millennium, their leaders must be ready to respond and adapt to radical changes. They must "trim the fat," as it were, reinventing existing structures, work across denominational lines with parachurch organizations and emerging groups, and, most importantly, go back to the Great Commission.

A Hinge of History

In my (Richard) seminars and classes, the question comes up, "Why is change so much a part of our life?" You and I live at a hinge point in history, a time when the world is moving in rapid and irreversible cultural change. Like seismic shifts in the culture, the tectonic plates of social, economic, and global interaction are grinding against one another: quakes and aftershocks are certain; the specifics are unpredictable. Saul lived at such a time, but he could not envision the future nation that the people would need. Jesus also came at such a moment of great cultural change. "When the time had fully come" (Gal. 4:4), Jesus ushered the kingdom of God into a new era. We live at such a moment in history. We were born into it. For forty years our society has experienced change on a grand scale. I don't know anyone that expects the next forty years to be any different. Change is here and change is hard. If you are a leader, you are called to lead in a changing time and a time that demands we change.

Group Discussion and Personal Reflection

Group Discussion

Types of Change

Review the chapter and note the various types of change that are mentioned—for example, a technical change, a culture change, an informational change, a generational change, etc. Discuss how each type of change is reflected in changes you are considering in your organization.

Explaining Resistance

Leaders must deal with resistance to change. As Richard Parrott says in his book *Leading Change*, "Stop and work on the resistance or the resistance will stop your work."[41] This chapter has two lists, one from John Maxwell and the second from James O'Toole. Each list details different ways leaders explain resistance to change. Discuss which explanations of resistance appeal to you and why.

Experiencing Change

Followers often forget and leaders often ignore that leaders also experience change. I (Richard) worked with an online cohort of students who had been together for six months. For legitimate reasons, the group was being divided at the end of my class. My class was on organizational culture and change. I challenged the group, "Don't waste the pain and the learning from this change. What does it teach you about leading an organization through transition?" Discuss what your experiences of change have taught you about leading change.

Leading Change

Discuss two questions: 1) What is the most significant change that I need to lead my organization through? 2) How do I need to change in order to lead the organization through change?

Personal Reflection

No one changes just because it is a good idea; we change because we struggle. Read the story of Jacob in Genesis 32:22–32 as he struggled through the night and became a new person, Israel.

Assess

The self-assessment for this chapter is a single question. It is a significant and challenging question for a leader. It is a question you must consider carefully:

➢ What is the most significant change needed in the organization I lead?

Analyze

Once you, the leader, determine the deep change that needs to take place in your organization, there are two additional questions you must ask yourself:

➢ Am I the one to lead the change?

➢ Am I willing to pay the price to lead the change?

Act

Read, read, read! There are many excellent books that will help you implement change. The following are especially good:

___ *Managing Transitions* (William Bridges). William Bridges is one of the world's experts on dealing with the human side of change. I (Richard) have recommended, taught, and given away this book time and time again.

___ *Leading Change* (John Kotter). From a Harvard professor, eight steps in a model for leading change. This book is a classic and has stood the test of time.

___ *The Fifth Discipline* (Peter Senge). Beyond the steps for leading change, there are the dynamics of systems thinking. Change is dealing with multiple moving parts and learning as you go. Senge's book is the source for understanding systems thinking.

___ *Leading Congregational Change* (Jim Herrington). This book and its accompanying workbook (Mike Bonem, James Furr, and Jim Herrington) bring the best of Kotter and Senge into the unique challenges of change in a local congregation.

Chapter 9

Saul Failed to Love the People

Despite Saul's noble beginnings, his continued authoritarian leadership, his rankism, and his tendency to isolate himself sabotaged his leadership. One of the root problems—and one of his greatest failures—was that he failed to love the people whom he was to lead. As a result, the people gradually transferred their own love to other, better leaders.

In earlier chapters, we looked at the occasion when Saul almost slew Jonathan for his son's violation of the oath to which Saul had so foolishly bound his troops (1 Sam. 14:24–52). Here, Saul put his belief in a superstitious oath before his love for his son. And it cost him in terms of the loyalty of his troops.

Later, once Jonathan and David had become friends, the two men entered into a covenant with one another. Following David's victory over Goliath, David reported back to Saul and conveyed his allegiance to the king and to the nation. The text then reports:

> When David had finished speaking to Saul, the soul of Jonathan was bound to the soul of David, and Jonathan loved him as his own soul. Saul took him that day and would not let him return to his father's house. Then Jonathan made a covenant with David, because he loved him as his own soul. Jonathan stripped himself of the robe that he was wearing, and gave it to David, and his armor, and even his sword and his bow and his belt. (1 Sam. 18:1–4 NRSV)

In verses 1 and 3, the word *love* is used to describe the relationship between Jonathan and David. As we noted in chapter 3, in this kind of setting, this word can mean a lot more than simple friendship; it can have political connotations. When the word *love* is used in the context of the making of treaties or the establishment of covenants, it always has political overtones.[1] In 1 Kings 5:1, for example, we are told that King Hiram of Tyre had "always loved David" (RSV). The NIV appropriately translates this as, "He had always been on friendly terms with David." That is, he and David were on friendly political terms. In another example, King Jehoshaphat is rebuked for having cultivated "love" with those who hate Yahweh (2 Chron. 19:2). In other words, he had made treaties with foreign nations that worshiped other gods. In these contexts of covenants, treaties, and international politics, the word *love* has to do with international friendship or cooperative politics between potentially hostile parties.[2]

Jonathan transferred his allegiance from his father, Saul, to David. Jonathan was a man who had seen the inability of his father to lead the nation. He recognized God's call on the life of David, and even though he was the rightful heir to the throne, he came to love David. In other words, he committed his allegiance to David. Jonathan gave David his robe and, since a man's robe may symbolize his authority and power, it may be that Jonathan was, in effect, transferring his own status as heir to him.[3]

Later in 1 Samuel 18, we are told that David continued in his devoted service to the people. After becoming a commander of a thousand, he "marched out and came in, leading the army" (v. 13 NRSV). In terms of the political meaning of *love* that we've been discussing, David was showing his love for the people of Israel through his service to them. And because of his devotion to the people, "all Israel and Judah loved David" (v. 16). Because of David's devotion to the nation, his leadership of the army, and his continued victories on Israel's behalf, the nation began to transfer its own allegiance away from Saul and onto David.

A few verses later, we are told how Michal, Saul's daughter, came to love David as well (v. 20). This "love" was like that of Jonathan and, while no doubt it was real love—in an emotional sense—it probably also carried the same covenantal shades of meaning mentioned before. It seems clear that these two siblings had come to show more love and loyalty to their father's competitor—David—than to Saul himself.[4]

The word *love*, then, which refers both to personal attachment and public commitment, is used of Jonathan (vv. 1, 3), of all Israel and Judah (v. 16), and of the king's daughter, Michal (v. 20). The term is like a thread that runs through this chapter, and it is surely no accident. The author was trying to show his readers that, because of Saul's failure to love the people, they gradually transferred their love to another, better leader—one who loved them.

Begin Leading by Loving

We believe that love is the foundation of great leadership. This theme is, to us, conspicuously absent from most books on leadership. And yet, loving your people is a crucial component to effective leadership. John Maxwell and Jim Dornan write:

> You may be wondering why you should take on a nurturing role with the people you want to influence, especially if they are employees, colleagues, or friends. You may be saying to yourself, "Isn't that something they can get somewhere else, like at home?" The unfortunate truth is that most people are desperate for encouragement. If you become a nurturer in the life of another person, then you have an opportunity to make a major impact on them.[5]

We had the honor of attending a leadership conference recently where Rudolph Giuliani was one of the featured speakers. He spent much of his time telling stories of how the 9/11 terrorist attacks on the World Trade Center impacted him and his understanding of leadership. Prior to 9/11, he had written a book entitled *Leadership*, which went to press before the terrorist attacks. After the attacks, the publisher asked him if he would go back through the manuscript, considering ways he might change the material or add to it based on his experiences following the crisis. Giuliani added a chapter entitled "Weddings Discretionary, Funerals Mandatory." In his presentation, he shared how he had attended hundreds of funerals in the years immediately following the attacks, and how families continually expressed their gratitude to him for being there in their time of crisis. He explained that people seldom thanked him for attending weddings, bar mitzvahs, baptisms, or parties. The point Giuliani made was that people are always happy for you to be at a party with them, but it's not near as meaningful to them as when you are there for them in a crisis. It was only after the 9/11 attacks that Rudolph Giuliani came to believe that loving the people is a crucial component of leadership.

Leadership gurus tout values, vision, structures, systems, potential, and risk. All are needed for leadership. But the issue of loving people is more subtle and often overlooked. In a classic article published in the May-June *Harvard Business Review*, 1955, O. A. Ohmann, who at that time was assistant to the president of Standard Oil Company of Ohio, deals with the human factor. Specifically, he deals with the relationship between leader and followers. He observes that even the best management techniques don't work in the hands of the wrong manager.

> We observe again and again that a manager with sound values and a stewardship conception of the role of boss can be a pretty effective leader even though the techniques used are unorthodox. I am convinced that workers have a fine sensitivity to spiritual qualities and want to work for a boss who believes in something and in whom they can believe.[6]

People need to know the boss cares. Love is finding its way into the business world. John Hope Bryant writes of the need for love-based leadership in a fear-based world.[7] Drawing on his remarkable success story, Bryant outlines the five laws of love-based leadership:

- Loss creates leaders. There can be no inner growth without the pain of legitimate suffering.
- Fear fails. Leading through fear is antiquated and self-defeating, a crippling indulgence that we can no longer afford.
- Love succeeds. The expression of love in business—creating long-term relationships with customers and employees based on caring for others and doing good—makes everyone wealthy.
- Vulnerability is power. When you open up, people open up to you. Real leaders know that vulnerability is not a weakness, but rather their greatest strength.

- Giving is getting: Leaders give, followers take. Giving inspires loyalty, attracts good people, confers peace of mind, and lies at the core of true wealth.

The power of love is the way a person in authority—whether he or she is a boss, a business owner, a manager, or a director—works with other people to value, inspire, respect, and always lift the humanity and dignity of each person.

Love, Fear, and Leadership

One can make a strong argument that the root of leadership grows either in fear or love. Frederick the Great,[8] King of Prussia (1772–1786), modernized his army by treating the soldiers as machine parts: "If my soldiers were to begin to think, not one would remain in the ranks." He treated the masses with contempt, even as he reformed and modernized the nation: "My people and I have come to an agreement which satisfies us both. They are to say what they please, and I am to do what I please." Frederick the Great believed that if the soldiers were more afraid of their officers than the enemy, they would attack the enemy rather than retreat. This was leadership built on fear. In opposition to leadership through intimidation, Jesus leads from love: "If you love me, you will keep my commandments" (John 14:15 NRSV).

In addition to outright intimidation, there is a more subtle form of fear that a bad leader might employ. In fact this is the easiest way for a leader to gain the unquestioning blind allegiance of followers—create a sense of fear and offer followers the leader's protection (in exchange for loyalty, long hours, and heretofore unknown duties that will be assigned). Despotic leaders from the ancient to the modern (Hitler and Saddam Hussein are two examples) have raised the phantom of fear and then offered a safeguard from the evil. All that is asked in return is that followers simply obey without question. The tactic is still in use.

The opposite approach was taken by Franklin Delano Roosevelt during the Great Depression and World War II. He recognized and acknowledged the real dangers, and then inspired the people with the memorable words, "The only thing we have to fear is fear itself." At another time he went on to say, "The point in history at which we stand is full of promise and danger. The world will either move forward toward unity and widely shared prosperity, or it will move apart."[9]

We should note FDR's approach to leadership. As leaders, we need to expose the real fears and provide an optimistic course of action in the confidence that we will prevail. This is in great contrast to creating dangers and fear and then using those to solidify the leader's position and power.

The Quiet Agenda

To love as a leader is to respect the quiet agenda of followers. Followers have lives to live, children to raise, homes to protect, family to help, friends to share, and dreams to pursue. Frederick Herzberg asks the question, "What do people want from their jobs?"[10] He observes that it is the factors that help an individual reach his or her personal aspirations that satisfy most deeply. Leaders express love through what Herzberg calls the "hygiene" factors, which are the concerns that keep hazardous elements away from work. These include good supervision, healthy interpersonal relations, good physical working conditions, a fair salary, benefits, and security. Leaders also express love through the "motivating" factors that help a person experience respect, personal growth, and self-fulfillment. Respecting and honoring a person's quiet agenda, a person's hope for the life he or she is trying to create, is a deep expression of love between leader and follower.

How Love Impacts Leadership

Perhaps the most practical lesson in leadership love was voiced by Zig Ziglar in a book that is now thirty years old, *Secrets of Closing the Sale*. He said, "You can have everything in life you want if you just help enough other people get what they want."[11] However, the act of giving must be free of expectation to truly be a gift. Mother Teresa said, "It is not how much we do, but how much love we put in the doing. It is not how much we give, but how much love we put into the giving."[12]

Can the principle of giving in love really work in the world of business? Bob Burg and John D. Mann have made an impact in the business world with the story of the Go-Giver.[13] The book appeared on *BusinessWeek*'s best-seller list in October 2008. The story is about a salesman named Joe. Joe longed for success. He was a true go-getter. However, despite how hard he tried and how fast he worked, he saw his dreams and goals disappearing into a future in which one day looked like the next.

The sales quarter was about to end and Joe needed to close a big sale. Seeking help, he asked the advice of Pindar, a mysterious tutor whom many disciples referred to as "The Chairman." Rather than receiving advice on how to close the deal, Joe was introduced to a series of successful "go-givers" who had been networked together by "The Connector." Together, they introduced Joe to the power of giving, rather than living and working with a blind focus on getting. What emerged from the series of conversations were the *Five Laws of Stratospheric Success*:

1. The Law of Value: *Your true worth is determined by how much more you give in value than you take in payment.*

2. The Law of Compensation: *Your income is determined by how many people you serve and how well you serve them.*

3. The Law of Influence: *Your influence is determined by how abundantly you place other people's interests first.*

4. The Law of Authenticity: *The most valuable gift you have to offer is yourself.*

5. The Law of Receptivity: *The key to effective giving is to stay open to receiving.*

The law that applies most directly to the work of the leader is the law of influence. John Maxwell declares, "All leadership is influence." Michael McKinney presses the thought, "Leadership is intentional influence." A leader who gives in love is a leader who grows in influence. What gifts can a leader give? Here are three gifts a leader can give to the team:

1. *The gift of inclusion.* The theory and research of Graen and Uhl-Bien[14] demonstrate the difference between employees and

volunteers who feel they are part of the in-group or the out-group. In-group members give extra effort while out-group members focus primarily on what is required. The difference between the in- and out- groups is the relationship with the leader. Ethical leaders treat everyone fairly, but there is a difference with the in-group. Here is the gift: treat each person with a special uniqueness that nurtures a high quality, professional relationship with that person. Here are specific ways to make each person part of the in-group:

- Let each person know how satisfied you are with his or her work.
- Understand the problems and needs associated with each person's job.
- Recognize and express the potential in each person.
- Use your power and influence to help solve work problems for your team.
- Come to the defense of an employee or volunteer, even when it costs you.

The simplest acts of favor and support create significant change in a person's relationship with the leader. The qualities of a unique, productive, and professional relationship between a leader and a member of the team are 1) mutual trust, 2) mutual respect, and 3) mutual commitment. The gift of a healthy, strong, and professional relationship with a leader brings untold benefits. When someone feels he or she is part of the in-group, that person will go the extra mile, put in the extra effort, and do what is above and beyond the requirements of the contract. For the leader of a church or volunteer organization, creating an inclusive in-group with as many people as possible is a secret of success.

2. *The gift of transformation.* Traditional leadership in the command and control model focuses on the rewards and punishments distributed by the leader to employees. This is a system of carrot and stick with, at various times, leaders providing a little more carrot or stick. There is another form of leadership—transformational leadership. It is leadership that transforms the tit-for-tat model of command and control into personal motivation for a grander vision and personal significance.[15]

You, the leader, can give a gift that transforms the motivation of employees and volunteers. You can be a leader that transforms your team. You can help them see the importance of the value and the mission of the organization, as well as specific goals and challenges. You can help them rise beyond self-interest to a greater interest in the greater good. You can help them move from the daily grind of work to the potential for professional and personal fulfillment. This gift of leadership, transformational leadership, is a gift of love that influences the vision, motivation, and emotions of others. What are specific ways a leader can give the gift of transformation?

- Be a role model of high standards and ethical conduct who does the right thing.
- Engage in conversations about the higher meaning of the organization's vision and values.
- Communicate and encourage high expectations for all team members.
- Use symbols and stories to communicate the value of working for the greater good of all.
- Praise creativity, innovation, new approaches, and unique solutions to problems.
- Listen to individual needs, concerns, and problems with consideration and care.
- Be a coach and adviser who provides individualized structure and direction.

You can give the gift of transformation. You need not be a motivational speaker, a professional therapist, or an organizational guru. However, you need to believe deeply in the mission of your organization. You need to sacrifice your own self-interest for the greater good. And, you need to invest yourself significantly and personally in the lives of your team members. It is only when you, yourself, are transformed that you may give the gift of transformation.

3. *The gift of authenticity.* The gifts we have discussed, inclusion and transformation, are valuable if, and only if, the leader also gives the gift of authenticity. Authenticity can be defined as

being genuine, valid, truthful, faithful, and dependable. Bill George introduced this type of leadership gift in his books *Authentic Leadership* and *True North*.[16] An authentic leader is true to her core values. She also empowers and inspires employees.

How can you develop your authenticity as a leader? First, authentic leadership begins with your self-knowledge, self-regulation, and self-concept. Reflect on your own experience. Your life story is the textbook of authentic leadership.[17] Reflect on your successes and regrets. The lessons of authenticity are found in your own experience. Second, authenticity is forged in life's difficulties and expressed in optimism and a positive outlook. Moral convictions, balance, and appropriate transparency are signs of authenticity.[18] Third, authenticity in leaders is relational.[19] Indeed, it is a reciprocal relationship where the leader affects the followers and the followers affect the leader. This expression of authenticity is appropriately vulnerable and is a great and risky gift from the leader to the team.

Let me (Richard) share a story. A decade ago I consulted with a manufacturing company in a small town. The plant was part of a national organization. The home office in Chicago was preparing to outsource the work of the local plant to China. The head of the local plant asked me to help him strategize a way to save the jobs of the employees and keep the plant open. I would like to report that our efforts were successful, and due to the love and dedication of the leader, the plant is still in operation.

What I want to share with you is the heart of the leader who fought for the people in his manufacturing plant. In that experience, I came face to face with a leader who loved his people. If the plant closed, he would receive reassignment. But this was not so for his workers.

I remember standing with him in his office that was perched over the plant floor, with windows as walls on three sides. He had read every book I suggested, shared his inner thoughts genuinely, and carried the concerns of his people in his mind and heart. Standing beside him as he looked from his office to the floor of the plant, I heard a deep sigh, almost a groan. "These people have families and mortgages. I must do everything I can to help them, no matter the cost to me." This is a leader who loved his people.

The Necessity of Self-Love

The ways of doing business described above are impossible if we don't first love ourselves. If we do not love ourselves, if we are plagued by self-doubt and a low self-esteem, then we will not be able to put others first. We will not be able to truly love others.

In his book *Empires of the Mind,* Dr. Denis Waitley tells the story of *Beauty and the Beast,* which, although it is a fairy tale, powerfully illustrates the ways that a low self-image can keep a person in bondage, unable to share love with others. In the fairy tale, a young prince lived in a fantastic castle but was spoiled, self-ish, and unkind. One dark night, an old beggar woman knocked on the door and asked for shelter. The only thing she had to offer as payment was a single rose. The prince was disgusted by her hag-gard appearance and, sneering, tried to send her away. The old woman warned the prince not to be deceived by appearances, but he angrily insisted that she leave.

The old woman finally shed her disguise, revealing that she was, in truth, a beautiful enchantress. Though the spoiled prince tried to apologize, the lovely sorceress had already seen that there was no love in his heart and, as punishment, she turned him into a repul-sive beast, and cast a spell on the castle and everyone who dwelled within its walls.

The prince was humiliated and, as the Beast, he hid himself within his castle. The rose, left by the sorceress, would bloom until he turned twenty-four and, if he could learn to love before its last petal fell, he would be freed from the spell. Otherwise, he would remain a beast forever. As the years went by, the Beast despaired of ever being able to love or be loved. If he found someone *he* could love, how could he win *her* love in return? Who would love him, a hideous beast?

When a beautiful young woman from the village offered to trade her freedom for the release of her father, whom the Beast had cruelly taken captive in his castle, the Beast selfishly accepted. He thought that if he could keep the woman captive in the cas-tle, she might eventually learn to accept him as her master. This was his unloving, selfish interpretation of love. Beauty resisted his belligerent advances, of course, and the Beast went on a rampage. Dr. Waitley compares insecure people to the Beast:

> Attacking those who disagree with their beliefs, the selfish and insecure try to prove they're right with might. Have-nots release their resentment by attacking the haves, demanding their fair share. Haves exhibit disdain for the have-nots who can't control their rage. This vicious, no-win cycle will continue until human beings, who must have a sense of consideration and responsibility for others' well-being, stop roaring and start listening.[20]

Ultimately, the Beast began to treat Beauty with respect, eventually letting her go to be with her father. It was only when the Beast had begun to truly love Beauty that he was able to do what was in her best interest—let her go—and, in doing this, he empowered her return. When you feel secure enough about yourself, then you are able to put others first—you are able to truly love them. This, Dr. Waitley explains, is your greatest gift to them:

> When others sense you have their interests rather than only your own at heart, they begin to trust you. That foundation of all friendships and healthy marriages is also the key to customer service and satisfaction. You never just close a sale. What you do is open a long-term relationship based on mutual disclosure and mutual trust.[21]

When you love yourself, it enables you to love others. And this, in turn, transforms your ability to lead.

Conclusions

Saul failed to love his people, and so they gradually transferred their allegiance elsewhere. Love is central, and we will never be effective leaders if we fail to love the people.

When leaders love their people, it does not mean that they allow themselves to be continually abused or treated like doormats. What it does mean is that they will have the best interests of their people at heart. It means they will put their people before themselves. It means they will serve, praise, and reward their people. And in so doing, they will earn the loyalty of those they lead—maybe even those who resist their leadership.

Group Discussion and Personal Reflection

Group Discussion

Love and Leadership

Read Mark 10:35–45. Discuss the difference between the two styles of leadership outlined in the passage: 1) "rulers of the Gentiles lord it over them"; and 2) "whoever wants to be first must be slave of all." Suggest practical examples of each type of leadership.

Love Is Giving

The chapter suggests three gifts of love a leader can give. Discuss each:

> *The gift of inclusion*: Treat each team member as part of the in-group.

- When would this gift be effective? When might it be ineffective?

> *The gift of transformation*: Help shift team members' motivation to one of working for the greater good.

- When would this gift be effective? When might it be ineffective?

> *The gift of authenticity*: Be genuine and real with your team.

- When would this gift be effective? When might it be ineffective?

Love and Self-Assessment

Read Psalm 8. Discuss how a leader can keep up confidence without coming across as arrogant. Discuss what you do to keep up your confidence in yourself and your ability to lead, especially in difficult situations.

Personal Reflection

Assess

➤ I listen carefully to the ideas of others before making a decision.

        Strongly Agree 5   4   3   2   1 Strongly Disagree

➤ I ask for feedback in a way that helps me understand myself.

        Strongly Agree 5   4   3   2   1 Strongly Disagree

➤ I know my greatest weaknesses and strengths.

        Strongly Agree 5   4   3   2   1 Strongly Disagree

➤ I admit my mistakes to others.

        Strongly Agree 5   4   3   2   1 Strongly Disagree

➤ I follow my core values and principles when I make decisions.

        Strongly Agree 5   4   3   2   1 Strongly Disagree

Analyze

Jesus gave the essence of love and leadership in this verse:

> "For the Son of Man came not to be served but to serve, and to give his life a ransom for many." (Mark 10:45 NRSV)

Reflect on the three challenges in the verse and analyze how you are doing at leadership love:

➤ Not to be served

➤ But to serve

➤ And to give

Act

Learning to love, as a leader, is challenging. It may feel odd at first. Here is a place to begin. It is a simple challenge I (Richard) have given to hundreds of leaders. It is called "a human moment," a phrase advanced by Edward Hallowell:[22]

The human moment has two prerequisites: people's physical presence and their emotional and intellectual attention. That's it. Physical presence alone isn't enough; you can ride shoulder-to-shoulder with someone for six hours in an airplane and not have a human moment the entire ride. And attention alone isn't enough either. You can pay attention to someone over the telephone, for instance, but somehow phone conversations lack the power of true human moments.

Human moments require energy. Often, that's what makes them easy to avoid. The human moment may be seen as yet another tax on our overextended lives. But a human moment doesn't have to be emotionally draining or personally revealing. In fact, the human moment can be brisk, businesslike, and brief. A five-minute conversation can be a perfectly meaningful human moment.

To make the human moment work, you have to set aside what you're doing, put down the memo you were reading, disengage from your laptop, abandon your daydream, and focus on the person you're with.

___ Intentionally engage in three human moments each day for the next month.

Chapter 10

Saul Failed to Be True to His Own Ethics

Another area in which Saul failed was in upholding the traditional ethics of the nation of Israel. While many modern readers may be overly influenced by the "separation of church and state," Saul would not have understood this kind of compartmentalism. In fact, in ancient Israel, the office of king was analogous to that of priest. Before Samuel anointed Saul king (1 Sam. 10:1), he led him into a hall in a building on the high place outside Ramah where he made a peace offering to Yahweh. During the feast that was eaten as part of the peace offering, Saul and his servant were seated at the head of the table as guests of honor (1 Sam. 9:22). Saul was given the leg of the beast they were eating (v. 24), which was not just a large portion, but it was a priestly portion.[1] Peter Leithart explains that "giving Saul the thigh thus announced that the king-designate was receiving an office analogous to the priest's. A priest was essentially a household servant of the Lord, a caretaker of God's house, and the king served in a similar way in the national house, the people-house."[2]

The King as Arbiter of God's Law

Indeed, the king did have a role similar to that of the priest in that he was to hold himself and the people of the nation accountable to God's law. This was made clear when the secret anointing of Saul was publicly confirmed (1 Sam. 10:17–27). When he was chosen by lot and the people had received him, Samuel then "told the people the rights and duties of the kingship; and he wrote them in a book and laid it up before the LORD" (v. 25 NRSV). This verse refers to a document, deposited at the shrine, where the priests probably looked after it. It has been described as the royal "constitution." We are given practically no details about its content, but it was probably an expanded version of Deuteronomy 17:18–20.[3] In that passage, Moses taught about the nature of the kingship:

> When he has taken the throne of his kingdom, he shall have a copy of this law written for him in the presence of the levitical priests. It shall remain with him and he shall read in it all the days of his life, so that he may learn to fear the LORD his God, diligently observing all the words of this law and these statutes, neither exalting himself above other members of the community nor turning aside from the commandment, either to the right or to the left, so that he and his descendents may reign long over his kingdom in Israel. (NRSV)

The "words of this law" and "these statutes" probably included both the "rights and duties" of the king.

> In other words, this was a document which told the king what he had a right to expect from his citizens, and what his duties were, under God, towards them. It seems, then, that the king and the people were in a covenant relationship with each other.[4]

The "words of this law" probably refer to the various laws contained in Exodus, Leviticus, and Numbers.

After Samuel explained the regulations of the king to the people, he wrote them down on a scroll, and deposited it in a safe place "before the LORD" (1 Sam. 10:25 NRSV), which probably means he put it in the tabernacle. It seems likely that he did this for two reasons:[5] First, to preserve it for future reference. The Deuteronomy passage cited above instructed that the king was to consult it frequently throughout his reign. Secondly, it was written down and preserved so that it could serve as a witness against the king and/or the people if its provisions were ever violated.[6]

It is clear, then, that Israel's king was to be an arbiter of God's law. As Israel's first king, God's law was to be Saul's highest standard. He, himself, was to follow it, and he was to mold his leadership around it.

Saul's Ethical Failures

Murder

One of the incidences we have already looked at—in chapters 3 and 4—was an extremely serious violation of the ethical standards that Saul would have been expected to uphold. This was the occasion when Saul slaughtered the eighty-five priests of Nob and then destroyed the entire city as well (1 Sam. 22:6–23). In chapter 7, we discussed the concept of *herem*, the "ban" under which Israel was to place the Canaanite tribes as they entered the land. After Israel had settled the land, the Law made provision for Hebrew towns to be placed under the ban if they were to lapse into idolatry.

> If you hear it said about one of the towns that the LORD your God is giving you to live in, that scoundrels from among you have gone out and led the inhabitants of the town astray, saying, "Let us go and worship other gods," whom you have not known, then you shall inquire and make a thorough investigation. If the charge is established that such an abhorrent thing has been done among you, you shall put the inhabitants of that town to the sword, utterly destroying it and everything in it—even putting its livestock to the sword. All of its spoil you shall gather into its public square; then burn the town and all its spoil with fire, as a whole burnt offering to the LORD your God. It shall remain a perpetual ruin, never to be rebuilt. Do not let anything devoted to destruction stick to your hand, so that the LORD may turn from his fierce anger and show you compassion, and in his compassion multiply you, as he swore to your ancestors, if you obey the voice of the LORD your God by keeping all his commandments that I am commanding you today, doing what is right in the sight of the LORD your God. (Deut. 13:12–18 NRSV)

Saul's slaughter of the priests of Nob is shocking in its heinous and brutal defiance of the sixth commandment.[7] But this is not the full extent of the transgression. While the Law made provision for a town being placed under the ban when it went astray after other gods, this is not what Saul suspected of Nob. Instead, Saul destroyed this city because he thought it had been unfaithful to *him.* "Like the kings of the nations, Saul had put himself in the place of God."[8]

Consulting the Witch of Endor

Another infamous example comes much later in the story of Saul, and involves his seeking out a witch for consultation. These events followed the death of Samuel, which meant that the prophet was no longer available for consultation, and the story begins by noting that "Saul had expelled the mediums and the wizards from the land" (1 Sam. 28:3 NRSV). A medium was, in the technical sense, one who consulted the dead on behalf of the living.[9] Early in his career, Saul had probably expelled the mediums in obedience to the law of Moses.[10]

The Philistines initiated an attack and mustered their forces in strength. Most of the battles between Israel and the Philistines had taken place in the southern part of the country, but now the Philistines changed their strategy and mustered in the north, at Shunem. They were probably trying to cut Israel in two, separating Saul from his northern tribes. Saul could not ignore this threat, and it seems that he was forced to fight on level ground, where Philistine chariots gave them a great advantage. Usually the Israelites had been able to fight in the hills, where chariots could not be used. One commentator notes:

> Israel was, therefore, in a dangerous situation, and Saul was desperately in need of military advice. Although the story is told in personal terms, it is important to realize that Saul was seeking guidance as king of Israel, not as a private individual.[11]

The problem Saul faced, of course, was that he could not get any prophetic help. First Samuel 28:6 says that Saul "inquired of the LORD," and mentions the three usual means for learning Yahweh's will: "dreams," "Urim,"[12] and "prophets."[13] Saul became so desperate that he "said to his servants, 'Seek out for me a woman who is a medium, so that I may go to her and inquire of her'" (v. 7 NRSV). His servants found him a witch in a town called Endor.

Saul and his men made the trip to see the witch in the dark. This may have been to avoid Philistine detection, or he may have been using the darkness to aid in disguising himself. Or possibly necromancers preferred to do their work at night.[14] In any case, when Saul and his men arrived, he asked the medium to consult a "spirit" on his behalf (v. 8). The medium did not yet recognize Saul, and so she reminded him that Israel's king had "cut off" all the land's mediums and spiritists (v. 9). Spiritism, witches, mediums, and necromancers[15] were forbidden in the Torah, and there are a number of stern passages that warn against any involvement with or practice of these arts. For example:

- Deuteronomy 18:9–12 includes these practices in a list of nine abominations that stand in opposition to revelation from God through his prophets.
- Exodus 22:18 denies sorceresses the right to live.
- Leviticus 19:26 and 20:26–27 also sternly caution against consulting a medium, a sorceress, or anyone who practices divination.

Those who cultivated these arts were to be put to death—the community was not to tolerate them, because what they did was so offensive that it was the very opposite of the revelation that came from God.[16] It was a sign of Saul's desperation that he now consulted a medium, and that in order to do so he had to go as far north as Endor, which meant a journey to the far side of the Philistine camp.

Despite the prohibition against such practices, Saul urged her on and promised her that she would not be punished. He used the most solemn of oaths by swearing in Yahweh's name (v. 10). Incidentally, this is the last time that Saul is recorded as having spoken the name of Yahweh.

The woman asked Saul who he wanted her to bring up, and he answered "Samuel" (v. 11). We are not told how or whether the woman's necromancy was effective here, whether she actually engaged the dead by means of her necromancy. Walter Kaiser, President Emeritus at Gordon-Conwell Theological Seminary, suggests that God must have brought up Samuel's spirit to give Saul one more warning about the evil of his ways. He explains:

> The medium must not have been accustomed to having her necromancies work, for when she saw Samuel, she cried out in a scream that let Saul know that something new and different was happening. That night her so-called arts were working beyond her usual expectations.[17]

If this was the case, then this may have been God's final means of bringing a word to a king who insisted on going his own way.

Whatever happened, it seems that the apparition was not visible to Saul, because he asked the woman what she was seeing. She answered that she saw a "spirit." The Hebrew literally says that she saw a "god." A living prophet could be compared to God in the sense that he was God's mouthpiece and therefore spoke with God's authority (Ex. 7:1–2; Deut. 18:17–18). It does not seem likely, though, that this is what the medium meant. In ancient times many people referred to the deceased as "gods," since they were believed to live in the realm of the supernatural.[18] This may be why the place where the medium practiced her dark arts was called Endor, which probably means "Spring of the Assembly of the Gods."[19] In any case, the woman described the "spirit" as "an old man wearing a robe" (v. 14), confirming that the apparition was Samuel, who always wore the characteristic robe of the prophet.[20]

Samuel complained at being disturbed, but Saul complained that he was in great distress because Yahweh would no longer answer him and he therefore needed his help (v. 15). Samuel answered by reminding Saul that Yahweh had already torn the kingdom away from him and given it to another (1 Sam. 15:28), and here he specifies that it is to be given to David (v. 17). The apparition went on to predict that Israel would be handed over to the Philistines and that "tomorrow you and your sons will be with me" (v. 19).

Though the consultation did result in this bizarre experience,[21] it was less than helpful for Saul. With his strength gone, since he had not eaten all day and all night, he fell onto the ground full length (v. 20).

The medium persuaded Saul to eat something and, although he initially refused, his servants finally persuaded him. They ate, and then Saul went out into the night (vv. 22–25). The next day, the Philistines mustered their forces at Aphek (1 Sam. 29:1). After a great deal of hard fighting, the Israelites were put to flight, and many fell on Mt. Gilboa (1 Sam. 31:1). Three of Saul's sons were killed there, and he himself was mortally wounded (vv. 2–3). Saul instructed his armor-bearer to finish killing him, so these "uncircumcised [Philistines] may not come and thrust me through, and make sport of me" (v. 4 NRSV). Saul's cumulative ethical failures were severe, and they contributed to the destruction of his kingship and, ultimately, to his own death. The author of 1–2 Chronicles sums up the story of Saul with a simple but poignant description:

> Saul died because he was unfaithful to the LORD; he did not keep the word of the LORD and even consulted a medium for guidance, and did not inquire of the LORD. So the LORD put him to death and turned the kingdom over to David son of Jesse. (1 Chron. 10:13–14)

The Crisis of Ethics Today

In recent years, scandals in companies such as WorldCom, Global Crossing, Tyco, and others have convinced many that there is an ethical crisis in the business world. One of the most public scandals has been the bankruptcy of Enron—the second largest bankruptcy in American history. In a recent book, *The Tao of Enron*, Chris Seay has written:

> With zero regard for how their aggressively self-obsessed and immoral actions would bankrupt the retirement and investment portfolios of thousands of investors and put thousands of unknowing employees out of work, key executives at Enron enriched themselves through a complicated series of sham partnerships and bogus accounting procedures. The second largest bankruptcy in American history offers more than a lesson in economics.[22]

Seay is convinced that 99.9 percent of Enron employees are basically fine and honest people, including former chairman Ken Lay. But, at the same time, the Enron fallout:

destroys a common assumption that man is basically good and warns us that a diseased form of capitalism feeds on corruption and greed and almost certainly leads to the collapse of personal ethics. The survival of the fittest means that someone must suffer for our gain.[23]

Seay points to business schools as one of the sources of ethical erosion among young executives. Another writer has suggested that "the current wave of business corruption is, at least in part, the consequence of some very bad ideas that dominate the larger society."[24]

These ideas have recently been explored in a number of studies. In 2002, Zogby International surveyed 401 college students and reported that 73 percent of students said that their professors taught that "what is right and wrong depends on differences in individual values and cultural diversity." Only a small minority of professors reportedly taught any kind of objective standard of right and wrong:

> The result of such teaching is a skewed view of business priorities. When the poll asked students to rate the importance of various business practices, "corporate diversity" outpolled basic corporate honesty. Thirty-eight percent said "recruiting a diverse workforce in which women and minorities are advanced and promoted" was most important. Only 23 percent picked "providing clear and accurate business statements to stockholders and creditors."[25]

Ethical standards have clearly been relativized and politicized, and it is in this climate that the business scandals have occurred.

For pastors, ethical issues may be more cloudy. Pastors are seldom caught up in embezzling (since they usually have finance committees and treasurers who manage their church's money) or other outright corrupt practices. However, pastors are faced with challenges to ethical living. In a recent interview, Erwin Lutzer outlined four ways pastors are often tempted to cross ethical lines.

1. *Manipulation.* Lutzer explains that "some pastors want a certain agenda so badly that they're willing to forgo consensus,

to ignore credible objections . . . They run roughshod over the feelings and the aspirations and maybe the wisdom of others."[26] This is unethical leadership, and it "creates hard feelings and erodes trust because people immediately think, 'Oh yeah, that's his agenda. He's deaf to other voices.'"[27]

2. *Spin.* In cases of spin, a pastor might use personal illustrations in the pulpit in ways that falsely magnify his own leadership, wisdom, and ability. In some cases, the pastor might use the podium as a "bully pulpit," glorifying his own ideas and belittling others'.

3. *Inappropriate behavior.* This could include the handling of finances, the abuse of relationships, or the cultivation of inappropriate intimacies.

4. *Self-promotion.* Sometimes pastors can be tempted to take credit for the ideas of others, using the pastorate as a means of self-promotion. The pastor who is tempted in this way may only adopt and promote ideas when he is able to take credit for them.

Lutzer's conclusion about these four challenges to ethical living is very insightful. He writes:

> Interestingly, none of these cases involved outright lying or flagrant improper behavior. But it's a personality, a lifestyle that erodes people's trust. At the end of the day, trust isn't just that we believe what a pastor says; it's that we can actually look into his life and believe that he really wants what the Almighty wants, which therefore encourages a spiritual bonding.[28]

Trust is the foundation of everything pastors do. And once a pastor loses a congregation's trust, he may not ever be able to get it back.

The Origins of Ethical Failure

An ethical breakdown in leadership is tragic and complex. It is tragic for the leader and the organization. It is complex in its origins and consequences. Let's look at the origin of ethical failure.

Such a failure does not happen in a vacuum, but as a small drip that breaks into a flood (James 1:13–14).

Leadership literature notes three sources of ethical failure. The first are personality disorders such as the narcissistic,[29] the Machiavellian,[30] and the sociopath.[31] The common element in these disorders is a lack of empathy. The narcissistic believes the rules do not apply to him. The Machiavellian disguises evil intent and manipulates the situation. The sociopath has no conscience or fear and, thus, will do whatever it takes to get ahead. While there are times when these traits serve the advancement of the organization, they eventually destroy people. These types of personality disorders are difficult to change and require extensive therapy. For most leaders and followers, the challenge is to learn to work with people who possess these personality disorders without resorting to their behavior patterns. This could have been Saul's problem. The Word of the Lord, while difficult and disturbing, nevertheless reports, "Now the Spirit of the LORD departed from Saul, and an evil spirit from the LORD tormented him" (1 Sam. 16:14 NRSV). The evil spirit may have been a deep personality disorder.

The second source of ethical failure is leadership success.[32] This seems to be the source of David's ethical failure with Bathsheba. Leadership itself presents a unique challenge to ethical choices. Ludwig and Longenecker[33] analyze the by-products of successful leadership that can seriously strain a leader's motivation to act in an ethical manner. First, if the leader is successful, the leader may become complacent and lose focus. Second, it is normal and appropriate for a leader to have access to privileged information. Third, successful leaders often have a great deal of control over resources, time, and money. Fourth, a successful leader's success can inflate his belief in his own ability to control outcomes. In combination, these leadership by-products are especially liable to give birth to unethical behavior.

A third explanation of ethical failure in leaders is a lack of emotional wisdom.[34] Anger, fear, and sadness are the primary emotional colors that hijack human passions. This seems to have been the case with Saul. He lived and ruled on a boiling caldron of fear and anxiety (1 Sam. 13:7; 17:24; 18:12). With David's victory over Goliath, Saul's fear of David (1 Sam. 18:12, 15) morphed into a dark, self-destructive pattern. He became angry (18:8), jealous (18:9), and "still more afraid of him, and he remained his enemy the rest of his days" (18:29). He used three negative tools of the leader's arsenal: attack, distract, and deceive (18:10–11, 17–21). What began on the battlefield of fear as a foolish action (1 Sam. 13:13) moved into acts of evil: "Saul told his son Jonathan and all the attendants to kill David" (1 Sam. 19:1). From there it was a short distance to murdering the priests of the Lord (1 Sam. 22), and consulting with the witch of Endor (1 Sam. 28).

Do the Right Thing

The most common way leaders guide themselves and their organizations toward ethical behavior is with inspiration and motivation. "Do the right thing" is the battle cry. Here are words of inspiration that challenge us to do the right thing:

- "A true hero is not one who thinks about doing what is right, but who does what is right without thinking." Kevin Heath, CEO, More4Kids

- "I never had a policy; I just tried to do my best each and every day." Abraham Lincoln

- "To know the right thing to do and not do it is the worst cowardice." Confucius

- "Have the courage to say no. Have the courage to face the truth. Do the right thing because it is right. These are the magic keys to living your life with integrity." W. Clement Stone, Founder, Combined Insurance Co.

- "The old law about 'eye for an eye' leaves everyone blind. It is always the time to do the right thing." Martin Luther King Jr.

Human beings, including leaders, need motivational inspiration that draws them toward integrity and ethical behavior. But human beings need more. They need to personalize a credo of behavior. High-quality organizations have meaningful and actionable mission statements that evoke high ethical values. Steve Jobs, for example, described the mission of Apple as "contributing to this world by making tools for the mind that advance mankind." As leaders, we should develop a mission/values statement, an ethical credo, and a statement of commitment to integrity. These are useful processes for personalizing and internalizing ethical behavior.[35]

A few years ago, John Maxwell wrote a book, *Ethics 101*,[36] in which he based all ethics on the golden rule: "So in everything, do to others what you would have them do to you, for this sums up the Law and the Prophets" (Matt. 7:12). Expressions of the golden rule are found across time and around the world.[37] Maxwell expanded his work on the golden rule in *There's No Such Thing as "Business" Ethics: There's Only One Rule for Making Decisions*.[38] Starting with the golden rule, John Maxwell draws out a series of principles for guiding ethical behavior:

- We want to be valued.
- We want to be appreciated.
- We want to be trusted.
- We want to be respected.
- We want to be understood.
- We don't want to be taken advantage of.

The golden rule may not be the panacea for all ethical behavior. One can always find a few philosophers who find fault with it. However, Jesus did not give the rule as a quip, like a saying in a Chinese fortune cookie. Jesus gave the rule as a summation of the Law and Prophets—that is, the rule is a way to interpret all other rules. He did not mean we could keep the golden rule and toss out the rest of the Bible. The golden rule is a foundation for ethical thinking and behaving. It is a demand not only for consistency but also for fairness. The rule places on you the requirement to put yourself in someone else's position and to show others the kind of respect and understanding you hope to receive yourself.

Tough Choices

There is another level to the discussion of ethics and leadership. Not all decisions are clear choices between right and wrong. In many instances, the choice is between two good options; sometimes the leader has the difficult task of choosing between two imperfect solutions, or worse, choosing the lesser of two evils. While leaders may downplay the moral component of these decisions and say, "It's only business," the truth is it is more than that—it is ethical business. When a client doesn't want to deal with a person of a certain ethnic group, how does a leader respond to the client and/or the salesperson who has been passed over because of his or her ethnicity? When must the job come first, and when do we let the job suffer for the sake of the family? These are tough questions. The deeper and more challenging ethical dilemmas for leaders involve critical choices that touch the lives of people and the values that matter the most.

Critical ethical choices, according to Joseph Badaracco, John Shad Professor of Business Ethics at Harvard Business School, are defining moments.[39] The ethical choices of the leader reveal, test, and shape both the leader and the organization. Defining moments do not come with clear consensus on right and wrong. Indeed, a defining moment is found not on the high, hard ground of ethical certainty but down in the swampy lowlands where choices are not clear and problems come in the form of a mess.[40] It is here that leaders make decisions with imperfect information and while under pressure and stress. This is the cauldron of ethics for leaders.

Leaders are faced with tough ethical choices. Common ones include balancing family obligations and work demands; respect for diversity and the bias of a client; openness in business and secrecy from competitors; opportunities of church outreach and the stated expectations of the "pillars of the church"; and the exceptional needs of an individual against consistency in procedures and expectations. How you, the leader, make these choices *reveals* your character, *tests* your character, and *shapes* your character. However, there is more. Because you are the leader, your choices affect the lives of others. Others watch how you make your choices. As you choose, you reveal your true expectations and priorities; test the publicized credo, mission, and values of the organization; and shape the way the organization will understand, embrace, or ignore these values in the future. King Saul's choices affected more than just himself. And your choices (like his) affect the future of the organization you lead.

When choices are tough, it is not a simple matter of doing the right thing, it is figuring out the best way to do the right thing. When choices are tough, we must not simply follow the golden rule but also discern where the golden rule leads in a specific and messy situation. How can you face tough decisions? There are four questions that will help you think through a tough ethical crisis. I encourage you to reflect on all four questions. In a tough situation, it is rare that there is only one option or solution that allows you to remain faithful to God's law and love. In all likelihood, there are several answers that allow you to remain faithful to the rule of God and the law of Love. These questions are designed to help you listen for the best answer:

1. *The test of heart.* What does your own intuition tell you? The French mathematician and philosopher of the seventeenth century Blaise Pascal observed, "The heart has its reasons that reason does not know." Sort out what you are feeling. Then, sort out why you are feeling as you are. Feelings can help make sense of tough choices. What wisdom do your emotions and intuition bring to this crisis? Because we cannot rely on feelings alone, we must proceed to the next test.

2. *The test of roots.* Ask yourself, where does this crisis come from in me? You know the issues in your organization. Now, trace back the issues in your own story, your experience, and the challenges that have shaped your life and leadership. Become what Marcel Proust called "a reader of yourself." What does your story tell you about what is good and right and best in this tough choice? Learn from your own wisdom, the wisdom God has placed in you. Again, we cannot stop here. We must proceed to test three.

3. *The test of your way.* What is *your* way to lead with integrity and effectiveness in this crisis? This test invites you to open the knapsack you carry, which includes the expectations of others as well as your own lofty expectations. It is amazing what we have all picked up on the journey of life: expectations, disappointments, resentments, unforgiveness, hidden sin, unrealistic prospects, etc. What needs to be unpacked

and left behind in order to move forward? You can learn from your emotions, your own story, and by seeking the path forward, despite what you must leave behind. There is one more test to complete this process.

4. *The test of reality.* What is possible in the reality of the situation? I (Richard) taught a class in which the opening line was, "It is far better to base your decisions and plans on the way things actually work than on the way they ought to work." This is not an excuse for taking the easy way or the slippery, sleazy slope but an encouragement to make a choice of integrity that works.

Loving Your Enemies

Ethical choices are not simply about logical thinking. People don't necessarily do the right thing because it is a good idea. Doing what's right takes *inspiration*, a word that originally meant divine guidance. In addition, ethical choices require a credo, a set of principles for guidance and direction. The golden rule is foundational for an ethical life. And ethical choices are put to the test in the swampy lowlands of messy problems that require self-reflection expressed in actions of courage and wisdom. Finally, there is one more level of ethical challenge for the leader: How do you deal with your enemies?

As we have discussed in earlier chapters, leaders inevitably face criticism and hostility. Oftentimes, this opposition comes from members of their own team, and the natural response is to assume a posture of defense against our critics. Defensiveness often leads to rumination on the injustice we have received. Such rumination, running the negative thoughts through the mind again and again, can lead to resentment. In resentment, it is amazing how the mind can justify the most cruel and wretched behavior. Good leaders do terrible things when possessed by hatred of an enemy. To protect your ethical behavior, follow the most demanding of all ethics, the ethic of Jesus Christ, the call to love your enemies.

Jesus said to "love your enemies and pray for those who persecute you" (Matt. 5:44). This is the foundational ethic of Christianity.

To many, this sounds like an impossible teaching. However, Jesus was not instructing people to have warm, fuzzy feelings for their enemies. To understand his teaching, we have to look at the original language of the New Testament (Greek), which had several words for love.

- *Eros*. The English word *erotic* comes from *eros*. This kind of love has to do with romance and affection.
- *Phileo*. We get the idea of filial love from the Greek *phileo*. Filial love refers to the concern friends have for one another.
- *Storge*. This is the love family members have for one another.
- *Agape*. In the classical Greek world, *agape* referred to an almost dispassionate love. If you were going to buy an animal, for example, you would inspect it for blemishes—you would evaluate it with a dispassionate, or an impartial and objective, eye.

The apostle Paul adopted the word *agape* to try to capture what he believed was the highest and most noble form of love. When he instructed people to love one another, he meant for them to love one another regardless of their natural emotional response. He called us to see past a person's shortcomings and to treat that person in a way that is in his or her best interest. Wanting the best for someone, despite his or her shortcomings, or hostility toward you—this is *agape* love. *Agape* does not depend on warm, friendly feelings toward someone. Instead, it wants what is best for the other person.

Agape love is a potent force because it means you seek the good of the other person, regardless of that person's feelings toward you. Martin Luther King Jr. explained the important effects that loving one's enemies could have:

> Love is the only force capable of transforming an enemy into a friend. We never get rid of an enemy by meeting hate with hate; we get rid of an enemy by getting rid of enmity. By its very nature, hate destroys and tears down; by its very nature, love creates and builds up. Love transforms with redemptive power.[41]

In 1957, when bus segregation was overturned by the Supreme
Court, many leaders in the south fought against the high court's
decision. On the evening of the Supreme Court's decision, forty car-
loads of Ku Klux Klan members invaded black neighborhoods, the
White Citizens Council warned that "any attempt to enforce this
decision [would] inevitably result in violence and bloodshed," and
the city commissioners took no action. Even so, Dr. King preached
that night:

> I want to tell you this evening that I believe that Senator Engel-
> hardt's heart can be changed. I believe that Senator Eastland's
> heart can be changed! I believe that the Ku Klux Klan can be
> changed into a clan for God's kingdom. That's the essence of
> the gospel.[42]

Later that same month, Dr. King spoke about love, reconciliation,
and redemption, and explained, "It is this type of understanding
goodwill that will transform the deep gloom of the old age into the
exuberant gladness of the new age."[43] Members of the movement
were instructed to "be loving enough to absorb evil and understanding enough to turn an enemy into a friend."[44]

The kind of love Dr. King was talking about was not a sentimen-
tal, emotional love, but the *agape* love that wanted the best for
all parties involved. In his masterful sermon on "Loving Your Enemies," King described the long-term effects he believed this kind of
love would have on even the harshest opponents of freedom and
equality for black Americans:

> To our most bitter opponents we say: "We shall match your
> capacity to inflict suffering by our capacity to endure suffering.
> We shall meet your physical force with soul force. Do to us what
> you will, and we shall continue to love you. We cannot in all good
> conscience obey your unjust laws, because noncooperation with
> evil is as much a moral obligation as is cooperation with good.
> Throw us in jail, and we shall still love you. Send your hooded
> perpetrators of violence into our community at the midnight hour
> and beat us and leave us half dead, and we shall still love you.
> But be ye assured that we will wear you down by our capacity to

suffer. One day we shall win freedom, but not only for ourselves. We shall so appeal to your heart and conscience that we shall win *you* in the process and our victory will be a double victory."[45]

If King had encouraged a violent response on the part of the nation's oppressed black citizens, America would have seen a bloody civil crisis. Instead, he taught love, and he eventually transformed a nation.

Love of enemies is the unique and demanding ethic of Jesus. Michael Hart, in his book *The 100: A Ranking of the Most Influential Persons in History*, lists the most influential people in history, ranking them from one to one hundred. To the shock of many Christians, Dr. Hart lists Jesus Christ as third, after Mohammad and Newton. What is significant for our discussion in this chapter is the reason he gives for listing Jesus in a place other than number one. Dr. Hart explains as he discusses the ethic of Jesus:[46]

> Does this mean that Jesus had no original ethical ideas? Not at all! A highly distinctive viewpoint is presented in Matthew 5:43–44:
>
> *Ye have heard that it hath been said; Thou shalt love thy neighbor, and hate thine enemy. But I say unto you, Love your enemies, bless them that curse you, do good to them that hate you and pray for them which despitefully use you, and persecute you.*
>
> And a few lines earlier: ". . . resist not evil: but whosoever shall smite thee on the right cheek, turn to him the other also."
>
> Now, these ideas—which were not a part of the Judaism of Jesus' day, nor of most other religions—are surely among the most remarkable and original ethical ideas ever presented. If they were widely followed I would have had no hesitation in placing Jesus first in this book. But the truth is that they are not widely followed.

The most demanding ethic is to love the enemy. In order to distinguish yourself as a leader who is a consecrated follower of Jesus Christ, you must pass the test of loving your enemy. When living out your Christianity in your everyday life, far beyond the value of a framed verse on your office wall or a Bible on your desk is your demonstration of the highest ethic of love, the love of enemies. It is this level of ethic that was unknown to King Saul. It required another day and another King to reveal this law of loving compassion: Jesus prayed, "Father, forgive them, for they do not know what they are doing" (Luke 23:34).

Group Discussion and Personal Reflection

Group Discussion

Why Good Leaders Go Bad

King Saul did not set out to be an angry, vengeful, out of control leader who finally looked to the dark arts of witchcraft for solace and succor. Discuss why good leaders go bad.

1. What turns healthy relationships into bastions of mistrust and disrespect?

2. What are the steps of a leader of good character who turns to bad choices?

3. What causes a leader's sense of clear purpose to dissolve into survival mode?

4. When does a leader begin to disrespect the person he or she is becoming?

Building Integrity in the System

What are ways a leader can build an expectation for ethical behavior into the organization? What boundaries and accountability does a leader need to guard his or her integrity and ethical choices?

Making the Tough Choices

What makes a choice tough for you? How do you go about making a tough choice?

Love Your Enemies

Read Luke 6:27–36. Discuss how to deal with enemies. In what ways can the words of Jesus be applied to an individual who is responsible only for him- or herself versus a leader who is responsible for the whole organization? What are the practical applications of Jesus' words for leaders who must deal with enemies?

Personal Reflection

Assess

Ethics are both personal and corporate, especially for a leader. The issue is not only doing the right thing but having followers who know you do the right thing. For this assessment,[47] how do you believe your followers would rate you?

> ➤ My followers would say I take credit for other people's ideas and suggestions.

Strongly Agree   5   4   3   2   1   Strongly Disagree

➤ My followers would say I would try to hurt someone's career because of a grudge.

　　　Strongly Agree　5　4　3　2　1　Strongly Disagree

➤ My followers would say I would let others take the blame for my mistakes.

　　　Strongly Agree　5　4　3　2　1　Strongly Disagree

➤ My followers would say I allow gender or ethnic bias to influence my decisions.

　　　Strongly Agree　5　4　3　2　1　Strongly Disagree

➤ My followers would say I put my personal interests above the organization's.

　　　Strongly Agree　5　4　3　2　1　Strongly Disagree

Analyze

If you gave yourself *a score of 10 or more*, it means you have a perception problem with your integrity and you know it. Seek a mentor or friend who will be honest with you. Apply the four tests to discern how to handle the problem:

1. *The test of your heart.* What does your intuition tell you?
2. *The test of your roots.* Where does this pattern of behavior come from?
3. *The test of your way.* What do you need to unpack and off-load before you can move forward with a solution?
4. *The test of reality.* What will work to fix the problem?

If you gave yourself a *score of 9 or less*, check out your perception with the help of trusted and honest colleagues. Personal perceptions can sometimes be at odds with the perceptions of others. In some organizations, the perception that "leaders are scoundrels" is so pervasive in the culture that you must be intentional and persistent to overcome the cultural bias.

Act

___ Enhance your inspiration for ethical leadership. Seek out and participate in organizations that promote and inspire ethical leadership.

___ Develop a credo of ethical principles. Write your own credo of ethical behavior. Lead your organization in developing a statement of ethical principles and values.

___ Study ethical organizations and leaders. Look at the life of ethical leaders and the policies of ethical companies to find models and inspiration.

___ Seek out advisers for tough choices. Create your own list of advisers. It is best to have the list before the tough choice hijacks you.

Chapter 11

Saul Failed to Admit Failure or Concede to David

When it became clear that God had rejected Saul and chosen David instead, Saul did everything in his power to try to prevent David from surviving long enough to ascend the throne. Saul threw spears at him on at least two occasions, sent a cohort of troops to kill him as he lay in bed, and hunted him throughout the wilderness. But what if Saul had, instead, cooperated with God by relinquishing his claim to the throne and preparing David to succeed him? If such a course of action had been possible, it would have saved the nation seven years of divided rule.

Transitions often bring difficult times, and leaders who fail to prepare for their eventual departure invite trouble. This chapter deals with the problem of prolonged position holding, as well as the failure to concede to new leadership. Successful leaders must be attuned to signs within their organizational culture, they must be the greatest supporters of the next generation of leadership, and they must give their blessing to the emerging generation of leaders.

Saul's Refusal to Concede Leadership

Much of Saul's reign was during wartime situations. Israel's primary enemy during this period was the Philistines, and Saul actually had many victories against them. First Samuel chapters 13–15 tell us about some of the early successes. Chapter 15 gives details about a victory over a smaller enemy, the Amalekites. Other victorious campaigns are summarized in 14:47, which reports that Saul delivered the Israelites from their enemies. In the midst of the reports of these important victories, however, are also the accounts of Saul's two most profound failures. First, he made an unlawful sacrifice

(1 Sam. 13:8–10) and, second, he refused to obey Yahweh and spared the Amalekite king, Agag (1 Sam. 15:8–9). We have studied these incidences in earlier chapters, and observed how they led to Yahweh's rejection of Saul as Israel's king (1 Sam. 13:13–14; 15:23, 26). We want to emphasize here, though, the permanence of that rejection. After Saul's unlawful sacrifice, Samuel said to Saul:

> You have done foolishly; you have not kept the commandment of the LORD your God, which he commanded you. The LORD would have established your kingdom over Israel forever, but now your kingdom will not continue; the LORD has sought out a man after his own heart; and the LORD has appointed him to be ruler over his people, because you have not kept what the LORD commanded you. (1 Sam. 13:13–14 NRSV)

Later, when Saul spared King Agag in the Amalekite war, Samuel twice accused Saul of having rejected the word of Yahweh (1 Sam. 15:23, 26); therefore, Yahweh had rejected him as king. When Samuel turned to go, Saul desperately "caught hold of the hem of his robe, and it tore" (1 Sam. 15:27). Samuel used the tearing of his robe as an illustration of the finality of Yahweh's rejection of Saul as Israel's king:

> The LORD has torn the kingdom of Israel from you this very day, and has given it to a neighbor of yours, who is better than you. Moreover the Glory of Israel will not recant or change his mind; for he is not a mortal, that he should change his mind. (1 Sam. 15:28–29 NRSV)

These passages make it clear that Yahweh's rejection of Saul was categorical; there was no chance beyond this point that Saul could retain his hold on the throne or pass it to his descendents; the possibility of a Saulide dynasty had been completely forfeited.

It is at this point that the storyteller introduces David into the narrative. He was quietly anointed as king (1 Sam. 16:13) and then brought into Saul's service as his personal musician (v. 21). The text reports that Saul "loved him greatly" and, because of his deep affection for him, Saul also made David his armor-bearer (v. 21 NRSV).

However, after David defeated Goliath, and his popularity began to grow among the people, Saul became "very angry" with David and suspected that he must be aspiring to take over the kingdom (1 Sam. 18:6–8). The text says that "Saul eyed David from that day on" (v. 9 NRSV).

The next day, while David was playing the lyre for him, Saul threw his spear at David in a mad effort to kill him (vv. 10–11). The text states that "David eluded him twice" (v. 11). It is not clear whether this means that Saul had two spears on hand and threw them both in rapid succession, or whether Saul attacked David in this way on two different occasions. What is clear is that "Saul was afraid of David, because the LORD was with David" (v. 12).

The text goes on to say that, for this reason, "Saul removed him from his presence" (v. 13 NRSV). The Hebrew literally says that Saul "caused him to be taken away from him." It was almost as if having David near was too painful for Saul, since the more David succeeded, the more it highlighted Saul's own rejection (1 Sam. 15:28; 16:13–14). And so Saul wanted to get David out of his sight. He accomplished this by making David a commander of a "thousand" (1 Sam. 18:13), which "roughly corresponds to a modern battalion,"[1] and which was the largest of the different military divisions. In this position, David "marched out and came in, leading the army" (v. 13 NRSV), and he "had success in all his undertakings; for the LORD was with him" (v. 14 NRSV). David had such success that Saul "stood in awe of him" (v. 15 NRSV) and "all Israel and Judah loved David; for it was he who marched out and came in leading them" (v. 16 NRSV).

The biblical author's comments in 1 Samuel 18:16 are extremely important for two reasons. First, in saying that all Israel loved David the biblical writer shows that the Israelites actually shifted their allegiance from Saul to David. In chapters 3 and 9, we discussed in detail how the nation began to transfer its allegiance away from Saul and onto David. Second, the writer explains the reason for this transfer in allegiance was that David "went out and came in before [them]" (RSV). To "go out and come in" is an expression of military security and success in the Bible and other ancient Near Eastern literature.[2] The New Revised Standard Version text says that David went out and came in, "leading the army" (v. 13), and that "all Israel and Judah loved David; for it was he who marched out and came in *leading them*" (v. 16 emphasis mine). In verse 16, the subject of the verb "lead" is "all Israel and Judah." The text is saying that, although Saul was still on the throne, it was David who was really "leading" the people of Israel. Even though Saul still reigned as the official king, David was the *de facto* leader of all Israel and Judah.

Saul had already been rejected by Yahweh, but did he know of Yahweh's intention to put David on the throne in his place? This is not clear in the text. The impression we get from 1 Samuel 16:1–13 is that the anointing of David occurred in secret, unbeknownst to Saul. It appears that David's fame was a result of his defeat of Goliath (1 Sam. 18:6–7). Saul's appointment of David as a commander of a battalion only increased his popularity, causing the people to transfer their allegiance to him. Whether Saul knew about the anointing of David or not, he clearly began to suspect David of aspiring to the throne (1 Sam. 18:8). Later, when David married Saul's daughter, Michal, he became Saul's son-in-law (vv. 20–27), which made him a member of the royal family. Saul realized how close this brought David to the throne, and he became "still more afraid of David" (vv. 28–29 NRSV). Still later, when Saul began to try to kill David, forcing David to flee from the house of Saul into the wilderness of Ziph, Jonathan met him there, "strengthened his hand through the LORD" (1 Sam. 23:16 NRSV), and encouraged him with these words: "Do not be afraid; for the hand of my father Saul shall not find you; you shall be king over Israel, and I shall be second to you; my father Saul also knows that this is so" (v. 17 NRSV). The king pursued David deep into the wilderness, and David was presented with an opportunity to kill Saul when he found him in a position of great vulnerability (1 Sam. 24:1–4). But David refused to raise his hand against the Lord's anointed, and instead cut off a corner of Saul's cloak in order to demonstrate that he had no hostile intentions against the king (v. 4). When from a safe distance David revealed what had happened to the king, Saul tearfully acknowledged his awareness that David would inevitably be the king, admitting, "the kingdom of Israel will be established in your [David's] hands" (v. 20). Even as Saul had been unaware of David's anointing by Samuel, he came to see "the handwriting on the wall": David would rule over Israel.

However, a major theme of 1 Samuel is that David was not a usurper of the throne, and that the Davidic covenant was established by God and not man. The text goes to great lengths to show that David painstakingly avoided taking any action against the house of Saul and that it was God who placed David on the throne, lest anyone think of David as a renegade who plotted to seize the throne, assassinated the king and his rightful heirs, and then tried to excuse his crimes by claiming divine right.[3] Some scholars have even argued that one of the main purposes of the book of 1 Samuel is to advocate for the innocence of David in the face of rumors of usurpation.[4] There is no doubt that this is a key theme in 1 Samuel, as many of the aforementioned passages demonstrate. Jonathan advocated for David to his father, saying:

> The king should not sin against his servant David, because he has not sinned against you, and because his deeds have been of good service to you; for he took his life in his hand when he attacked the Philistine, and the LORD brought about a great victory for all Israel. You saw it, and rejoiced; why then will you sin against an innocent person by killing David without cause? (1 Sam. 19:4–5 NRSV)

In advocating for David, Jonathan said David was "innocent." His point was that David was innocent of the accusation of aspiring for the throne and should be absolved of any such charges. John Maxwell proposes that "Saul could have been a hero had he cooperated with God in preparing David to succeed him. He didn't have a more submissive staff person in his entire palace than David."[5]

However, Saul did not react well to David's meteoric rise to fame in Israel and, even after it became clear that Yahweh had categorically rejected Saul, he had no intention of relinquishing his throne. After having personally tried to kill David by throwing spears at him in his throne room, Saul appointed David to the leadership of a "thousand," an appointment that actually served two purposes. First, as we already mentioned, it got David out of Saul's sight, but, second, it also regularly put David in the dangerous position of being in the thick of combat when the Israelites went into battle against the Philistines. In all probability, Saul was hoping that the Philistines would manage to do what he failed to do with his own spear. Later, when Saul's daughter Michal fell in love with David, the king attempted to use her affections as a "snare" for David (1 Sam. 18:21) by requiring one hundred Philistine foreskins as a bride-price. His plan was that David would be struck down by the Philistines as he sought to meet these demands (v. 25). After David's marriage to Michal, Saul again threw his spear at David while David was playing music for him (1 Sam. 19:9–10). Later, Saul sent messengers to kill David in his bed, but his wife Michal helped him to escape through the window (vv. 11–17). David joined Samuel in Ramah (vv. 18–19). And when David missed a festival he was required to attend and Jonathan made excuses for him, Saul exploded in foul-mouthed rage and hurled his spear at his son (1 Sam. 20:30–33). These events made it clear to both Jonathan and David that King Saul was intent on killing David and that David must flee the court for good (1 Sam. 20).

David fled into the wilderness, and at this point Saul's longest war began—his war against David. What followed was a desperate "cat-and-mouse game" in which David fled from one place to another, with Saul hot on his heels. David first fled to Nob, which was probably located only a couple of miles southeast of Gibeah and a mile-and-a-half northeast of Jerusalem (1 Sam. 21:1–2). After the episode at the Nob sanctuary (1 Sam. 22:6–23), David fled to Gath, Adullam, and Mizpah (1 Sam. 21:10–15). He fled further and further south, toward more barren terrain, hiding out first at Keilah and then in Ziph (1 Sam. 23:1–28). Saul was determined to track David down no matter where he went or what it took (1 Sam. 23: 22–23), and he instructed the Ziphites to pinpoint every potential hiding place that David might use and then report back to him with definite information. Saul was given the location of David's hideout, and he pursued him into the wilderness of Maon. This particular episode concluded in a hair-raising episode in which Saul closed in on David:

> [Saul] pursued David into the wilderness of Maon. Saul went on
> one side of the mountain, and David and his men on the other side
> of the mountain. David was hurrying to get away from Saul, while
> Saul and his men were closing in on David and his men to capture
> them. Then a messenger came to Saul, saying, "Hurry and come;

for the Philistines have made a raid on the land." So Saul stopped pursuing David, and went against the Philistines; therefore that place was called the Rock of Escape. (1 Sam. 23:25–28 NRSV)

Saul had apparently divided his forces into two groups, so that they could attack both flanks of David's men on the other side of the mountain. In the end, God used the distraction of the Philistines to rescue David from the clutches of Saul.

From there, David went and lived in the strongholds of En-gedi, on the west coast of the Dead Sea (1 Sam. 23:29). After Saul had finished fighting the Philistines, he took three thousand men and went to look for David yet again in the wilderness (1 Sam. 24:1–2). It was here that David had the opportunity to kill Saul but refrained from doing so while the king relieved himself in a cave (vv. 3–7). A similar occasion occurred later, after the death of Samuel, when David was hiding out in the wilderness of Ziph, and David had the opportunity to kill the king while he slept (1 Sam. 26). Instead, David took the king's spear and water jar to show that he had been near enough to strike the king but did not, and later confronted the king from a distance, asking:

> Why does my lord pursue his servant? For what have I done? What guilt is on my hands? Now therefore let my lord the king hear the words of his servant. If it is the LORD who has stirred you up against me, may he accept an offering; but if it is mortals, may they be cursed before the LORD, for they have driven me out today from my share in the heritage of the LORD, saying, "Go, serve other gods." Now therefore, do not let my blood fall to the ground, away from the presence of the LORD; for the king of Israel has come out to seek a single flea, like one who hunts a partridge in the mountains. (1 Sam. 26:18–20 NRSV)

Saul poignantly replied, "I have done wrong; come back, my son David, for I will never harm you again, because my life was precious in your sight today; I have been a fool, and have made a great mistake" (v. 21 NRSV). David returned Saul's spear, but then they each went their own way—David into the wilderness and Saul back to his palace (v. 25). At this point, it was far too late for reconciliation.

Saul finally died on Mount Gilboa in a battle with the Philistines (1 Sam. 31). His death was followed by a long, drawn-out conflict over who would become Israel's next king. Abner, the commander of Saul's army, crowned Ishbaal, Saul's one remaining son (2 Sam. 2:8–9). The house of Judah, however, followed David (v. 10). This meant that there were now two royal houses, that of Saul and that of David. In their struggle with one another, these two houses engaged in violent conflict (2 Sam. 12:12–23; 3:1, 6), betrayal (2 Sam. 3:6–20), and murder (2 Sam. 3:26–27; 4:5–7). After seven years, the elders of the tribes of Israel came to David at Hebron and accepted him as their king over all Israel (2 Sam. 5:1–3). Although David went on to reign for forty years (vv. 4–5), nearly a decade had been lost due to the problems of succession.

The Importance of Succession

A transition in leadership can be the most painful event an organization experiences, and surrendering the reins of power to a successor can be one of the most difficult tests for a leader. Many times, after a leader has supposedly "passed the baton," he will linger, sit on the board, keep an office, or consult for the company. David Ulrich notes that "very often these well-intentioned efforts backfire."[6] Henry Ford, founder of the Ford Motor Company, tasked his son Edsel with finding a successor to take over the company. Ford was famous, however, for his stubbornness and his refusal to listen to advice, and he rejected virtually every recommendation his son made. Edsel became so discouraged that he developed a cancerous stomach ulcer that ultimately killed him. At his funeral, Edsel's widow confronted her father-in-law and accused him of having killed her husband.[7] Many people in leadership have tremendous difficulty handing over the baton to a successor. The psychoanalyst Otto Rank said that "leaving [one's] office means a loss of heroic stature, a plunge into the abyss of insignificance, a kind of mortality."[8] But leaders with honor recognize when they have made their most valuable contributions, and then they graciously hand over the reins of leadership to the next generation.

Career Change and Personal Transition

Personnel changes come in three forms—moving up, moving on, and moving out. In the course of a career, most people are subjected to all three. *Moving up* results in a larger office and paycheck, but the political and personal challenges may be painful and demanding. *Moving on* to a new position, reduced assignment, or another organization means starting again, learning new networks, and figuring out "how things are done here." *Moving out* is painful and frightening, whether it is from job loss or from retirement.

"It is not the changes that get you, it is the transitions," reports William Bridges,[9] a world-renowned guru in transitional psychology. He continues, "Change is not the same as transition. Change is situational: the new site, the new boss, the new role, or the new policy. Transition is the psychological process people go through to come to terms with the new situation. Change is external, transition is internal." Without the internal work of transition, change accomplishes little. The old French saying addresses this phenomenon, "The more things change, the more they remain the same." Changes—even multiple changes—make little lasting difference unless and until the soul-searching work of transition is completed.

In Israel's history, the national leadership shift from King Saul to King David was a change for both men and for the nation. The difficult, painful, and destructive issues coming out of the change emerged during the thwarted process of transition. Unless transition occurs, change will not work. Change starts with an outcome, such as "David will be king." In contrast, transition begins with an ending: "Saul will not be king."

To illustrate from another time in Israel's history, moving into the promised land was *change*, while letting go of Egypt was *transition*. The old country preacher was right in saying, "God's big challenge was not gettin' Israel out of Egypt, but gettin' Egypt out of Israel." This was the purpose of the wilderness wanderings. A spiritual and psychological change had to take place in the hearts of the people and the heart of the nation before they could enter the new land as free men and women. The change was in geography. The transition was in their self-perception—once slaves but now free!

In modern organizations, personnel changes come fast, be it moving up the ladder or out the door. Matt Paese and Richard Wellins, both vice presidents of DDI International, conducted a study of 385 leaders in transition.[10] The group included CEOs, heads of business units, and individuals moving into first-time management assignments. The results of the study apply to those who are moving up, moving on, or moving out:

- Making a transition is among life's most difficult personal challenges.
- Transitional challenges are characterized by changes in political networks, job complexity, and human dynamics.
- Few leaders report making the transition effectively.
- The transition required a shift of effort in communicating, planning, and building a team.
- Very few leaders in transition feel organizations are doing the right things to help make the transition successful.

The study concludes that the difficulties in leadership transitions are due to politics, complexity, and loss of control. Politics are difficult in transition because of "competing agendas, egos, reputations, and a great deal of intellect."[11] The complexity of the task increases because "accountability is ill-defined, competition for resources is fierce, and routes to success must be determined anew."[12] The first-time leader who moves from personal production to managing for results through other people will experience a loss of control. A person moving out, through job loss or retirement, experiences loss of control in a different way, but it is loss just the same. Even the individual pushed up the ladder discovers that those at the top do not have nearly as much control as those at the bottom of the ladder imagine.

The transition King Saul experienced is a case study in politics, complexity, and loss of control. King Saul handled it badly. How can you avoid the pitfalls of King Saul as you move up the ladder, on to your new position, or out to a new career or retirement? Dealing with politics, planning, and the personal, soul side of transition are required.

Politics: Power and Ego. In their book *The 48 Laws of Power*, Robert Greene and Joost Elffers suggest that the first law of power is "never outshine the master." In full, the law reads:

> Always make those above you feel comfortably superior. In your
> desire to please and impress them, do not go too far in display-
> ing your talents or you might accomplish the opposite—inspire
> fear and insecurity. Make your masters appear more brilliant than
> they are and you will attain the heights of power.[13]

To put the law another way, the duke must never outshine the king if the duke wants to keep his head. This observation of power was played out in the political battles between Saul and David. Perhaps David's rise to prominence was too threatening for Saul. David unwittingly allowed his star to shine too brightly in the presence of the king. Saul's fear and insecurity resulted in his determination to put David to death. Arrogant insecurity in high places of power and influence can bring down havoc.

The harsh dynamics of politics are played out in organizations in diverse ways depending on the political culture of the organization. There are organizational cultures that tend to hide the political jockeying and gamesmanship beneath smiles and polite banter. Other organizations are openly and viciously political. Recognition, ego, reputation, influence, and resources are the chips of political competitions. Political maneuvering is at a peak when there is the potential for a major personnel change in the air. People will trade on promises, secrets, gossip, rumors, and lies. The one moving up the ladder where the politics are more blatant will be surprised, even shocked, by how things get done. Moving on requires learning a new set of political rules and developing a new network of allies. Moving out may be the most difficult; letting go of political influence, networks, and clout can shatter personal identity. In transition, everyone must deal with political reality and the inner, deeper challenge of personal transition.

Planning: Upside and Downside. Due to the increased number of leadership changes and the complexity of these changes, organizations are moving toward succession planning. The process of planning depends on the organization. As a response to the corporate and accounting scandals of Enron, Tyco International, Adelphia, Peregrine Systems, and others, new legislation was enacted. Called the Sarbanes-Oxley Act of 2002,[14] the legislation set standards for all public company boards, management, and public accounting firms. As a result, most public corporations have a succession plan (few would admit they don't). Family corporations and businesses are often fraught with personal difficulties as they shift from one generation to the next. Many nonprofits and ministries have boards to guide the transition. However, sorting out who has the influence on the board to guide the process can be difficult. Churches have a variety of methods for making changes depending on the denomination or independent by-laws.

Stephen Miles of *Forbes Magazine* writes for larger corporations, but his wisdom on planning succession applies to all organizations, regardless of size.[15] His advice is to plan in advance and keep the plan before the board. The organization must engage the stakeholders in creating the plan. With the plan clearly in view, the decision makers must then look carefully at internal candidates. When evaluating potential leaders, decision makers must assess the candidates under stressful circumstances that present significant challenges, and be careful not to evaluate them just when they are succeeding. Finally, an organization must have a plan to support the selected incoming leader.

A major challenge with planning succession is found in the unanticipated consequences. When a potential change in leadership is whispered, the rumor mill begins churning, and those rumors can create a horse race between internal candidates, a roller derby at lower levels of management, and bookies on the sidelines taking bets. The mission of the organization is bruised or lost in the melee. When a new leader is finally selected, the board often feels that their job is done (they have completed the change) and leaves the new leader in a "sink or swim" dilemma (navigating the transition). In summary, one cannot move through a major personnel transition without some fallout due, in part, to the planning process. This, however, is not an excuse to avoid planning. Indeed, good planning can mitigate negative outcomes. In most cases, a plan, even a poor one, is better than no plan at all.

Personal Issues: Stress and Change. Deeper than the political shenanigans, more significant than the corporate succession plan, is the soulful challenge of working through personal transition. Indeed, the corporate plan only succeeds to the extent that those experiencing transition are willing to engage in the accompanying personal and psychological work. The rancorous politics can be stunted by mature responses from those dealing with the transition personally. Wise boards and bosses give people time to work through the stress and change that is the heart of the psychology of transition.

Our understanding of the psychology of transition was born in studies of bereavement, especially the work of Kubler-Ross,[16] first published in 1969. These studies identified and listed a consistent, identifiable process that all people experience when dealing with loss. Their conclusions became commonly known as the five stages of grief. The stages are 1) denial, 2) anger, 3) bargaining, 4) depression, and 5) acceptance. It was later observed that people experiencing transition also must go through these five stages in order to successfully complete the transition. Specifically, the psychology of grief was applied to Peace Corps volunteers experiencing the transition to new cultures to help deal with the inevitable "culture shock."[17] The Peace Corps continues to utilize worksheets based on this five-step process today. Interestingly, social scientists observed that significant transition in the workplace feels very much like culture shock to those who are experiencing it.[18] Because of these multiple successful applications of the psychology of grief, within a decade of its development the application was made to career transitions.[19]

What are the personal issues associated with moving up, moving on, and moving out? John Fisher developed a detailed and complex curve of transition[20] that can be summarized as 1) the first mountain, 2) the valley of despair, and 3) the new path. The *first mountain* is an uneasy mix of fear and happiness. Fear, because you cannot grasp a clear picture of the future. Happiness, because something, at last, is happening. Happiness, because your expectations are high (perhaps too high). Fear, because you know you need to make changes and people are watching. The great danger at this moment is to slip into denial. Denial is a tempting substitute for the work involved in a personal transition. It is hard to accept the effect that the change has on your inner life. The opportunity on the first mountain is to embrace this as a defining moment[21] and engage in discovering how the moment tests you, what the moment reveals about you, and how the moment will shape your future.[22] The way that you embrace or ignore this defining moment has some bearing on the way you will deal with the next stage, the valley of despair.

Once over the first mountain, you enter the *valley of despair*. The experience is felt differently by everyone, but the fundamental issues are similar. You experience the shock of discovering that you are not who you once were, at least in your career. This is a challenge to the way you understand yourself, your future, and your choices. It can be compared to Paul's "Damascus Road" experience, when he heard God's voice and was struck blind, at least for a while.[23] We, too, may feel blinded by the new challenges the transition brings. We may experience feelings of shame and depression as we struggle to make sense out of what has happened and why. The valley takes time to traverse. "He who lacks time to mourn, lacks time to mend."[24]

The most common dangers in the valley are slumping into disillusionment, burning up with hostility, or giving up in defeat. As you are faced with these dangers, you must remember that while traveling through this valley, your perception of reality may be distorted, your motivations could be misguided, and your emotions may not be adequately restrained. Again, your hope is to participate fully, maturely, and authentically in this defining moment in your life. Rather than be overwhelmed by your emotions, strive to let your inner feelings teach you valuable lessons that will make this journey through the valley worthwhile. Take the time and emotional energy to trace back what is happening today to past events in your own story. The goal of your quest must be to find *your* way through, and to follow it with dignity and grace. While feeling, processing, and sorting your emotions is vital to this transition process, a concurrent and equally important part of the valley walk is to keep your feet on the ground. Remember, while your vision of reality or motivation at this stage may not be entirely trustworthy due to the emotional nature of transition, the counsel of trusted friends can help you stay in touch with reality.

At the end of your valley walk is your payoff for the mixture of fear/happiness of the first stage and the emotional upheaval of the second stage. At last, there is *the new path*—acceptance and moving forward. When you diligently follow through in the work of your transition, you will find that one day—and then, over the course of many days—you will begin to exert more control, you will make things happen in a positive way, and you will begin to feel like yourself again, albeit a new and improved self. You will find yourself able to make sense of what has happened and why. Your confidence will increase. You will feel good about what you are doing and assured that you are doing the right things in the right way.

Transitions are hard. John Kenneth Galbraith, an economist, put it well: "Faced with the choice between changing one's mind and proving that there is no need to do so, almost everybody gets busy on the proof."[25] You cannot move through a change, whether it is a change of leadership or a change of mind, without dealing with transition. You must slog through the personal stuff. In facing real and personal transition, avoid the pitfalls of King Saul, his overriding fear, his deep-seated resentment, his long-term depression, and his ultimate defeat. Face your moment of transition as a defining moment. Embrace it as a time that will test who you are and as one that will shape who you will become.

Group Discussion and Personal Reflection

Group Discussion

Saul and David

Look over the chapter and discuss how Saul and David each handled the transition from "King Saul" to "King David." What did each do that helped the transition? What did each do that potentially harmed the transition? What are the "takeaways" from the story that fit the transition you are facing now?

The Politics of Change

What do you see as the political nature of your organization? How does your organization handle transition? How do you handle the politics of change in your organization?

Have a Plan

How does your organization manage personnel changes? Does your organization have a succession plan or procedure for making changes in top leadership? If so, what is it? What can you do to help with the transition of a new leader?

The Personal Stuff

What time in your life has been a "defining moment" of transition for your career? Can you apply the stages of change outlined in the chapter?

- The first mountain—fear and happiness, the danger of denial
- The valley of despair—threat and shame, the danger of hostility and defeat
- The new path—acceptance and moving forward with confidence

How did this time in your life help to shape your future?

Personal Reflection

Assess

One of the key tasks of a leader is to help individuals and the organization through transition. Assess your competency in the following key leadership behaviors associated with leading through transition: Rate yourself on a 3, 2, 1 scale with 3 = high competency, 2 = fair competency, and 1 = low competency.

____ Analyze how individual behavior and attitudes need to change in order to have a successful transition.

____ Analyze who stands to take a loss as the change unfolds in the organization.

____ Exert sufficient energy into helping the team understand the problem that the change will address.

____ Help team members experience the problem firsthand so they understand why the change is needed.

____ Talk about what transition means both strategically and personally for people and intentionally guide the transition.

Analyze

> ➤ How have you handled your defining moments of personal transition in your career?

> ➤ How do you help your team handle the defining moments of team transition in organization?

Act

To become a better leader in times of transition, you can take the following actions:

___ Study the psychology of transitions. Begin with William Bridges' book, *Managing Transitions*.

___ Study how you have dealt with transition and how others helped you; learn from your own experience in order to better serve your team.

___ If possible, start by intentionally managing a small transition:

- Think about who gains and who suffers loss in the change.
- Present the problem that creates the need for change.
- Help the team experience the problem by talking with clients, etc.
- Think about what behaviors and attitudes need to change.
- Present the dynamics of transition so the team understands.

Chapter 12

Saul Failed to Consult God

No one would accuse Saul of being too spiritual. Indeed, the Bible only notes a few occasions when he sought God's counsel. At the beginning, Saul was a "choice" candidate for the kingship when God selected him. According to 1 Samuel 13:13, the Lord had planned to "[establish his] kingdom over Israel forever" (NRSV). Yet, once he was crowned king, Saul began to lose sight of God's call on his life. He began to deteriorate spiritually.

In this regard, Saul is like many leaders. They begin with vision, values, and, many times, a zeal for God. However, the hard road of leading others—the disappointments, the betrayals, and the ambiguity of it all—takes its toll. It is common for a leader to either turn away from the spiritual reality of life or to compartmentalize his or her life with spiritual stuff reserved for Sundays only. The temptation is to divide life between the hard realities of leadership at work and the soft escape of spiritual thoughts that ease the tension. We might call this "leadership with a side of spirituality."

In 1 Samuel 14:16–23, we glimpse a picture of Saul dividing spiritual guidance from the hard realities of leadership. To grasp the full measure of the story, remember that Joshua had led the Israelites into the promised land and encouraged them to settle in that land. However, the book of Judges tells us that the Israelites didn't follow through with Joshua's instructions. The Israelites were hill people and instead of settling throughout the land, they confined their settlements to the hill country. The low land at the coast was open. This is where the Philistines migrated and settled. A clash was inevitable. Indeed, it was this conflict that led the Israelites to cry out for a king. The Philistines were one of the major groups Saul fought against throughout his reign.

A key point in the conflict is recorded in 1 Samuel 14. The Philistines had built a new garrison on an important pass, and Saul was unsure about what to do. Unbeknownst to Saul, his son Jonathan went out with his armor-bearer and attacked this garrison, and killed about twenty Philistine soldiers there. Verse 15 says that, because of what he had done, "there was a panic in the camp, in the field, and among all the people; the garrison and even the raiders trembled; the earth quaked; and it became a very great panic" (NRSV).

Saul's indecisiveness and uncertainty continued. Verse 18 tells us that he called to the priest, Ahijah, and said, "Bring the ark of God here" (NRSV). Some translations say, "Bring the *ephod* of God here." The *ephod* was part of the priestly garment in the Old Testament that was used to discern the will of God. In any case, whether Saul was calling for the ark or the *ephod*, it's clear that his desire was to seek direction from God as to how to respond to the developing situation. However, as he was talking with the priest, "the tumult in the camp of the Philistines increased more and more; and Saul said to the priest, 'Withdraw your hand'" (v. 19 NRSV). In other words, Saul told the priest not to bother about inquiring of God.

In this narrative, Saul was playing the part of a modern manager, devoid of higher callings, deeper values, or spiritual sensitivity. Henry Mintzberg, noted management expert and professor, describes the work of the manager-leader: "The pressures of the job drive the manager to take on too much work, encourage interruptions, respond quickly to every stimulus, see the tangible and avoid the abstract, make decisions in small increments and do everything abruptly."[1]

The chaotic nature of leadership takes its toll on the inner life of the leader. Max De Pree, a deeply spiritual and wonderful Christian leader, describes leadership as an art,[2] like the improvisations of a jazz band.[3] While spiritually grounded leaders can create incredible harmony, many other leaders look like they are impulsive and disorderly. Abraham Zaleznik writes:

> Leaders often experience their talent as restlessness, as a desire to upset other people's apple carts, an impelling need to 'do things better.' As a consequence, a leader may not create a stable working environment; rather she may create a chaotic workplace, with highly charged emotional peaks and valleys.[4]

Leadership is spiritually demanding. Leaders must live with ambiguity rather than certainty. They are the recipients of criticism. Often, it is unjust criticism. At the same time, they receive more credit than their due, simply because they have the position of leader. A leader serves as a warehouse of conflicting goals and aims, each vying for attention and resources. To face the daunting task of leadership without the resources of God's presence and guidance is not only arrogant but also foolhardy.

Saul was deep in a crisis with the Philistines. Yet he turned away from the counsel of God. Once the Philistines were on the run, Saul suggested that the Israelite armies pursue them and finish them off. His soldiers agreed, but it took the priest to suggest that they consult God before taking any further action (1 Sam. 14:36). Saul asked God whether he should lead the Israelites in pursuit of the Philistines, but God "did not answer him that day" (v. 37). God did not answer the man who had pushed aside his counsel just a few hours earlier.

Saul construed that some sin must have been committed in the army, and he vowed, "Even if it is in my son Jonathan, he shall surely die!" (v. 39 NRSV). The sacred lots were cast and fell on Jonathan. He confessed to having violated the fast that his father had enjoined upon the army before the battle had begun (1 Sam. 14:24–30). As we discussed in earlier chapters, Saul had required his troops to abstain from food during the course of a lengthy battle. It was a rash and foolish decision, motivated, perhaps, more from superstition than any real religious sensibilities. His inquiry of God was, in this instance, based on his desire to uphold this rash oath.[5] It was more about making Saul look good than seeking God's plan that Saul might follow.

These are the only times before his rejection as king that we are specifically told that Saul inquired of God. In the first instance, Saul stopped the inquiry before it was completed. In the second case, his inquiry served only to identify who had violated his rash oath. In neither case was Saul seeking the heart of God in order to know the Lord or submit himself to Yahweh's leadership in his life and reign.

The Pretense of Spirituality

Saul had a pretense of spirituality, but it did not hold up under pressure. When the rubber met the road, his real lack of reliance on God was exposed. And the danger of shallow or even false spirituality in a spiritual leader is certainly not confined to ancient times. Many stories could be told of leaders—including pastors and other spiritual leaders—whose spirituality went awry. Back in the early 1990s, I (Ralph) attended a conference at Heritage USA, the Christian theme park and residential complex that had originally been built in Fort Mill, South Carolina, by PTL Club founders Jim and Tammy Faye Bakker. The Bakkers had gone from working at Pat Robertson's Christian Broadcasting Network in 1966, to developing a variety show called *The 700 Club*, which became one of the longest-running televangelism programs ever aired. In the early 1970s, they launched their own show, *The PTL Club*, which was eventually carried by about a hundred stations and had around twelve million viewers. In 1978, they opened Heritage USA, which became one of the top US vacation destinations by 1986, second only to Walt Disney World and Disneyland. During this time, Jim and Tammy Faye Bakker began to be criticized in national venues for their conspicuous consumption, and PTL's fund-raising activities began to come under scrutiny. The next year, it was revealed that Bakker had had a sexual encounter several years earlier with Jessica Hahn, a staff secretary at the Heritage Village Church, and that she had been paid $265,000 to keep it a secret. In the face of those allegations, Bakker resigned from PTL on March 19, 1987. A Federal grand jury probe was carried out over sixteen months, which concluded that, by offering lifetime partnerships in Heritage USA, the Bakkers were actually selling securities. In 1989, Jim Bakker was sentenced to forty-five years in federal prison and a $500,000 fine. When I visited the park in the early 1990s, Bakker was in prison serving his sentence and the park was virtually empty. It looked like it was frozen in time, with the heavy equipment still parked around the Heritage Grand Towers and the arm of the crane still poised at some of its upper floors, right where it had been when construction had stopped with Bakker's resignation.

Bakker received parole in August 1994, after serving nearly five years of his sentence. He went on to write a moving account of his experiences entitled *I Was Wrong*, in which he reflected on his career, his original vision for Heritage USA, and the reasons for his downfall.[6] He explains that PTL was not selling securities by offering lifetime partnerships in Heritage USA, and a Federal jury reached that same conclusion on July 22, 1996, after which the case was overturned and the judge was dismissed from the case.

My interest here, however, is not in the details of the case but in Bakker's personal reflections on his experiences. He recalls how, as he languished in prison, he struggled to understand why God had allowed him to be imprisoned. It occurred to him that he had become so busy building Heritage USA—"ostensibly for God"[7]—that he had lost his intimate relationship with Him. He recalls weeping in his cell when he looked at a photo someone sent him in which he was standing at a construction site with a bodyguard, while his son, Jamie, looked on from a distance. He felt he had been so busy with Heritage USA that he had missed his son's growing up. While Jamie's constant companion was a bodyguard, Bakker himself recounts that he "hardly remembered Jamie Charles's childhood." He recalls:

> He had just been born when we had started PTL in an old furniture store in Charlotte. Then we moved to a twenty-five-acre site we called Heritage Village, and our ministry began to take off, multiplying exponentially. Analysts from IBM Corporation estimated that we grew 7,000 percent over the next year and a half. We could barely keep up—things were happening so quickly. Before long, we were building Heritage USA and sending gospel programming to fifty-two nations. In the midst of the swirl of spiritual activity, I lost touch with my family, and especially with Jamie. . . . Like many other ministers, I had made a tragic mistake: I had confused the *work* of God for God Himself.[8]

Bakker explains that "it happened so subtly, imperceptibly, while I was busy doing what I thought was important work for God."[9] He goes on to review a massive list of responsibilities he had at Heritage USA. He was the president of the Inspirational Television Network, which was seen on two hundred stations and on over eight thousand cable systems, and served as executive producer of numerous television programs, including *The PTL Club*, *The Jim and Tammy Show*, and others. He was also senior pastor of the Heritage Village Church and Missionary Fellowship, which had several thousand people in attendance each week. He preached the services and supervised a staff of twenty-five assistant pastors. He had nearly three thousand employees and thousands of volunteers who worked at Heritage USA, and supervised a dozen or more parachurch ministries run out of Heritage USA. He goes on to explain:

> In addition to these responsibilities, I was president of Heritage USA, the world's largest Christian retreat center. At the height of our efforts, our dedicated staff provided eighty-six religious services each week. According to PTL security figures, more than six million visitors came through the gates at Heritage USA in 1986, the last full year I served as president. We had seven restaurants, three swimming pools, three trains, 3,336 lodging rooms and campsites built or being developed, Mainstreet USA shops and religious bookstore, a dinner theater where inspirational musicals and plays were performed with a full orchestra, Heritage Island, a huge, $13 million, state-of-the-art water park staffed by seventy lifeguards per shift, the Heritage Passion Play, a dramatic presentation of the life of Christ in a multimillion-dollar outdoor amphitheater, and much more. We also had time-share lodgings and a retirement village, which included single-family homes, high-rise condominiums, apartments, and duplexes, in various stages of construction.[10]

Bakker goes on to note that Heritage USA also had a five-hundred room Heritage Grand Hotel, which I mentioned earlier. After reviewing this staggering list of responsibilities, Bakker concludes, "It was little wonder that I burned out. Although my intentions were good, I was obsessed with building what some might call a modern-day Tower of Babel."[11]

Bakker recalls that, as he sat in his prison cell, he had already repented, again and again, for his sexual indiscretion and for having misled people with the prosperity gospel. As he racked his brain and examined his heart, he asked God to reveal to him the areas in which he still needed to repent. It finally occurred to Bakker that he had issues that went beyond repentance, back to the issue of his very *relationship* with God. He says:

> God had been showing me in many ways that the primary reason He had allowed me to be imprisoned was not to punish me, nor was it so I could minister to other prisoners; I was in prison so I could get to know Him. Some people might find it ironic that a preacher who had spoken to millions of people about how to find God needed to be sent to prison to renew a relationship with Him himself. But I am convinced there was no other way God could have gotten my attention. God wanted me to quit worshiping bricks and mortar, programs and talents, and get back to worshiping Him.[12]

Every leader faces the danger of forgetting his or her relationship with God in the hustle and bustle of day-to-day leadership. We can get so caught up in the external matters with which we are dealing that we forget the internal matters. We must, therefore, learn to lead from the inside out.

Lead from the Inside Out

The task of leadership requires spiritual resources. The recognition of this is apparent in the ever-increasing emphasis on spirituality and leadership. Look at the excellent writings of authors such as Margaret Wheatley, Warren Bennis and Burt Nanus, Stephen Covey, Peter Block, John Gardner, James Kouzes, and Barry Posner. There are vast differences in their writings, but note these common themes, themes that evoke the spiritual reality of life and the spiritual nature of leadership:

- Leadership potential is in everyone.
- Leadership is shared throughout the organization.
- Servant-leadership is the preferred paradigm.
- You should lead with vision and purpose rather than positional power.

- Leadership is a transformational task.
- Leaders are to model the way for others.
- Leaders should engage in reciprocal relationships.
- Leaders are to empower others.
- You should lead with values and integrity.

Note that this list would not describe King Saul. Perhaps, near the beginning, the potential for spiritual leadership was within his grasp. However, Saul turned away from the counsel of God.

Avoid the pitfall. Learn to hear, trust, and follow God. Leadership is a spiritual task. Christ is our source of spiritual vitality. We must turn to him and cooperate with him in the challenge of leading others. He calls us to lead with purpose and mission, his mission. We have the Scriptures, and we have a life of prayer to cultivate. He has promised guidance and discernment. It is our firm belief that the human spirit, your spirit, was created to join with the Holy Spirit. When you bring your full being, your "true and best in Christ,"[13] to the task of leadership, it stands to reason that the Spirit of Christ, the Holy Spirit, is with you. We believe this is the most important chapter in the book.

Leadership Is Spiritual

For a leader to hear, trust, and follow God, she must first learn to engage in leadership as a spiritual practice. For many, describing leadership as spiritual may sound odd. Let's look at a list of spiritual activities that relate to realistic leadership.[14] For each, assess your own level of spiritual practice in these leadership competencies:

- Competent leaders are intentional in their decisions and actions. Spiritual leaders rely on faith to compel ethical decisions so they act with integrity.
- Competent leaders must engage in self-reflection. Spiritual leaders' self-reflection leads to greater depth, self-understanding, and leadership insights.
- Competent leaders participate in self-assessment. Spiritual

leaders have the openness and courage to receive feedback and make corrections as needed.

- Competent leaders build healthy teams. Spiritual leaders create faithful communities that work and learn together in mutual trust and respect.

- Competent leaders demand intellectual integrity. Spiritual leaders call on courage to see the world as it is rather than the way they wish it might be.

- Competent leaders demand ethical integrity. Spiritual leaders tell the truth, keep promises, and raise the vision for ethical integrity in others.

- Competent leaders serve their followers. Spiritual leaders are servant-leaders who treat followers with compassion, coaxing out the best within them.

- Competent leaders continue to develop. Spiritual leaders know that leading requires learning, honing, and improving their skills as a leader.

Some of the most popular teaching and reading on leadership has a spiritual basis. Stephen Covey's *Seven Habits* is based on faith in the goodness of people and an individual's ability to do the right thing. Lee Bolman and Terrence Deal mix a variety of spiritual perspectives in *Leading with Soul: An Uncommon Journey of Spirit*. "We must learn to be true to ourselves, and our whole selves"[15] is the spiritual advice of Russ Moxley in *Leadership and Spirit: Breathing New Vitality and Energy into Individuals and Organizations*. Peter Vaill takes the next step in *Spirited Leading and Learning*, when he startles the reader with the observation that "leadership is not a secular enterprise . . . it forces us to rethink the boundary between the secular and the sacred, the natural and the transcendental . . . to think and communicate theologically— something, unfortunately, that is not presently contemplated at any known MBA program."[16]

The task of leadership is spiritual. I would dare say that these writers from outside the church take the spiritual calling of leadership more seriously than many business, academic, and government leaders who sit in the pews each Sunday morning. It is a plain and painful fact that you cannot consult with God about your leadership until you embrace and embark on leadership as a spiritual practice.

Once you accept leadership as a spiritual practice, the bottom line is faithfulness.[17] Faithfulness is not an excuse for shoddy leadership or dipping profits. Faithfulness is a call to a higher and more challenging form of leadership. Saul drifted away and then turned away from the spiritual demands of leadership. You can choose to sail toward and turn into the Spirit of God who desires to lead you as you lead your organization.

Attention and Authenticity

Once you accept the truth that leadership is a spiritual enterprise, it is time to develop the two competencies of the inner life: attention and authenticity. The spiritual practices have value if, and only if, you learn to pay attention and are authentic. By this I mean that you pay attention to your perceptions, your motivation, and your emotions. When I say authentic, I mean that you are true to your best in Christ. Leaders are measured by outcomes, but what is inside drives the leader.

Saul seems to have retreated from his inner life. I (Richard) remember being called in on an intervention for the leader of a large organization. I was one of a team of consultants that invested a twelve-hour day with this one leader. The organization was full of angst and rebellion. Our task, as a team of consultants, was to help the leader identify and work though his part in the problem.

It was an amazing day. The team members were open, genuine, and gentle when needed, but probing as required. The leader seemed to want to "fix the problem" or at least the blame, which he considered the first step in fixing a problem. Through the day, we all participated in a number of exercises, discussions, and silent times for reflection.

After a full day of self-probing, I counted only one time when the man expressed a statement of self-awareness. He said he was angry with his team. After a full day, I did not hear even one expression of empathy for any member of his organization. Without self-awareness and empathy, it is impossible to lead from a spiritual core, impossible to consult with God about your leadership.

The twin competencies of paying attention to the inner life, yours and others', along with personal and professional authenticity, keep you in touch with yourself. You ask, "Why do I need to be in touch with myself?" To lead in consultation with God, it is essential. Reflect upon the writing of John Calvin, a leader of the Protestant Reformation, from the opening of his ten-volume work *The Institutes*:

> Nearly all wisdom we possess, that is to say, true and sound wisdom, consists of two parts: knowledge of God and of ourselves. But while joined by many bounds, which one precedes and brings forth the other, is not easy to say.[18]

You cannot truly know yourself until you come to know God; you cannot know God until you are willing to know your true self. In our modern world, it is tempting to place knowledge of self in the armchair of the psychologist and the knowledge of God in the pew on Sunday morning. However, this is not how the spiritual life works. To consult with God requires attention and authenticity.

Pay spiritual attention. W. H. Auden, a British and American poet, is regarded by many as one of the greatest writers of the twentieth century.[19] Think about this penetrating thought from Auden: "Choice of attention—to pay attention to this and ignore that— is to the inner life what choice of action is to the outer. In both cases, a person is responsible for their choice and must accept the consequences."

I often explain this to leaders by holding up a fist of folded bills, currency. Money is the currency of the marketplace. You pay money and receive goods and services. You can pay for a cup of coffee, a new car, or a castle on a mountain top. The market deals in the currency of money.

Leaders deal in the currency of attention. Your task is to focus the attention of your team on the important problems, the right goals, the best procedures, and the big picture. You lead with the currency of attention. If your team (or you) is distracted, your organization will pay a price. As a leader, you know that where you focus your attention is also where your team will focus their attention. You must pay attention to the proper issues and objectives.

Apply the same lesson to your inner life. Will you focus on what your inner life is teaching you? Do you believe God wants to speak to you through your inner life? What can you learn from your emotions? This is more than knowing what you feel and why, but what do your emotions teach you about yourself and your challenge? These same questions can be applied to the inner attention of motivation and perspective.

If you are willing to know yourself, you will be open to hear the voice of God through Scripture and prayer. God's approach to you is clear: "If you are going to know me, we are going to deal with you." That's how it works. Learn to pay attention to your inner life. God is speaking.

Be spiritually authentic. The phrase I (Richard) use to describe spiritual authenticity is "living true to your best in Christ." Did you know your soul was created to collaborate with heaven's throne? The two, your soul and heaven's throne, are determined to bring your true and best to life every day. You are invited to collaborate in this grand and eternal scheme. In another place, I expressed it this way:

Authentic Christian spirituality is living true to my best in Christ.

1. *To be true* is to be genuine, honest, open, and real about what I 1) understand and 2) feel at any giving moment, and 3) what is driving my thoughts, emotions, and actions.

2. *To be my best* is to submit my understanding, feelings, and motives to the acceptance, assessment, correction, cleansing, forgiveness, and empowerment of the Spirit of Christ.[20]

An error leaders make is in thinking that the part of their life that belongs to God exists to provide an escape from the rest of their life, which is the tough part, the part where they lead others. This creates the false reality of doing leadership work during the week and the escaping to gentler things on Sunday in the sanctuary. There are two things wrong with this thinking. First, God will not take just part of you; he is interested in a "whole-person program." You will not find one place in Scripture where God was satisfied with a part-time commitment. God wants all of you.

Second, God does not provide you an escape from the reality of the world but expects you to soldier up and face the reality of the world in him. God intends to go to work with you on Monday and every day. And, when you bring your work home, he is right there. Here is how God works: There is a grand moment of forgiveness and faith when your life begins in God, but that is only the beginning. What follows is a lifelong journey. God has designs on you. True, he loves you as you are, but he is not content to leave you as you are. In essence he says, "If you are going to live in me, we are going to work on you."

Spiritual Authenticity and Church Leadership

Spiritual authenticity can be a special problem for those who hold leadership roles in the church, especially pastors. It is very easy for pastors and other church leaders to assume that they have given attention to their spiritual lives and that they are in an authentic relationship with the Lord, since they are doing the Lord's work. Surely if you are leading others in worship and prayer, administering the sacraments of Baptism and Holy Communion, then things must be perfect between you and God. It is because pastors and other church leaders are engaged in these activities that it is so easy for them to delude themselves about their relationship with God.

Twenty years ago, Donald Hands and Wayne Fehr wrote a little book entitled *Spiritual Wholeness for Clergy: A New Psychology of Intimacy with God, Self and Others*,[21] in which they made an extremely insightful study of the ways that pastors may relate to God. In their study, Hands and Fehr designed a diagram that can be used as a diagnostic tool for understanding intimacy with God and its counterfeits on the basis of two polarities, which are personal power, indicated on the y axis, and one's capacity for relationships, indicated on the x axis (Fig. 1). By "personal power," they mean "the power to be," which is a basic sense of self-affirmation.[22] This person has a healthy sense of his or her right to be here. He

Intimacy with God

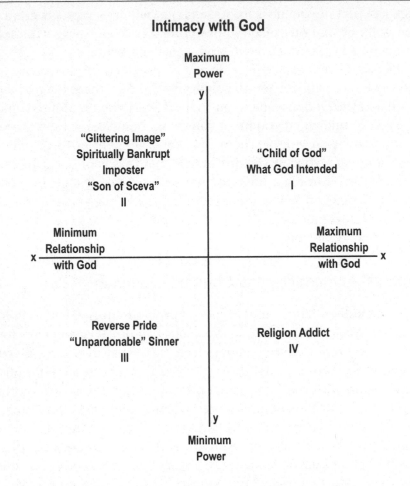

Maximum
Power

y

"Glittering Image"
Spiritually Bankrupt
Imposter
"Son of Sceva"
II

"Child of God"
What God Intended
I

x ——— Minimum
Relationship
with God

Maximum
Relationship
with God ——— x

Reverse Pride
"Unpardonable" Sinner
III

Religion Addict
IV

y

Minimum
Power

has experienced what psychologists call individuation or integration. He is a healthy individual who is comfortable with himself. The other polarity, one's capacity for relationships, refers to the need to be with another or others. The two axes create four quadrants, each of which illustrates one possible orientation of the self toward God.

Quadrant I represents the fulfillment of God's intention for people. This person has a maximum sense of power as well as a maximum capacity for relationship, and feels secure as a "child of God," which is what God intends for his children. By contrast, the person in Quadrant II has a maximum sense of personal power but, because he has a minimal openness for relationship, he has a nominal relationship with God. This person may be doing "the Lord's work," but he is spiritually bankrupt. Hands and Fehr note the title of Susan Howatch's novel, entitled *Glittering Images*, which was about a pastor named Charles Ashworth who presented a "glittering image" on the outside, but who was spiritually impoverished on the inside.[23] They also note the case of the seven sons of a Jewish high priest named Sceva, who tried to drive out evil spirits by calling on the name of the "Jesus whom Paul preaches," but who failed because they did not know Jesus themselves (Acts 19:13–17). In Quadrant III, we see someone who has both a minimal sense of personal power and a minimal relationship to God. This person has little sense of worth and may feel unworthy of God's grace. They may feel that they are an "unpardonable" sinner. Lastly, Quadrant IV identifies another kind of person with a false spiritual stance. This person has little sense of personal power and has not experienced personal individuation, and clings to God in a compulsive way. He may appear to be maximally related to God, but he is more likely "addicted" to religion as a means of trying to achieve self-worth. The reality for this person is probably that "all this religiosity is actually a substitute for that genuine intimacy with God that liberates from self-contempt and all anxiety."[24]

Hands and Fehr powerfully illustrate that, while pastors and other church workers may be doing "the work of the Lord," that alone is not an indicator of their level of intimacy with God. A pastor may be fully integrated as a child of God, but it is also possible to be a pastor and be spiritually bankrupt, in spiritual despair, or be a "religion addict." I (Ralph) think Saul may fit best in Quadrant IV. He was charged with leading Israel as its covenant mediator, and he engaged in many religious activities. But, as time went on, it seems that he carried out many of these religious activities in an effort to meet requirements, rather than to know and rely upon God. Pastors and other church leaders can fall into this same trap without even realizing it. In this respect, pastors and other church leaders are no different from business leaders. They must both work to develop the two competencies of the inner life: attention and authenticity.

God's Gifts: The Bible, Prayer, and the Community of Faith

Leadership is a spiritual task that calls you to know God and yourself through paying attention and being authentic. However, you are not left to your own devices and imagination in this challenge. God is with you and speaks to you through Scripture, prayer, and the community of faith. But how does a leader read the Bible, pray, and benefit from being part of a community of faith? How can you hear, trust, and follow God in your leadership?

The way of prayer and Scripture is certainly not the way of the Pharisees, for "they love to pray standing in the synagogues and on the street corners to be seen by men" (Matt. 6:5). Scripture and prayer bring a unique temptation for leaders. One of the tasks of leadership is to manage reputation, the way others see you. It is possible to interpret Saul's turning to God, as demonstrated by the Pharisee praying on the street corners to be seen, as a way of managing his own reputation. As a Christian leader, it is possible to use the disciplines of prayer and the study of Scripture as a means of self-aggrandizement or a tool to manage your leadership reputation. Be careful, your soul weighs in the balance.

Authenticity and attention are prerequisites for Bible understanding and prayer. So, how can you approach the Scripture and your inner prayer life? As a leader, you are practical. Therefore, make your Bible study and prayer practical. Start with a real issue in your leadership challenge. Then ask two questions:

1. How can this challenge open me up to God?
2. How can I respond to this challenge in a way that is true to my best in Christ?

With these two questions in your mind and heart, search the Scriptures and pray with all your strength. And do this as a discipline, regularly, not just in a moment of crisis. Search the Scripture; pray from your heart; and expect God's guidance.

Search the Scripture. When Moses was leading the Hebrews, God knew that, one day, the people would cry out for a king.

Realizing that one day the office of king would emerge in Israel, God set down guidelines for what the king was to be like and how he was to operate. Those guidelines are in Deuteronomy 17:14–20:

> When you have come into the land that the LORD your God is giving you, and have taken possession of it and settled in it, and you say, "I will set a king over me, like all the nations that are around me," you may indeed set over you a king whom the LORD your God will choose. One of your own community you may set as king over you; you are not permitted to put a foreigner over you, who is not of your own community. Even so, he must not acquire many horses for himself, or return the people to Egypt in order to acquire more horses, since the LORD has said to you, "You must never return that way again." And he must not acquire many wives for himself, or else his heart will turn away; also silver and gold he must not acquire in great quantity for himself. When he has taken the throne of his kingdom, he shall have a copy of this law written for him in the presence of the levitical priests. It shall remain with him and he shall read in it all the days of his life, so that he may learn to fear the LORD his God, diligently observing all the words of this law and these statutes, neither exalting himself above other members of the community nor turning aside from the commandment, either to the right or to the left, so that he and his descendants may reign long over his kingdom in Israel. (NRSV)

Now, why shouldn't the king have had a lot of horses? That's how you build an army. Soldiers ride horses into the field. But God said, "I don't want you to rely on constantly building up military arms for your national survival."

What about wives? Why shouldn't the king have had several wives? Kings normally sealed international treaties with marriages. But God was saying, "I don't want you to put all your faith in partnerships with foreign kings for your security."

So what was the king's job? If he was not supposed to focus on building up arms or on making international treaties, then what was he supposed to be doing?

Look at Deuteronomy 17:18–19. Here's what the king was supposed to do: pore over God's Word every day, "so that he may learn to fear the LORD his God, diligently observing all the words of this law and these statutes" (NRSV).

Here is how the king was supposed to know what to do: consult the Word of God day-in and day-out, poring over it and meditating on it. And this is the way spiritual leaders and other Christians should seek the Lord today, through his Word. Henry and Richard Blackaby say:

> True spiritual leaders recognize their utter dependence on God. So they regularly fill their heart and mind with his Word. When leaders' minds are filled with Scripture, they find themselves thinking according to biblical principles. When a difficult situation arises, the Holy Spirit will bring appropriate Scriptures to mind. When they prepare to make a decision, the Holy Spirit will bring to memory a Scripture verse that provides relevant guidance.[25]

Pray from your heart. Sometimes when people face a situation, they'll analyze it and reason through it, and only consult with God after they've made the decision. I (Ralph) am reminded of a board of elders at a well-known church in Alabama that was having some conflict several years back. The elders had been unable to come to agreement on a particular issue. They had analyzed it and written out the pros and cons, and they had had several very intense meetings in which voices and blood pressures had been raised. Finally, in the midst of some very intense debate in one of the meetings, one of the ministers interrupted and asked if they could just stop and pray. One of the elders was irritated and said, "Has it come to that?" as if prayer should only be a last resort.

No, it should be a first resort! And it should be ongoing. Henry and Richard Blackaby offer six reasons that prayer is so critical in the life of a leader:[26]

1. Leaders can only accomplish God's will through their organizations if they are connected to God (John 15:5).

2. People can only be spiritual leaders when the Spirit is present in their lives, and prayer is conducted by and through the Spirit (Rom. 8:26–27).

3. God's wisdom comes through constant contact with God (1 Cor. 2:9–13).

4. God is all-powerful and can accomplish far more than a leader could ever hope to by his or her own power.

5. Prayer is the leader's best remedy for stress (Matt. 11:28–30; 1 Pet. 5:7).

6. God reveals his agenda through prayer, a truth that Jesus modeled in his own life (Mark 1:35–39).

At every juncture of his own ministry, Jesus constantly prayed. He often got up while it was still dark, and would go out to a deserted place, where he would pray (Mark 1:35; 6:46; 14:32, 35, 39–40). And he taught his disciples—you and me—that we, too, should be praying always. The apostle Paul was the same way. He constantly sought the Lord's guidance about where he should go next in his missionary work (Acts 16:6–10), and he counseled believers to "pray without ceasing" (1 Thess. 5:17 NRSV). Leaders need to be spending time in prayer every day, seeking the Lord's face, seeking his guidance with regard to the details of their lives.

Share your spiritual life. Human beings were created for community, and we are not meant to live lives of isolation. In order to have health and well-being, we need to participate in a genuine spiritual community. We must have a venue where we can be honest about own lives, give and receive affection and forgiveness, and express our personal faith as well as our faith struggles. For pastors, this presents a special challenge, since they are employed as "the facilitators and focal points of Christian community for their congregations," which means that they often do not have access to this kind of community participation.[27] Pastors can easily fall into emotional and spiritual isolation and will need to "take the initiative to find or create the kind of peer spiritual community in which they can live and grow."[28] This could include involvement in a group outside the church but, even if it includes other pastors, it should be a place where pastors can develop and keep relationships that are personal instead of professional. These are relationships in which the pastor is not functioning in a pastoral role or exercising pastoral responsibilities. Such a group can help a pastor remain authentic and accountable. On the other hand, as Gary McIntosh and Samuel Rima observe in their book *Overcoming the Dark Side of Leadership,* even when we maintain such relationships, "it is possible for us to withhold important information and subtle motives that hinder our accountability group from performing their task."[29] They note that "we need to subject our goals and motives to much more than a superficial inspection by those we count on to hold us accountable to biblical principles and godly leadership practices."[30] A pastor may need a close group of peers with whom he or she can agree to be open and accountable to one another. A pastor may want to enter into a relationship with another pastor as his or her spiritual director. However you go about it, the spiritual life must be shared, and you must have a place where you can share yourself in authentic ways.

Expect God's guidance. God gives discernment and guidance. However, you must listen. You must know how to listen. Here are three principles for discerning God's guidance:

1. Discerning God's guidance comes from being open to him rather than trusting in your moral or intellectual superiority.

2. Discerning God's guidance requires that you submit your perceptions, motivations, and emotions to God's mercy and judgment.

3. Discerning God's guidance is most likely to take place when you seek his presence first and, then, allow his answer to come to you.

God's guidance comes through the clear words of Scripture. God's guidance comes in the sanctified imagination of the heart in times of prayer. God's guidance echoes through the words and actions of others. Remember that discerning the guidance of God can mean finding his will in a specific situation, but more often it is discerning his way as revealed in Scripture, that is, applying the truth of the Bible to the challenge. Finally, his guidance may come as his wisdom, wisdom from your own experience or the experience of others, as he places the responsibility to make the decision in your hands. God gave you a brain and he expects you to use it.

God has an investment in you. He has placed you in a position of leadership. He wants to guide you. Seek his guidance. Phillip Yancey is quoted by Priscilla Shirer in *Discerning the Voice of God*:

> I know the Lord is speaking to me when I stop listening to sounds from the world that feed my sense of pride and ambition. Instead, I fall quiet, tune in to God's great world around me, and actively listen. Sometimes nature speaks, telling me of God's majesty and glory. Sometimes God's Word speaks, reminding me of what God wants me to know. And sometimes the Spirit speaks, awakening my conscience, reminding me of failures, stirring my compassion and my sense of justice, aligning me with God's will. I cannot control the voice of God or how it comes. I can only control my "ears"—my readiness to listen and quickness to respond.[31]

It's Not About You

As a leader, called by Christ, the bottom line is faithfulness to him. Of course a business must make a profit. Profit to a business is like breathing to a human body. If you are a small business, especially, you can't hold your breath very long. It is never "only money" unless you are talking about someone else's money. Money is the means of a dream, the dream of paying your employees, providing a worthy product and service, putting children through college, supporting a worthy cause, retiring with dignity. Jesus spoke of money far more than you may realize. Read the Gospels and count the references. He understood and understands.

However, money is a means to an end. What is the end? For the Christian leader, the organization must align with the mission of God on earth. This doesn't mean just sending missionaries overseas, helping young people gain a theological education, and investing your tithes and offerings in a local church. Yes, these are important, but there is more—the actual work you do, the service your organization provides, and the products you produce.

Let me (Richard) tell you a story:[32]

At a country club on the east side of Cleveland, I sat across the table from the founder and owner of a company that makes T-bolts for furniture. A T-bolt is a small piece of hardware that holds furniture together. I wondered how this wonderful Christian man aligned his company with the grand mission of God. I asked him a series of questions:

Question: What is it about making T-bolts for the last forty years that is important to you?

Response: Well, it's not the hardware but the people who work at the plant.

Question: What is it about the people at the plant that is significant to you?

Response: We have been through a lot together. Most of them have been with me a long time. I guess we are like a family.

Question: What is it about being like a family that's significant to you?

At this point, he caught on to my pattern of questions. He saw the seriousness of what I was doing and answered honestly and from the heart.

Response: Let me think about that (pause). I think it's that we are helping each other have better lives.

Question: What is it about having a better life that is significant to you?

Response: My, you are getting down deep with me (pause). I think it's that I want to give people a sense of hope, especially when life is hard.

In a few, short sentences, this man had moved from the everyday challenges that occupied his mind—producing T-bolts for the market—to the values and mission that aligned with God's will on earth. In his business, he was living out the prayer, "Your kingdom come, your will be done on earth as it is in heaven" (Matt. 6:10).

Robert Fritz has stated the challenge of commitment and cooperation with God that serves as a call to all Christian leaders:[33]

> Many people have chosen the religious path, without making
> the fundamental choice to live in accordance with their highest
> spiritual truths. There are many people who have chosen to be
> married, without making the fundamental choice to live from
> within a committed relationship. Fundamental choices are not
> subject to change in internal or external circumstances. If you
> made the fundamental choice to be true to yourself, then you will
> act in ways that are true to yourself whether you feel inspired or
> depressed, whether you feel fulfilled or frustrated, whether you
> are at home, at work, with your friends, or with your enemies. . . .
> When you make a fundamental choice, convenience and comfort
> are not ever at issue, for you always take action based on what is
> consistent with your fundamental choice.

Christian leaders are called to consecrate their lives to God and
cooperate fully with him. To consecrate is to surrender each and
every thing to God. In short, consecration means to "give it to God."
To cooperate means to align your life with God's purpose and plan.
To put it in a phrase, in all you do, follow God's purpose, "go with
God." This is the rhythm of leadership for the Christian, to give all
to God and to go with God's purpose. To only give the problem to
God and then walk away is irresponsible. To tighten your lip and
vow to go with God but never surrender to him is futile. "Give and
go" is the way of Christian leadership. Give it to God because at the
core, the spiritual issues are what count for eternity. Give it to God
by paying attention and being authentic in your inner life. Go with
God as you search the Scriptures and pray from the heart. Go with
God as you discern his will, his way, and his wisdom.

The call for more leadership, better leadership, and superhero
leadership is a false cry that, in many cases and places, bypasses
the head of all, God in Christ. The spiritual quest for a leader, at
last, leads to the deep and troubling truth: *this is not about you.*
This is about God. It is a troubling truth, but lean into it, live with it,

embrace it, and you will find this truth to be wonderfully liberating. Indeed, it may make you a better leader.

To take an example from the church rather than the business world, in his important new book *I Am a Follower: The Way, Truth, and Life of Following Jesus*,[34] Leonard Sweet makes the case that the trendy fixation with leadership in today's church is a result of the fact that we live in a culture that worships success—he calls it the "leadership myth." The influence of twenty-first-century corporate-obsessed culture has led to a focus on leadership techniques and tactics that will theoretically enable pastors and other church leaders to turn congregations into well-oiled, smoothly functioning machines. "Somewhere back in the past half century," Sweet writes, "we diagnosed the church's problem as a crisis of leading," as if getting leadership right was the key to the success of the church.[35] Sweet explains:

> Over the last three decades, there has been a seismic shift across the landscape of the church. The advent of church-growth theory, coupled with exponential advances in technology, has created a hyper-pursuit for leadership muscle that has never been seen before. Seminars and conferences have become trendy leadership fitness centers. Titans of business and mega-church pastors serve as leadership fitness trainers, while books and periodicals deliver leadership steroids and growth hormones.[36]

The assumption of the leadership myth is that if pastors, elders, deacons, and church workers will only become leaders—or better leaders—then their churches will succeed.

Sweet bristles at this leadership myth, and argues: "Contrary to what you may have heard or assumed, everything doesn't rise and fall on leadership."[37] And he goes on to insist that "the church is led not by leaders but by Christ. The head of the church is Christ. Everyone else is a follower."[38] Sweet is not decrying leadership *per se*, but he is highlighting a paradoxical dimension of Christian leadership that has been lost: Christians *lead* by *following*.[39] His whole book is devoted to cultivating not leadership but followership. And this is our emphasis in this chapter, that true Christian leadership is based on our own efforts to follow the leading of our Lord, who is the ultimate Leader of the church. God reveals his agenda through his Word and through prayer. Tune your heart, open your mind, and seek the counsel of God as a leader.

Group Discussion and Personal Reflection

Group Discussion

Saul Turned Away

Why did Saul turn away from the counsel of God? What are the stresses and temptations that pull Christian leaders away from seeking the counsel of God?

Leadership and Spirituality?

For some, it is difficult to see the spiritual side of leadership. For others, the spiritual challenge of leadership is self-evident. List the reasons why leadership may be seen as devoid of spirituality. List the reasons why leadership is seen as fundamentally spiritual. How do you see the connection between leadership and spirituality?

Facing Yourself; Finding God

Calvin wrote, "Nearly all wisdom we possess, that is true and sound wisdom, consists of two parts: the knowledge of God and of ourselves." How does this relate to your spiritual life? How does this apply to your leadership?

The Lord's Prayer for Leaders

Read the Lord's prayer in context—Matthew 6:5–14. What petition of the prayer or piece of the context particularly speaks to a leadership issue you are facing at this time? How do you practice Bible reading and prayer? Tell of a time when you have discerned God's guidance for your leadership.

Personal Reflection

Assess

➣ I believe that leadership involves a spiritual foundation.

I fully agree 5   4   3   2   1 I fully disagree

➤ I am learning be attentive and authentic in a life in God.

I fully agree 5　4　3　2　1 I fully disagree

➤ The Bible and prayer help me discern God's guidance.

I fully agree 5　4　3　2　1 I fully disagree

➤ I integrate consecration to God with cooperation with God.

I fully agree 5　4　3　2　1 I fully disagree

➤ My purpose as a leader aligns with God's mission in the world.

I fully agree 5　4　3　2　1 I fully disagree

Analyze

➤ What is the condition of your spiritual life in God?

➤ What is the relationship between your spiritual life and your leadership?

➤ What would you like to change about your spiritual life?

Act

___ Implement a spiritual discipline such as Bible reading and prayer for thirty days.

___ Seek the counsel of Christian leaders you admire, and ask about their spiritual life and leadership.

___ Read about leadership and spirituality; below is a list to get you started:

David Baron and Lynette Padwa, *Moses on Management: 50 Leadership Lessons from the Greatest Manager of All Time* (A Liberal-Jewish approach to leadership)

Laurie Beth Jones, *Jesus, CEO: Using Ancient Wisdom for Visionary Leadership* (A para-denominational Christian approach to leadership)

Charles Manz, *The Leadership Wisdom of Jesus: Practical Lessons for Today* (An ecumenical Christian approach to leadership)

Max De Pree, *Leadership Is an Art*, and *Leadership Jazz* (A Reformed Christian approach to leadership)

Lovett Weems, *Leadership in the Wesleyan Spirit* (A Wesleyan approach to leadership)

Leighton Ford, *Transforming Leadership* (A Christ-centered approach to leadership)

Dr. J. Robert Clinton, *The Making of a Leader: Recognizing the Lessons and Stages of Leadership Development* (A Christian life story approach to leadership)

Part III

Turning Failure into Success

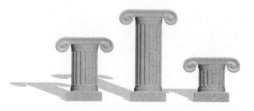

Chapter 13

Avoiding the Pitfalls of King Saul

Throughout *Leadership Lessons*, we have used the failures of King Saul as our starting point for studying leadership. As we noted in chapter 1, this approach is somewhat unique, since leadership books—in general, business, and church categories—have traditionally focused on "best practices." Our approach of using the "worst practices" of a historical figure in order to teach positive leadership habits may seem unusual to some. Some might not understand the value of reading and reflecting on someone else's leadership failures. Barbara Kellerman of the Harvard Kennedy School insists, however, that "to look at leadership through rose-colored glasses is a mistake for many reasons, not least because we tend to learn more from our failures than from our successes."[1] Will Rogers, humorist and political observer, is often quoted as saying, "Good judgment comes from experience, and a lot of that comes from bad judgment."[2] The most poignant lessons of leadership are carefully and often painfully extracted from our mistakes and our poor judgment. To learn from one's mistakes and failures is a differentiating competency in effective and ethical leaders. It is a most painful thing to be forced to learn from your own mistakes and regrets. However, it is even more painful to not learn from them.

It is also easier to learn from *other people's* mistakes and failures. We are more objective. I (Richard) teach an ethics for educators class for undergraduates. I have the students scan the Web for stories of good and bad behavior in teachers. The Web is filled with such stories. I then require the students to analyze each story in order to discover a lasting lesson. This simple system of professional reflection involves four questions:[3]

1. What happened?

2. What caused it to happen that way?

3. What can you learn from what happened?

4. What will you do to apply what you have learned from what happened?

Students, especially when they work in pairs, are quick to pick up on the ethical lessons in the stories of failure. I have helped students analyze hundreds of these stories of good and bad behavior. In doing so, I have learned that it is far easier to pick out the lesson in the bad behavior rather than the good behavior. We learn from the mistakes and failures of others.

Our goal in *Leadership Lessons*, therefore, has been to help readers learn from the ashes of Saul's failures and aspire to greatness by learning from someone else's struggles with the difficulties of leadership. Throughout this volume, we have reviewed the failures and foibles of King Saul, and can now look back at his leadership with the advantage of hindsight. But how can the benefit of hindsight be converted into foresight? In this chapter, we'll take the lessons we have learned from the failures of King Saul and use them to identify some basic guidelines for becoming a better leader, a leader who is both effective and ethical. From our study we can identify a pattern of bad behavior in leadership that provides in-depth lessons for becoming a better leader:

1. Leadership degenerates into a persistent personal crisis.

2. The leader attempts to manage the personal crisis with the pervasive use of dysfunctional behavior.

3. The thoughts and emotions of the leader become an inner theater of angst.

4. At the core, the leader lives in a void of spiritual separation and loss.

This is the pattern we have found in Saul. The pattern is all too common and tragic today. Let's trace the negative pattern from the outside in.

The Path of Leadership Failure

1. *A persistent personal crisis.* Leaders deal with people, plans, and problems. Decisions often must be made in the absence of complete information, commitment, or confidence. This is the reality of leadership that produces nagging criticism and second-guessing for the leader. The ambiguity and anxiety of leadership wears on the leader; it becomes personal. When this pervasive leadership challenge degenerates into a pervasive personal crisis for the leader, poor judgments and mistakes proliferate (all leaders make mistakes), and the mistakes are defended, fortified, and repeated. The basic competency of learning from experience is lost. For such a leader, each day becomes a personal crisis where leading is no longer about the organization but about the leader.

Saul's leadership degenerated into a persistent personal crisis that focused on Saul rather than on the nation. It might be argued that Saul experienced too much success too early. The problem with success is that it doesn't teach you how to deal with failure. When failure came to King Saul at Micmash (1 Sam. 13), rather than reflect, learn, and respond with wisdom, he reacted and retreated. From that moment, the relationships in his life and leadership were poisoned. Blame, vengeance, defensiveness, and isolation grew like a cancer in him. Saul could not keep the challenge of leadership objective enough to deal with it rationally and spiritually. Everything became personal.

Healthy leadership is about the people, the organization, or the nation. The persistent personal crisis is when leadership becomes about the leader. In Saul's case, each person, plan, and problem became about him: his break with Samuel, his estrangement from Jonathan, his blame of the soldiers, his enmity with David, his slaughter of the priests, and his isolation from those who might have helped him. The way Saul dealt with people, plans, and problems was not to advance the nation but to defend and avenge himself as king. The servant focus of leadership became self-focus. This is leadership in persistent personal crisis.

How can leadership turn from a servant focus to self-focus for a leader? Leadership is a deeply personal task. This is why leadership is such a dangerous calling. Having worked with hundreds of young leaders in a diversity of fields, I know that with only the fewest exceptions, these leaders want to do what is good for the people, advance the mission of the organization, and be ethical and effective. However, the weight and weariness of the task takes a toll. The change in the leader is not a flip of a switch from serving others to self-preservation. The change is more like the dimming, flickering, and extinguishing of a light. Whatever the individual path, the end result is that leadership has ceased to be about the people and has become about the leader.

Even in daily crises, the leader may have the competency to maintain a "good" reputation by using the language of serving others: "For the good of all . . ."; "The mission must go on . . ."; "Best for the organization. . . ." However, the inner and quiet conversation takes a different bent: "How dare they treat me this way . . . ?"; "Why do they stop me . . . ?"; "I'll settle this score . . ."

On one occasion when I (Richard) consulted with an organization whose leader had moved from servant-focused to self-focused leadership, I interviewed the staff. Their resounding explanation of the change was, "He still says 'servant leadership,' but we know that means we are here to serve the leader."

The emergence of a persistent personal crisis in a leader takes time. It is not an isolated bad decision or even a solitary unethical judgment call made under undue stress and temptation. The crisis that turns a leader from leading the people to being lost in him- or herself is a process, a downward cycle:[4]

- The symptoms of decline begin in *relationships*. You are still effective but have less vitality. You hold slights and emotional hurts too long. Tension and conflict grow at home and at work. You may be tempted to isolate or attack. Both are ways to escape.

- The next symptom is tainted *character*. You begin to appear less capable and more harassed. You rationalize your distorted perceptions, justify your negative attitudes, and nurse your angry motivations. At this point, you do not receive criticism well. Your judgment, choices, and distractions are self-serving and border on unethical, often crossing the line.

- A clear and courageous sense of *purpose* is the next piece to go by the wayside. You keep up with work, but the behavior patterns you use to defend yourself are harming you and your organization. Resentful, discouraging, and self-defeating thoughts flood your mind and distract you from your work. You tell others you care about what happens, but tell yourself you "just can't help it."

You become a person you don't like. You lose respect for yourself. At the end, Saul sought the advice of a long-dead mentor through the aid of a witch. What self-respecting king of Israel would do such a thing? This king, Saul, was lost in a persistent personal crisis of leadership. The issues were not about Israel, but Saul.

2. *The pervasive use of dysfunctional behavior.* Every crisis calls for management behaviors. Rather than adopt healthy and effective leadership behaviors that promoted the nation of Israel, Saul developed behaviors that protected his distorted perspective, vindicated his angry, fearful emotions, and justified his self-protecting and avenging motivation. Rather than advancing his leadership, his pervasive use of these behaviors resulted in the dysfunction of his leadership:

- Saul failed to handle authority humbly.
- Saul failed to break out of his tendency to isolate himself.
- Saul failed to think before he spoke.
- Saul failed to act when the time was right.
- Saul failed to lead the people, but let them lead him instead.
- Saul failed to promote or make necessary changes.
- Saul failed to love the people.
- Saul failed to stay true to his own ethics.
- Saul failed to admit failure or concede to David.
- Saul failed to consult God.

The behavior patterns of the leader influence the strategy, culture, and structure of the organization to such a degree that it is impossible for an organization to succeed if the leader's behavior is organizationally dysfunctional.[5] Effective leaders are inspirational and instrumental. *Inspirational* behaviors include envisioning, empowering, and energizing. *Instrumental* function requires the behaviors of designing, controlling, and rewarding. When leaders adopt these competencies and do so in alignment with the needs of the organization, it is highly likely that the organization will advance.[6] However, if a leader fails at these functions, the organization will in all likelihood suffer.

Saul was a failure at both the inspirational and instrumental leadership behaviors. He failed to envision the changes that were needed. Rather than empower the next leader, David, he sought to destroy him. And Jonathan energized the troops to attack while Saul remained "under a pomegranate tree" (1 Sam. 14:2). Saul also failed in the instrumental behaviors. He did not design the systems needed for the young nation to advance. He did not take control, responsibility, and accountability for decisions, failures, or advancement. Rather than reward those who were his best help, he regretted and retrieved the honors he distributed. Each reward he gave David, he eventually turned into punishment and vengeance. The pervasive use of the dysfunctional leadership behaviors extracted a toll on the people of God as well as the leadership of the king.

Kurt Motamedi suggests several dysfunctional patterns of leadership behavior. We can spot these patterns in King Saul, and you may see the shadow of these patterns in yourself:[7]

Explosive behavior: moody, destabilizing, "I want it my way."

Implosive behavior: passive aggressive, "Don't let me down or else."

Impulsive behavior: unpredictable, "I want to do it this way now."

Apprehensive behavior: suspicious, defensive, "No one can be trusted."

A leader who has come to the point of engaging in leadership as a persistent personal crisis adopts a pattern of dysfunctional leadership behaviors that put the leader and the organization in jeopardy.

3. *An inner theater of angst.* Imagine a stage play of attitude and emotions going on inside each person, a theater of the inner life. The play can be helpful or harmful to the person. The dialogue and imagined actions so closely connected to life may energize a positive or negative perspective on life. The theater of the inner life whips up demanding emotions or emotional wisdom. When a person is full of inner vitality, the play is punctuated with the three "H's": humility, humanity, and humor.[8] Such a leader can grasp a clear picture of reality. He or she seeks the perspective of others, tests the waters, expects and absorbs ambivalence, and employs practical wisdom to make better decisions. The leader with a healthy inner life has control over his or her emotions. This leader has a clear sense of what motivates him or her and knows when an attitude/motivation adjustment is needed. This is the description of a person with a proper sense of self-respect.

In the inner theater, the lead player is the self. When the self is understood in healthy and realistic terms, the inner play promotes healthy and effective leadership. However, for someone caught in a leadership web of personal crisis and a pattern of dysfunctional leadership behavior, the inner theater plays out a disjointed story of angst, anger, and arrogance. The sense of self is distorted. Thus, the leader clings to a distorted perspective of the situation that fires the emotions and twists motivation into self-protection, defeatism, or aggrandizement. This leader has ignored the directive of Paul:

> For by the grace given me I say to every one of you: Do not think of yourself more highly than you ought, but rather think of yourself with sober judgment, in accordance with the measure of faith God has given you. (Rom. 12:3)

Self-image manifests itself in behaviors and decisions. But it is a most difficult thing for a leader to have a proper image of him- or herself. The difference between confident and arrogant is tough to discover in oneself even if it is rather easy to judge in another.

A leader must sort out a sense of self in the fray of the challenge of working with people, plans, and problems. The way the leader thinks about him- or herself impacts the leader's choices, judgments, and actions. The leader's followers know this. You see, they think about the leader, also. Everyone has opinions and positions on whether the leader is too much of this or not enough of that. Some folks know that the way they express their thoughts about the leader will influence the leader's decisions. Some will try to puff up the leader while others attempt to tear down the leader. They do this in order to try to advance their personal agendas. In this whirlpool of calculated opinions, the leader must stay centered with an accurate and emotionally healthy understanding of self. This is not an easy task.

A distorted sense of self drives the dysfunctional behavior that perpetuates the daily personal crisis. Kets de Vries, in his groundbreaking paper *The Leadership Mystique*, suggests five characteristics of how the leader's twisted understanding of self, the inner theater, is played out:[9]

- *Dramatic*. The leader needs attention, feels entitled, and has a tendency toward extremes. The inner theater is grandiose: "I want to get attention from and impress the people who count in my life."

- *Suspicious*. The leader vigilantly prepares to attack personal threats, is hyper-sensitive, cold, and demands loyalty. The inner theater is suspicious: "Some menacing force is out to get me; I cannot trust anybody."

- *Detached*. The leader is withdrawn, uninvolved, lacking interest, and sometimes indifferent, indecisive, and inconsistent. The inner theater is isolation: "Interactions with others will fail; it is safer to remain distant."

- *Depressed*. The leader lacks self-confidence, fails to take initiative, fears success, tolerates mediocrity or failure, and depends on others for rescue. The inner theater is passivity: "It is hopeless to change the course of events; I am just not good enough."

- *Compulsive*. The leader dominates others, insists on conformity, has a dogmatic or obstinate personality, and is a perfectionist who obsesses on details and rules. The inner theater is control: "I don't want to be at the mercy of events. I must be master and be in control of all things that affect me."

When leadership is a persistent personal crisis, when the behaviors adapted to manage the personal crisis are, in fact, damaging the leader and the organization, then an identity issue is at stake. The leader does not have a clear, accurate, and healthy sense of self. A sense of self that is either aggrandized or belittled will jeopardize the leader's ability.

At this point, psychologists stop the analysis. Yet, for the spiritual person, there is a deeper problem to address. Blaise Pascal, the philosopher and religious skeptic who experienced God in a most profound way, stated the problem thus: "There is a God-shaped vacuum in the heart of every man which cannot be filled by any created thing but only by God, the Creator, made known through Jesus." It is accepting and dealing with the deeper problem that gives hope for real and lasting change.

4. *Spiritual separation and loss.* What is it like to lose a consistent and healthy sense of identity as a leader? John Dominic Crossan, co-founder of the Jesus Seminar, describes the contemporary spiritual condition of our culture, a description that applies to leadership without identity in Christ: "There is no lighthouse keeper. There is no lighthouse. There is no dry land. There are only people living on rafts made from their own imaginations. And there is the sea."[10] Without a spiritual foundation for life and for leadership, the undulations of a sea of ambivalence, challenge, and crisis devolve into self-serving pessimism. Leaders need a spiritual foundation.

While nominal psychotherapists may not delve in the realm of the spiritual life, the gurus of leadership press forward in search of a solid foundation. Jay Conger, associate professor at McGill University in Montreal, Canada, and visiting professor at the Harvard Business School, describes the interest in spirituality among management professors:

> During the last several decades, my field of management—organizational behavior—has concerned itself directly with improving the quality of work life, with enhancing the sense of community in organizations. . . . We have written and taught

about empowerment and vision and motivation and transformational leadership. We have consulted with managers on how to implement these processes. And while our efforts have raised the consciousness among some organizations, there is a sense that much remains to be done. . . .

Some of us are coming to an interest in spirituality as a more profound solution. For spirituality, more powerfully than most other human forces, lifts us beyond ourselves and our narrow self-interests. When not misused, it is the most humane of forces. It helps us to see our deeper connections to one another and to the world beyond ourselves. . . .

. . . spirituality will not lend itself to management techniques. Rather, it presents the most complex challenge we could face in attempting to enhance workplace life, but also potentially the most rewarding.[11]

King Saul was weak in his spiritual life and his spiritual relationship with God. Only twice in the biblical record did he seek the counsel of God. Both incidences seem to have been motivated as much by politics and personal protection as authentic spirituality. In the increasingly complex issues of leading the nation of Israel, the king chose to divorce himself from spiritual reality. In contrast, David also faced challenge and crisis, often at the hand of King Saul. Yet, David turned to the spiritual resources and relationship he had in God. God knew David and sought for him because David was "a man after his own heart" (1 Sam. 13:14 NRSV). For Saul, spiritual resources served utilitarian purposes. For David, God was his source of life.

For a leader, a relationship with God is not a private affair but something that goes to the heart of the leader's identity as it relates to God's purpose or plan. From the beginning, David understood the Lord's heart; he understood God's purpose. But Saul never grasped God's heart or his design for Israel. The people asked Samuel for a king, saying, "Give us a king to lead us" (1 Sam. 8:6). God understood the eternal significance of the people's demand. To Samuel God replied, "Listen to all that the people are saying to you; it is not you they have rejected, but they have rejected me as their king" (1 Sam. 8:7). Samuel explained to the people that a king would take advantage of them, tax them, take their young men into battle and their young women into servitude, yet the people persisted in their demand:

> But the people refused to listen to Samuel. "No!" they said. "We want a king over us. Then we will be like all the other nations, with a king to lead us and to go out before us and fight our battles." (1 Sam. 8:19–20)

Here is the point, the deep failure of the nation and the failure of King Saul: the people wanted to "be like all the other nations," but Israel was not like all the other nations. Israel was God's plan to take back the world as his kingdom and temple. David understood the heart of God, and, in a way appropriate for his time in the plan of God, he cooperated with God in making the world ready for God's kingdom on earth. In complete contrast, Saul never seemed to understand that he was not to be a king like other kings, not to lead a nation like other nations. For Saul, the grand and eternal spiritual purpose of his life and leadership never made the connection to the life and purpose of God. Now you can see the full measure of Saul's failure:

. . . loss of God's purpose in life and leadership,
. . . creates confusion of identity, arrogance, or belittlement,
. . . which fosters dysfunctional behaviors
in order to manage the daily crisis of leadership . . .
which is about the leader rather than the people.

Saul's Failure Leads You to Better Leadership

Leadership has to be more than just about you, the leader. Leadership has to be about the people, the organization. Yet, at the spiritual level, the foundation of leadership for the Christian who leads, there is something more. You, a Christian leader, are to join the heart and purpose of God. The Christian leader's prayer is: "your kingdom come, your will be done on earth as it is in heaven" (Matt. 6:10). For the Christian, it is this spiritual partnership with God that "lifts us beyond ourselves and our narrow interests."[12] Collaborating with God's purpose gives you identity that is realistic and appropriate, empowering you to "think of yourself with sober judgment, in accordance with the measure of faith God has given you" (Rom. 12:3). From a strong foundation of God's purpose and your identity in Christ, a positive and healthy pattern of leadership competencies and behaviors is nurtured. These positive and healthy competencies empower you to take on the leadership challenge of dealing with people, plans, and problems.

We now come to the question of application: How can you experience this new reality of life and leadership? Your full engagement is required. John Wesley, the founder of the Wesleyan movement, called us to commitment and cooperation with God, saying, "He that made us without ourselves, will not save us without ourselves."[13] When God created the world, your cooperation was not required. When God knit you together in your mother's womb (Ps. 139:13), when your frame was woven together in the depths of the earth (Ps. 139:15), your commitment was not needed. However, now that you are here, now that you participate in your life, now that a change is called for in your life and leadership, your cooperation and commitment are essential. Full commitment brings access to God's best for you. Cooperation with God is the foundation of better leadership. Begin with the question, "What is God's purpose for my leadership?" The answer will not come in quarterly objectives and metrics laid out on an Excel spreadsheet. You will not receive God's purpose in a new organizational chart or job assignment. God's purpose in you is even greater than the vision and values of the company, as important as these are to leading an organization. God's purpose is not found out there in your leadership role; it is found within, in your partnership with him.

The answer to the question, "What is God's purpose for my leadership?" begins with what God wants *for* you rather than *from* you. He stands at the entrance of your heart. There, the almighty Creator God knocks on the door of your life. "If anyone hears my voice and opens the door, I will come in and eat with him, and he with me" (Rev. 3:20). God intends to set up housekeeping in your soul. His will is to make "his dwelling" (John 1:14) in you. Before God gets his purposeful hands on your leadership, he wants to place his creative hands on you.

God wants you as his child (John 1:13). With your full commitment and cooperation, the Lord of the universe has a purpose for your leadership. He has vision flashing in his eyes. He has eternal purpose in his mind. God is the King of the world. You are his servant. The Almighty's purpose is clear: God will use you to advance his kingdom on earth. God intends to employ you and your leadership in the work of his kingdom, advancing his reign over the earth: "For the kingdom of God is not a matter of eating and drinking, but of righteousness, peace and joy in the Holy Spirit" (Rom. 14:17). Your leadership is meant to promote what is right, what brings peace, what expands joy, all through the presence and power of the Holy Spirit. As the Latin motto of the Society of Jesus says, *Ad maiorem Dei gloriam*, abbreviated as AMDG, which means, "For the greater glory of God," all you do, including the way you lead, is for the greater glory of God. All work that is not evil, even work that less sensitive souls might consider inconsequential to the spiritual life, is of spiritual worth and power when preformed in order to give glory to God. God employs all such work and leadership for the advancement of his kingdom on earth. This is the foundation of "faith-full" leadership.

Saul just didn't get it. He led people who wanted to be like other nations and he retreated into acting like other kings. Jesus saw it lived out in the kings of his day:

> You know that those who are regarded as rulers of the Gentiles lord it over them, and their high officials exercise authority over them. Not so with you. Instead, whoever wants to become great among you must be your servant, and whoever wants to be first must be slave of all. For even the Son of Man did not come to be served, but to serve, and to give his life as a ransom for many. (Mark 10:42–45)

David understood. Before he was king, he had a heart for God (1 Sam. 13:14). With a full heart for God, your leadership task looks different. Your thinking is changed. The power of God's Spirit moves you from selfish intent to the heart of a servant. To be clear, the challenge of leadership does not change. You still face the issues of people, plans, and problems. Crisis will come. Place it in the heart of God. Ask, "Lord, what is your purpose in this leadership crisis?"

Group Discussion and Personal Reflection

Group Discussion

Review the Chapter

What did you find most encouraging in the chapter? What did you find most challenging in the chapter?

For the Glory of God

The motto *Ad maiorem Dei gloriam* means "For the greater glory of God." How does your leadership bring glory to God? What could you do to be more intentional about leading "for the glory of God"?

To Be Effective and Ethical

Barbara Kellerman suggests twelve steps by which leaders can "strengthen their personal capacity to be at once effective and ethical":[14]

1. Limit your tenure
2. Share power
3. Don't believe your own hype
4. Get real, and stay real
5. Compensate for your weaknesses
6. Stay balanced
7. Remember the mission
8. Stay healthy
9. Develop a personal support system
10. Be creative
11. Know and control your appetites
12. Be reflective

Look over Kellerman's list and answer the following questions:

➤ Which one(s) are you doing now?

➤ Which one(s) could you implement now?

➤ Which one(s) do you find especially challenging to implement?

To Lead as God's Servant

Read Matthew 20:24–28. How has this study of King Saul changed your outlook on leadership?

Personal Reflection

Assess

> ➤ I am fully committed to God's purpose for my leadership.

> Agree 5 4 3 2 1 Disagree

> ➤ I am fully cooperating with God in fulfilling his purpose through my leadership.

> Agree 5 4 3 2 1 Disagree

> ➤ I am leading so as to bring glory to God.

> Agree 5 4 3 2 1 Disagree

> ➤ I am growing in my ability to lead as a servant of God.

> Agree 5 4 3 2 1 Disagree

Analyze

> ➤ How would you characterize your relationship with God in your role as a leader?
> ➤ How would you like to change your relationship with God in your role as a leader?

Act

Here are seven action steps that you can employ to bring greater glory to God through your leadership:

___ *Pray.* The prayer of the righteous accomplishes much (James 4:2–3).

___ *Wait.* Trust the Lord to work in you and around you (Isa. 40:31).

___ *Reflect.* Reflect on your work as you study the Bible (2 Tim. 2:15).

___ *Mentor.* Invest in others to help them be their best (2 Tim. 2:2).

___ *Listen.* Listen for God's voice in the voice of others (John 10:27).

___ *Work.* Honor God with diligent work (Prov. 10:4; 21:5).

___ *Vision.* Vision God's best for your leadership (1 Cor. 2:9).

Notes

Chapter 1: Why Study a Failed Leader?

1. Sydney Finkelstein, *Why Smart Executives Fail: And What You Can Learn From Their Mistakes* (New York: Portfolio, 2003).
2. Quote from the Web site www.whysmartexecutivesfail.com.
3. Gary L. McIntosh and Samuel D. Rima, *Overcoming the Dark Side of Leadership: How to Become an Effective Leader by Confronting Potential Failures* (Grand Rapids: Baker Books, 1997, 2007).
4. John C. Maxwell, *Failing Forward: Turning Mistakes into Stepping Stones for Success* (Nashville: Thomas Nelson, 2000).
5. Barbara Kellerman, *Bad Leadership: What It Is, How It Happens, Why It Matters* (Boston: Harvard Business School Press, 2004).
6. David Dotlich and Peter Cairo, *Why CEOs Fail: The 11 Behaviors That Can Derail Your Climb to the Top—and How to Manage Them* (San Francisco: Jossey-Bass, 2003).
7. Hans Finzel, *The Top Ten Mistakes Leaders Make* (Colorado Springs, CO: Victor, 2007).
8. Paul B. Carroll and Chunka Mui, *Billion Dollar Lessons: What You Can Learn from the Most Inexcusable Business Failures of the Last 25 Years* (New York: Portfolio, 2008).
9. Donald Keough, *The Ten Commandments for Business Failure* (New York: Portfolio, 2011).
10. Gene Edwards, *A Tale of Three Kings: A Study in Brokenness* (Carol Stream, IL: Tyndale House, 1980), 23–24.
11. Barbara Kellerman, *Bad Leadership*, 226.
12. Ibid., 232.
13. Karl Barth, G. W. Bromiley, and T. F. Torrance, *Church Dogmatics, The Doctrine of Reconciliation*, Vol. 4, Part 3.1: *Jesus Christ, the True Witness* (London: T & T Clark, 2004), 253.
14. "Quotations from Chairman Powell: A Leadership Primer," www.govleaders.org.

Chapter 2: Introducing King Saul

1. See R. K. Hawkins, "The First Glimpse of Saul and His Subsequent Transformation," *BBR* 22.3 (2012): 353–62.
2. H. P. Smith, *The Books of Samuel* (International Critical Commentary; Edinburgh: T & T Clark, 1899), 59.
3. Sara Fudge, "1 Samuel," in M. W. Hamilton, ed., *The Transforming Word: One-Volume Commentary on the Bible* (Abilene, TX: Abilene Christian University Press, 2009), 277.
4. Rabbi Joseph Telushkin, *Biblical Literacy: The Most Important People, Events, and Ideas of the Hebrew Bible* (New York: William Morrow and Company, 1997), 197.

Chapter 3: Saul Failed to Handle Authority Humbly

1. This became Saul's policy (1 Sam. 14:52).
2. This was the practice of Absalom in 2 Sam. 15:1 and of Adonijah in 1 Kings 1:5.
3. R. F. Youngblood, "1, 2 Samuel," in F. E. Gaebelein, ed., *The Expositor's Bible Commentary*, vol. 3 (Grand Rapids: Zondervan, 1992), 614.
4. I. Menelsohn, "Samuel's Denunciation of Kingship in the Light of the Akkadian Documents from Ugarit," BASOR 143 (1956): 17–22.
5. See 1 Sam. 31:11–13.
6. E.g., Ex. 15:18; Num. 23:21.
7. Ex. 15:6, 11; Judg. 5:3–5; cf. also Judg. 8:22–23.
8. Robert W. Fuller, *Somebodies and Nobodies: Overcoming the Abuse of Rank* (Gabriola Island, BC, Canada: New Society Publishers, 2003), 8.
9. S. S. Yonick, "The Rejection of Saul: A Study of Sources," *AJBA* 4 (1971), 31, no. 2.
10. In ancient Sumer, for example, the kings supported the state religious institutions, portrayed themselves as gods, and used a prefix before their names that suggested deification. See, for example, J. Klein, "Sumerian Kingship and the Gods," in G. M. Beckman and T. J. Lewis, eds., *Text, Artifact, and Image: Revealing Ancient Israelite Religion* (Providence, RI: Brown University, 2006), 115–31.
11. P. Machinist, "Kingship and Divinity in Imperial Assyria," in *Text, Artifact, and Image*, 152–88.

12. Z. Zevit, "Israel's Royal Cult in the Ancient Near Eastern Kulturkreis," in *Text, Artifact, and Image*, 189–200.

13. It appears that the kings of the Northern Kingdom did not observe these restrictions. The text reports that Jeroboam I "ascended the altar" (1 Kings 12:32–33 NAB), and the eighteen kings who followed after him are said to have followed in his ways (e.g., 1 Kings 15:34; 16:7, 19). The northern kings apparently held to the ancient Near Eastern conception of the king as having a priestly role. This seems to have been in defiance of the Levitical prescriptions.

14. E. H. Peterson, *First and Second Samuel* (Louisville: Westminster, 1999), 82.

15. See Prov. 13:13.

16. W. Brueggemann, *First and Second Samuel* (Louisville: John Knox Press, 1990), 105.

17. 1 Sam. 22:11, 18–19.

18. Peter Northhouse, *Leadership: Theory and Practice*, 5th ed. (Los Angeles: Sage, 2010), 3.

19. Fuller's definition permeates the literature on rankism. His work is found in Robert W. Fuller, *Somebodies and Nobodies*, 8.

20. Finzel, *Top Ten Mistakes*, 22.

21. Ibid., 23.

22. Ibid., 22.

23. Robert W. Fuller, *Somebodies and Nobodies*, 26.

24. Ibid., 2.

25. Ibid., 3.

26. Ibid., 4.

27. Finzel, *Top Ten Mistakes*, 26.

28. Fuller, *Somebodies and Nobodies*, 6–7.

29. Finzel, *Top Ten Mistakes*, 26.

30. Robert Tannenbaum and Fred Massarik, "Participation by subordinates in the managerial decision-making process," *Canadian Journal of Economics and Political Science* (1950): 408–18.

31. Tom Peters and Nancy Austin, *A Passion for Excellence* (New York: Random House, 1985), 447–64.

32. Kurt Lewin, "Group Decision and Social Change," in Theodore M. Newcomb and Eugene I. Hartley, eds., *Readings in Social Psychology* (New York, 1947).

33. The quote is from the original essay that began the Servant Leader Movement. See Robert K. Greenleaf, *The Servant as Leader* (Indianapolis: Robert K. Greenleaf, 1970).

Chapter 4: Saul Failed to Break Out of His Tendency to Isolate Himself

1. Niccolo Machiavelli, *Discourses on the First Ten Books of Titus Livius*, Book 2, Translated by Christian E. Detmold (Cambridge: University Press, 1882), 295.
2. A. Rosengren, K. Orth-Gomer, H. Wedel, and L. Wilhelmsen, "Stressful Life Events, Social Support, and Mortality in Men Born in 1933," *British Medical Journal*, vol. 307, 1993.
3. Cf. 1 Sam. 23:6, 9; 30:7; 2 Sam. 8:17.
4. Barbara Green, *King Saul's Asking* (Collegeville, MN: Liturgical Press, 2003), 88.
5. Henry and Richard Blackaby, *Spiritual Leadership: Moving People on to God's Agenda* (Nashville: Broadman & Holman, 2001), 247.
6. James Thompson, *Equipped for Change: Studies in the Pastoral Epistles* (Abilene, TX: ACU Press, 1996), 14–15.
7. John Powell, *Why Am I Afraid to Love?* (Allen, TX: Tabor, 1982), 52.
8. Louis Untermeyer, *Robert Frost's Poems* (New York: Washington Square Press, 1971), 94.
9. Ibid., 95.
10. Powell, *Why Am I Afraid to Love?*, 52–53.
11. Rosabeth Moss Kanter, *Confidence: How Winning Streaks and Losing Streaks Begin and End* (New York: Random House, 2004), 97–98.

Chapter 5: Saul Failed to Think Before He Spoke

1. Ralph W. Klein, *1 Samuel* (Word Biblical Commentary 10; Waco, TX: Word Books, 1983), 108.
2. C.F. Keil and Franz Delitzsch, *The Books of Samuel, Commentary on the Old Testament* vol. 2 (trans. James Martin; Edinburgh: T & T Clark, 1865–1892), 440.
3. Hans Wilhelm Hertzberg, *I and II Samuel* (Old Testament Library; Philadelphia: Westminster, 1964), 175.

4. Carol Grizzard, "1 Samuel," in *The New Interpreter's Study Bible* (Nashville: Abingdon Press, 2003), 424.

5. As per Klein, *1 Samuel,* 209.

6. Grizzard, *1 Samuel,* 424.

7. Bruce C. Birch, *The First and Second Books of Samuel,* in *The New Interpreter's Bible,* vol. 2 (ed. L. E. Keck; Nashville: Abingdon Press, 1998), 1135.

8. Chris Argyris and Donald Schon, *Theory in Practice: Increasing Professional Effectiveness* (San Francisco: Jossey Bass, 1974), 3, 20.

9. Chris Argyris, *Integrating the Individual and the Organization* (New York: Wiley, 1964), 100–101.

10. Les Giblin, *Skill With People* (Wyckoff, N.J.: Les Giblin, 1985), 7–8.

11. See the discussion by Paul N. Anderson, "Word, The," in *New Interpreter's Dictionary of the Bible,* vol. 5 (ed. K. D. Sakenfeld; Nashville: Abingdon Press, 2009), 893–98.

12. Keith Ferrazzi, *Never Eat Alone: And Other Secrets to Success, One Relationship at a Time* (New York: Currency, 2005), 144.

13. Les Giblin, *Skill With People,* 3.

14. See Dale Carnegie, *How to Win Friends and Influence People* (reissue edition; New York: Simon & Schuster, 2009).

15. Many New Testament passages speak about encouraging one another as well. Cf., for example, Rom. 1:12; Col. 4:8; 1 Thess. 5:11, 14; Heb. 10:25.

16. Susan K. Hedahl, *Listening Ministry: Rethinking Pastoral Leadership* (Minneapolis: Fortress Press, 2001), 95.

17. Taylor Caldwell, *The Listener* (New York: Doubleday, 1960), 9–10.

18. Ibid., 162–63.

19. I first discovered this book as a reference in Susan Hedahl's work, cited earlier, p. xi.

20. James Garlow, *21 Irrefutable Laws of Leadership Tested by Time* (Nashville: Thomas Nelson, 2002), 135.

21. Jerald Brauer, *Westminster Dictionary of Church History* (Philadelphia: Westminster Press, 1971), 452.

22. Garlow, *21 Irrefutable Laws,* 135.

23. Walter Isaacson, *Benjamin Franklin: An American Life* (New York: Simon and Schuster, 2003), 56.

24. Ibid.

25. Ibid., 57.

26. Ibid.

27. Ibid., 326.

Chapter 6: Saul Failed to Act When the Time Was Right

1. D. F. Payne, "1 and 2 Samuel," in D. A. Carson, R. T. France, J. A. Motyer, and G. J. Wenham, eds., *New Bible Commentary: 21st Century Edition* (Downers Grove, IL: InterVarsity, 1997), 309–10.

2. Antiquities VI, 378 [xiv.9].

3. It was somewhat common for year dates to be left out of official royal documents. See K. A. Kitchen, *Ancient Orient and Old Testament* (Downers Grove, IL: InterVarsity, 1966), 75.

4. 1 Sam. 8:18–20.

5. Compare Samuel's warning in 1 Samuel 8:11–12.

6. Or three thousand, including Jonathan's troops, mentioned earlier (v. 2).

7. 1 Sam. 13:16; 14:2.

8. Cf. Num. 20:5; Deut. 8:8; Song 4:13; 6:11; 7:12; Joel 1:12; Hag. 2:19.

9. This is the kind of scene to be repeated in the "eschaton," or last days (Ezek. 38:21).

10. Green, *King Saul's Asking*, 51.

11. David Pratt, *Nobel Wisdom: The 1000 Wisest Things Ever Said* (RJ Books, 2008).

12. V. Vroom and A. Jago, "Decision Making as a Social Process: Normative and Descriptive Models of Leader Behavior," *Decision Sciences*, Vol. 5, 743–55.

13. N. Tichy and W. Bennis, *Judgment: How Winning Leaders Make Great Calls.* (New York: Penguin Group, 2007), 85, 127, 176.

14. Sarte, Jean-Paul (1963) *Essays in Aesthetics*, (Open Road Media, Jan. 17, 2012), 2.

15. Michael Useem, *The Go Point: When It's Time to Decide—Knowing What to Do and When to Do It* (New York: Three Rivers Press/Crown Business/Random House, 2009), 66–68.

16. Tichy and Bennis, *Judgment*, 18–40.

17. This story is found in Richard Leslie Parrott, *True & Best: Authentic Living* (Ashland, OH: Seize Your Life, Inc., 2006), 100.

18. G. Pervost, C. Marriott, (Trans.) (1893) *The Homilies of S. John Chryso-stom: Archbishop of Constantinople, on the Gospel of Saint Matthew.* Translated with Notes and Indices. James Parker and Company.

Chapter 7: Saul Failed to Lead the People, but Let Them Lead Him Instead

1. D. F. Payne, "1 and 2 Samuel," 312.
2. Num. 21:2–3.
3. Josh. 6:21.
4. Josh. 8:26.
5. Josh. 10:28.
6. Josh. 11:11.
7. Lev. 18:21.
8. Lev. 18:25, 27–30.
9. Walter C. Kaiser Jr., "Completely Destroy Them!" in *Hard Sayings of the Bible*, eds. Walter C. Kaiser Jr., Peter H. Davids, F. F. Bruce, and Manfred T. Brauch (Downers Grove, IL: InterVarsity Press, 1996), 206–7.
10. Deut. 25:18.
11. Youngblood, "1, 2 Samuel," 673.
12. Josh. 2:12–14.
13. Cf. 1 Sam. 30:1.
14. D. F. Payne, "1 and 2 Samuel," 311.
15. Youngblood, "1, 2 Samuel," 674.
16. Kaiser, *Hard Sayings*, 208. See also the comments of Youngblood, "1, 2 Samuel," 677.
17. Brueggemann, *First and Second Samuel*, 113.
18. Green, *King Saul's Asking*, 46. Emphasis mine.
19. Ibid., 57.
20. Ronald Heifetz, *Leadership Without Easy Answers* (Cambridge: Harvard University Press, 1998), 273–74.
21. Denis Waitley, *Empires of the Mind: Lessons to Lead and Succeed in a Knowledge-Based World* (New York: William Morrow and Company, 1995), 30.
22. Ibid., 211.
23. Dr. Denis Waitley, *The Winner's Edge: How to Develop the Critical Attitude for Success* (New York: Times Books, 1980), 37.

24. Benno Muller-Hill, "Science, Truth, and Other Values," *Quarterly Review of Biology* 68, no. 3 (September 1993), 399–407. Quoted in John C. Maxwell, *Thinking for a Change: 11 Ways Highly Successful People Approach Life and Work* (New York: Warner Books, 2003), 196.

25. Dr. Denis Waitley, *The Seeds of Greatness Treasury: A Priceless Gift of Poetry, Prose, and Proverbs of Inspiration* (Rancho Santa Fe, CA: International Learning Technologies, Inc., 2003), 12.

26. E. A. Ritter, *Shaka Zulu: The Biography of the Founder of the Zulu Nation* (New York: Penguin Books, 1978), 235–47.

27. Interview with Dr. John Shea conducted by Robert C. Tucker, 1984, as told by Denis Waitley, *Empires of the Mind*, 212.

28. John Mason, *Know Your Limits—Then Ignore Them* (Tulsa, OK: Insight Publishing Group, 1999), 21.

29. John C. Maxwell, *Thinking for a Change: 11 Ways Highly Successful People Approach Life and Work* (New York: Warner Books, 2003), 199.

30. Mason, *Know Your Limits*, 133.

31. Waitley, *The Winner's Edge*, 41.

32. Jane M. Healy, *Endangered Minds: Why Our Children Don't Think* (New York: Simon and Schuster, 1990), 47–55, 195–234.

33. Neil Postman, *Amusing Ourselves to Death: Public Discourse in the Age of Show Business* (New York: Penguin, 1985), 155–56.

34. Waitley, *The Winner's Edge*, 41.

35. Denis Waitley, *Timing Is Everything: Turning Your Seasons of Success into Maximum Opportunities* (Nashville: Thomas Nelson, 1992), 181–82.

36. Mason, *Know Your Limits*, 133.

Chapter 8: Saul Failed to Promote or Make Necessary Changes

1. William Pasmore, *Creating Strategic Change: Designing the Flexible, High-Preforming Organization* (New York: John Wiley and Sons, 1994), 15.

2. Leon J. Wood, *A Survey of Israel's History* (Grand Rapids: Zondervan, 1986), 201.

3. Ibid., 203.

4. John C. Maxwell, *Developing the Leader Within You* (Nashville: Thomas Nelson, 1993), 56–62.

5. Ronald A. Heifitz and Marty Linsky, *Leadership on the Line: Staying Alive Through the Dangers of Leading* (Boston: Harvard Business School Publishing, 2002), 11.

6. James O'Toole, *Leading Change: The Argument for Values-Based Leadership* (New York: Ballantine Books, 1996), 161–64.

7. Hiroo Onoda, *No Surrender: My Thirty-Year War* (New York: Dell, 1976), 50–51, 54.

8. Ibid., 146.

9. Ibid., 246, 251.

10. Peter Senge, *The Dance of Change* (New York: Doubleday, 1999), 16.

11. Heifetz and Linsky, *Leadership on the Line*, 123–39.

12. Some of the material in this section is borrowed by permission from Ralph K. Hawkins, *A Heritage in Crisis: Where We've Been, Where We Are, and Where We're Going in the Churches of Christ* (Lanham, MD: University Press of America, 2001), 11–13.

13. Glen Martin and Gary McIntosh, *The Issachar Factor: Understanding Trends That Confront Your Church and Designing a Strategy for Success* (Nashville: Broadman & Holman, 1993), 57.

14. Dr. Randall J. Harris and Dr. Rubel Shelly, *The Second Incarnation: Empowering the Church for the Twenty-First Century* (West Monroe, LA: Howard, 1992), 136.

15. Martin and McIntosh, *The Issachar Factor*, 11–12.

16. Gregg R. Allison, *Historical Theology: An Introduction to Christian Doctrine* (Grand Rapids: Zondervan, 2011), 678.

17. Marva Dawn, *Reaching Out Without Dumbing Down: A Theology of Worship for the Turn-of-the-Century Culture* (Grand Rapids: Eerdmans, 1995), 303.

18. Charles Denison, *Mainline Manifesto: The Inevitable New Church* (St. Louis, MO: Chalice Press, 2005).

19. Ibid., 35.

20. Ibid., 25–26.

21. *Constitution on the Sacred Liturgy* (December 4, 1963), 1.3.21, in Vatican Council II, vol. 1: *The Conciliar and Post-Conciliar Documents*, ed. Austin Flannery (New York: Costello, 1975), 9, cited in Allison, *Historical Theology*, 676.

22. Denison, *Mainline Manifesto*, 113.

23. Cf. Ralph K. Hawkins, "Is the Church Moving into a 'Postdenominational' Era?" in Ralph K. Hawkins, ed., *Simul Iustus et Peccator:*

Essays in Honor of Donald S. Armentrout (Sewanee, TN: University of the South, 2003), 239–61.

24. We do not know much about Generation Z yet, although we do know something about the environment in which they are growing up. Their parents are members of either Generation X or Y.

25. See Dan Cox, Scott Clement, et al., "Non-believers, Seculars, the Unchurched and the Unaffiliated," presented to the American Association for Public Opinion Research, May 2009, www.publicreligionresearch.org/objects/uploads/fck/file/ASPOR%20Paper%Final.pdf.

26. Thom S. Rainer and Jess W. Rainer, *The Millennials: Connecting to America's Largest Generation* (Nashville: Broadman & Holman, 2011).

27. Ibid., 231.

28. Ibid., 236.

29. Ibid., 244.

30. Ibid.

31. Ibid., 243.

32. Ibid., 259–69.

33. Ibid., 271.

34. Ronald M. Cervero, "Building Systems of Continuing Education for the Professions," in Robert E. Reber and D. Bruce Roberts, eds., *A Lifelong Call to Learn: Approaches to Continuing Education for Church Leaders* (Nashville: Abingdon Press, 2000), 282–83.

35. Jon Walker, "Online Churches—the Wave of the Future?" in *Religion Today* Feature Story, http://news.crosswalk.com/religion/item/0,,359710,00.htm.

36. Ibid.

37. As predicted by Anthony E. Healy, "Finding a Niche and Filling It: Congregations in a Postindustrialist Economy," in *Congregations* 27, no. 4 (July/August 2001), 27.

38. John R. Throop, "Church 2.0: Use the Internet to Boost Your Community-building Efforts," *Your Church* 53, no. 6 (November 2007): 34–38; Andrea Useem, "The New Connectivity: How Internet Innovations Are Changing the Way We Do Church," *Congregations* 34, no. 4 (Fall 2008): 22–28.

39. Esther Dyson, *Release 2.0* (New York: Broadway Books, 1997), 8.

40. Cervero, 285. See, for example, Dwight J. Friesen, *Thy Kingdom Connected: What the Church Can Learn from Facebook, the Internet, and Other Networks* (Grand Rapids: Baker, 2009); Jesse Rice, *The Church of Facebook: How the Hyperconnected are Redefining Community* (Colorado Springs: David C. Cook, 2009); Walter P. Wilson, *The Internet Church* (Nashville: Thomas Nelson, 2004).

41. Richard L. Parrott, *Leading Change* (Nashville: Seize Your Life, Inc., 2003), audio recording.

Chapter 9: Saul Failed to Love the People

1. Ernst Jenni, *Theological Lexicon of the Old Testament* (Peabody, MA: Hendrickson, 1997), 49.

2. Robert L. Alden, *Ahav*, in R. Lair Harris, Gleason L. Archer, Jr., and Bruce K. Waltke, eds., *Theological Wordbook of the Old Testament* (Chicago: Moody Press, 1980), 14.

3. Youngblood, "1, 2 Samuel," 707.

4. Ibid., 710.

5. John C. Maxwell and Jim Dornan, *Becoming a Person of Influence* (Nashville: Thomas Nelson, 1997), 39.

6. O. A. Ohmann, "Skyhooks: With Special Implications for Monday through Friday," *Harvard Business Review* (May–June 1955, reprinted Jan.–Feb. 1970).

7. John Hope Bryant, *Love Leadership: The New Way to Lead in a Fear-Based World* (San Francisco: Jossey-Bass, 2009).

8. Robert B. Asprey, *Frederick the Great: The Magnificent Enigma* (Lincoln, NE: iUniversity, 2007; original publication by Ticknor and Fields, 1986).

9. *New York Times*, February 12, 1945.

10. Frederick Herzberg, Bernard Mausner, and Barbara Block Snyderman, *The Motivation to Work* (New York: John Wiley & Sons, 1959).

11. Zig Ziglar, *Secrets of Closing the Sale* (Grand Rapids: Revell, 1984, updated in 2003).

12. Mother Teresa often shared the quote. A collection of written transcripts can be found at www.ascension-research.org/teresa.

13. Bob Burg and John Mann, *The Go-Giver: A Little Story About a Powerful Business Idea* (New York: Penguin, 2008).

14. G. B. Graen and M. Uhl-Bien, "The transformation of professionals into self-managing and partially self-designing contributions: Toward a theory of leadership making," *Journal of Management Systems* (1991): vol. 3, 33–48.

15. The term "transformational leadership" was coined by J. V. Dowton, *Rebel Leadership: Commitment and Charisma in a Revolutionary Process* (New York: Free Press, 1973). The concept advanced into the political leadership field in James M. Burns, *Leadership* (New York: Harper and Row, 1978). For an excellent treatment of the subject for organizations, see Bernard M. Bass, *Leadership and Performance Beyond Expectations* (New York: Free Press, 1985).

16. Bill George, *Authentic Leadership: Rediscovering the Secrets of Creating Lasting Value* (San Francisco: Jossey-Bass, 2003). And, by the same author, *True North: Discover Your Authentic Leadership* (San Francisco: Jossey-Bass, 2007).

17. B. Shamir and G. Eilam, "What's Your Story: A Life-Stories Approach to Authentic Leadership Development," *Leadership Quarterly*, no. 16 (2005): 395–417.

18. F. Walumbua, B. Avolio, W. Gardner, T. Wemsing, and S. Peterson, "Authentic Leadership: Development and Validation of a Theory-Based Measure," *Journal of Management* 34, no. 1 (2008): 89–126.

19. A. H. Eagly, "Achieving Relational Authenticity in Leadership: Does Gender Matter?" *Leadership Quarterly*, no. 16 (2005): 459–74.

20. Denis Waitley, *Empires of the Mind*, 232.

21. Ibid., 230.

22. Edward Hallowell, "The Human Moment at Work," *Harvard Business Review* (January 1999): 58–66.

Chapter 10: Saul Failed to Be True to His Own Ethics

1. Lev. 7:33–34.

2. Peter J. Leithart, *A Son to Me: An Exposition of 1 & 2 Samuel* (Moscow, ID: Canon Press, 2003), 74.

3. D. F. Payne, "1 and 2 Samuel," 307.

4. Ibid.

5. Youngblood, "1, 2 Samuel," 632.

6. Cf. similarly Deut. 31:26; Josh. 24:26–27.

7. Ex. 20:13.

8. Leithart, *A Son to Me*, 119.

9. Cf. Isa. 8:19.

10. Cf. Lev. 19:31; 20:6–7; Deut. 18:11.

11. D. F. Payne, "1 and 2 Samuel," 319.

12. The sacred lots stored in the priestly ephod.

13. First Chronicles 10:14 states that Saul "did not inquire" of the Lord. It may be that Saul's attempts at inquiry were of such an unworthy nature that it would be an abuse of language to speak of him as really "inquiring of the Lord." (Comments of John Haley, quoted in Youngblood, "1, 2 Samuel," 779).

14. Othniel Margalith, "Dor and En-Dor," *ZAW* 97 (1985), 111.

15. Necromancers are those who claim to communicate with the dead.

16. See Jer. 27:9–10.

17. Kaiser, *Hard Sayings*, 217.

18. Theodore J. Lewis, *Cults of the Dead in Ancient Israel and Ugarit* (HSM; Atlanta, GA: Scholars Press, 1989), 115–16.

19. Margalith, "Dor and En-Dor," 111.

20. e.g., 1 Sam 15:27.

21. Cf. Kaiser, *Hard Sayings*, 217.

22. Chris Seay, *The Tao of Enron: Spiritual Lessons from a Fortune 500 Fallout* (Colorado Springs: NavPress, 2002), 13.

23. Ibid.

24. Timothy Lamer, "Reaping the Whirlwind," in *World* 17, no. 27 (July 20, 2002), 15.

25. Ibid.

26. Erwin Lutzer in "Where Judgment Begins: Sorting the Tangled Elements of Ethics and Integrity: A Leadership Forum," in *Leadership* 24, no. 1 (Winter 2003), 27.

27. Ibid.

28. Ibid.

29. Michael Maccoby, "Narcissistic Leaders: The Incredible Pros, the Inevitable Cons," *Harvard Business Review* (February 2000) vol. 1:92.

30. Peter Heinze, Rhianon Allen, Carol Magai, and Barry Ritzler, "Let's Get Down to Business: A Validation Study of the Psychopathic Personality Inventory Among a Sample of MBA Students," *Journal of Personality Disorders* (2010) vol. 4: 487–98.

31. J. Cangemi and W. Pfohl, "Sociopaths in High Places," *Organization Development Journal* (Summer 2009) vol. 2 : 85–96.
32. Terry L. Price, "Explaining Ethical Failures of Leadership," *Leadership and Organizational Development Journal* (2000) vol. 4: 177–84.
33. Dean Ludwig and Clinton Longenecker, "The Bathsheba Syndrome: The Ethical Failure of Successful Leaders," *Journal of Business Ethics* 12 (1993): 265–73.
34. Daniel Goleman, *Emotional Intelligence* (New York: Bantam, 1995).
35. A comprehensive study of corporate ethics programs. R. Goodell, *Ethics in American Business: Policies, Programs, and Perceptions* (Washington, D.C.: Ethics Resource Center, 1994).
36. John C. Maxwell, *Ethics 101: What Every Leader Needs to Know* (New York: Warner Books, 2003).
37. http://www.teachingvalues.com/goldenrule.html.
38. John C. Maxwell, *There's No Such Thing as "Business" Ethics: There's Only One Rule for Making Decisions* (New York: Warner Books, 2003).
39. Joseph Badaracco, *Defining Moments: When Managers Must Choose Between Right and Right* (Cambridge, MA: Harvard Business School Press, 1997).
40. This thought is built on the ideas expressed by Donald Schon, *The Reflective Practitioner: How Professionals Think in Action* (New York: Basic Books, 1983).
41. Martin Luther King, Jr., "Loving Your Enemies," in *Strength to Love* (Philadelphia: Fortress Press, 1963), 54.
42. Stewart Burns, *To the Mountaintop: Martin Luther King, Jr.'s, Sacred Mission to Save America, 1955–1968* (New York: HarperSanFrancisco, 2004), 142.
43. Ibid., 144.
44. Ibid., 145.
45. King, "Loving Your Enemies," 56.
46. Michael H. Hart, *The 100: A Ranking of the Most Influential Persons in History* (New York: Carol Publishing Group, 1994), 20–21.
47. The five assessment questions are adapted from PLIS, a thirty-question assessment that appeared in Craig and Gustafson, "Perceived Leader Integrity Scale: An Instrument for Assessing Employee Perceptions of Leadership Integrity," *Leadership Quarterly* (1998) vol.2: 143–44.

Chapter 11: Saul Failed to Admit Failure or Concede to David

1. D. G. Schley, "Thousand," in D. N. Freedman, ed., *Eerdmans Dictionary of the Bible* (Grand Rapids: Eerdmans, 2000), 1304–5.

2. A. Betz, "Go Out and Come In," in *Eerdmans Dictionary of the Bible*, 510.

3. As postulated by B. Halpern, *David's Secret Demons: Messiah, Murderer, Traitor, King* (Grand Rapids, MI: Eerdmans, 2001); S. L. McKenzie, *King David: A Biography* (New York: Oxford University Press, 2002).

4. See the discussion in A. E. Hill and J. H. Walton, *A Survey of the Old Testament* 3rd ed. (Grand Rapids: Zondervan, 2009), 263–68; and T. Longman III, and R. B. Dillard, *An Introduction to the Old Testament* 2nd ed. (Grand Rapids: Zondervan, 2006), 138–39.

5. John C. Maxwell, *The Maxwell Leadership Bible* 2nd ed. (Nashville: Thomas Nelson, 2007), 374.

6. D. Ulrich, J. Zenger, and N. Smallwood, *Results-Based Leadership* (Boston: Harvard Business School Press, 1999), 214.

7. Ford is a case study in the refusal to listen to others. See R. S. Tedlow, *Denial: Why Business Leaders Fail to Look Facts in the Face—and What To Do About It* (New York: Portfolio, 2010).

8. Otto Rank, as quoted in Jeffrey Sonnefeld, *The Hero's Farewell: What Happens When CEOs Retire* (New York: Oxford University Press, 1988), 3.

9. William Bridges, *Managing Transitions: Making the Most of Change* (Reading, MA: Addison-Wesley Publishing, 1991), 3–5.

10. M. Paese and R. Wellins, "Leaders in Transition: Stepping Up, Not Off," Developmental Dynamics International, Inc. (2007), www.ddiworld.com.

11. Ibid.

12. Ibid.

13. Robert Greene and Joost Elffers, *The 48 Laws of Power* (New York: Penguin, 1998), 1.

14. A guide to the Sarbanes-Oxley Act is found at www.soxlaw.com.

15. Stephen Miles, "Succession Planning: How To Do It Right," Forbes.com, http://www.forbes.com/2009/07/31/succession-planning-right-leadership-governance-ceos.html.

16. Elizabath Kubler-Ross, *On Death and Dying* (New York: Simon and Shuster, 1997).

17. http://wws.peacecorps.gov/wws/publications/culture/pdf/chapter6. pdf.

18. Paul Pedersen, *The Five Stages of Culture Shock: Critical Incidents Around the World* (Westport, CT: Greenwood Press, 1995).

19. Nigel Nicholson and Michael West, "Transitions, Work Histories, and Careers," in Michael Arthur, Douglas Hall, and Barbara Lawrence, eds., *Handbook of Career Theory* (Cambridge, MA: Cambridge University Press, 1989), 181–201.

20. J. M. Fisher, "A Time for Change," in *Human Resource Development International* (June 2005) vol. 8, No. 2: 257–263.

21. Badaracco, ibid.

22. The three words *test*, *reveal*, and *shape* come from the writing of John Dewey, *Ethics*, 1908, revised 1932.

23. Acts 9.

24. Phillip Van Artevelde, (1852) "A Dramatic Romance in Two Parts," London, Edward Moxon, Dover Street. Part 1. Act 1, Scene 5.

25. Kenneth Galbraith, (1971) *Economics: Peace and Laughter*, New American Library, 50.

Chapter 12: Saul Failed to Consult God

1. Henry Mintzberg, "The Manager's Job: Folklore and Fact," *Harvard Business Review* (July–August 1975), 49–61.

2. Max De Pree, *Leadership Is an Art* (New York: Doubleday, 1989).

3. Max De Pree, *Leadership Jazz* (New York: Doubleday, 1992).

4. Abraham Zaleznik, "Managers and Leaders: Are They Different?" *Harvard Business Review* (March–April 1998).

5. Yahweh did not answer Saul's inquiry in this case (1 Sam. 14:37), and this is a clear indication that he was displeased. Does this mean that Yahweh was displeased that Saul's oath had been violated? If this is the case, then it would seem that Yahweh approved of Saul's oath. However, Saul's inquiry was based on his *assumption* that God was not answering him because his oath had been violated. However, Saul had already been told by Samuel that his dynasty would not continue (1 Sam. 13:13–14), and later, after his complete rejection by God, "Saul would understand that no approach or technique, however authorized in other contexts, would bring a divine response, however desperate his need" (Youngblood, "1, 2 Samuel," 667).

6. Jim Bakker, *I Was Wrong* (Nashville: Thomas Nelson, 1996).

7. Ibid., 295.

8. Ibid., 296.

9. Ibid.

10. Ibid., 298.

11. Ibid.

12. Ibid., 294.

13. Material in this section is adapted from and with the permission of Richard Leslie Parrott, *My Soul Purpose* (Nashville: The Woodland Press, 2009).

14. The list is adapted from Robert Banks and Bernice Ledbetter, *Reviewing Leadership: A Christian Evaluation of Current Approaches* (Grand Rapids: Baker Academic, 2004), 53.

15. Russ Moxley, *Leadership and Spirit: Breathing New Vitality and Energy into Individuals and Organizations* (San Francisco: Jossey-Bass, 2000).

16. Peter Vaill, *Spirited Leading and Learning: Process Wisdom for a New Age* (San Francisco: Jossey-Bass, 1998).

17. Thomas Jeavon, *When the Bottom Line Is Faithfulness* (Indiana University Press, 1994).

18. John Calvin, *Institutes*, book 1, chapter 1, translated by Henry Beveridge (Peabody, MA: Hendrickson Publishers, 2008), 4.

19. Stan Smith, ed., *The Cambridge Companion to W. H. Auden* (Cambridge, MA: Cambridge University Press, 2004).

20. This material is from Richard Leslie Parrott, *My Soul Purpose*. Used by permission.

21. Donald R. Hands and Wayne L. Fehr, *Spiritual Wholeness for Clergy: A New Psychology of Intimacy with God, Self and Others* (Bethesda, MD: The Alban Institute, 1993).

22. See Rollo May, *Power and Innocence* (New York: W. W. Norton & Co., 1972).

23. Susan Howatch, *Glittering Images* (New York: Fawcett Crest, 1987).

24. Hands and Fehr, *Spiritual Wholeness*, 54.

25. Henry and Richard Blackaby, *Spiritual Leadership: Moving People on to God's Agenda* (Nashville: Broadman & Holman, 2001), 182.

26. Ibid., 148–51.

27. Hands and Fehr, *Spiritual Wholeness*, 67.

28. Ibid.

29. Gary L. McIntosh and Samuel D. Rima, *Overcoming the Dark Side of Leadership: How to Become an Effective Leader by Confronting Potential Failures* (Grand Rapids: Baker, 2007), 208.

30. Ibid.

31. Philip Yancey, as quoted in Priscilla Shirer, *Discerning the Voice of God* (Chicago: Moody, 2007), 54.

32. I (Richard) first reported this story in Richard Leslie Parrott, *True and Best: Authentic Living* (Nashville: Seize Your Life, Inc., 2006), 37–38. Used by permission.

33. Robert Fritz, *The Path of Least Resistance: Learning to Become the Creative Force in Your Own Life* (New York: Fawcet, 1989).

34. Leonard Sweet, *I Am a Follower: The Way, Truth, and Life of Following Jesus* (Nashville: Thomas Nelson, 2012).

35. Ibid., 21.

36. Ibid., 19.

37. Ibid., 24.

38. Ibid.

39. Ibid., 21.

Chapter 13: Avoiding the Pitfalls of King Saul

1. Kellerman, *Bad Leadership*, 221.

2. www.cmgww.com/historic/rogers/about/miscellaneous.html.

3. The four questions are from Richard Leslie Parrott, *Better Answers to Tougher Questions: Unlock the Power of Wisdom* (Nashville: Seize Your Life, Inc., 2006). Used by permission.

4. A complete description of the cycle of decline is found in Richard Leslie Parrott, *My Soul Purpose*.

5. Kets de Vries, *The Leadership Mystique* (Fontainebleau, France: INSEAD, 1998).

6. Ibid.

7. Kurt Motamedi, "Seven Neurotic Styles of Management," *Graziadio Business Review* 8, no. 4 (2006), www.gbr.pepperdine.edu/2010/08/seven-neurotic-styles-of-management/.

8. Kets de Vries, *The Leadership Mystique*.

9. Ibid.

10. John D. Crossan, *The Dark Interval: Towards a Theology of Story* (Niles, IL: Argus, 1975), 44.

11. Jay Conger & Associates, *Spirit at Work: Discovering the Spirituality in Leadership* (San Francisco: Jossey-Bass, 1994), 16–17.

12. Ibid.

13. John Wesley, *Works*, vol. 6, p. 513.

14. Kellerman, *Bad Leadership*, 233–35.

About the Authors

Dr. Ralph Hawkins, a native of Birmingham, Alabama, is associate professor of Religious Studies at Averett University, in Danville, Virginia. He is a founding co-chairman of the Society of Biblical Literature Joshua–Judges Section, and is the author of *The Iron Age I Structure on Mt. Ebal* (Winona Lake, IN: Eisenbrauns, 2012) and *How Israel Became a People* (Nashville: Abingdon Press, 2013). Dr. Hawkins teaches Bible and archaeology courses, is an ordained minister, and speaks frequently to church audiences on the subjects of both biblical archaeology and biblical leadership.

* * *

Dr. Richard Leslie Parrott is a professor of education at Trevecca Nazarene University. He teaches classes in research, ethics, philosophy, and leadership. His publications include *When Pastors Pray* (Sandberg Leadership Center, 2001), *True and Best: Authentic Living* (Ashland, OH: Seize Your Life, Inc., 2006), *Essentials: The Proven Path of Effective Leadership* (Ashland, OH: Seize Your Life, Inc., 2007), and *My Soul Purpose* (Nashville, TN: Woodland Street Press, 2009). Dr. Parrott has thirty years of experience that he puts to good use as the founder and president of Seize Your Life, a corporation devoted to helping individuals and organizations take hold of life's full potential. He is a frequent speaker for businesses and churches.